LEARN PYTHON
THE HARD WAY

Fifth Edition

T0201071

LEARN PYTHON THE HARD WAY

A Deceptively Simple Introduction
to the Terrifyingly Beautiful World of
Computers and Data Science

Fifth Edition

Zed A. Shaw

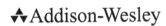

Addison-Wesley

Hoboken, New Jersey

Library of Congress Control Number: 2023950645

ISBN-13: 978-0-13-827057-5
ISBN-10: 0-13-827057-0

1 2024

Contents

Preface

This simple book is meant to get you started in programming. The title says it's the hard way to learn to write code, but it's actually not. It's only the "hard" way because it uses a technique called *instruction*. Instruction is where I tell you to do a sequence of controlled exercises designed to build a skill through repetition. This technique works very well with beginners who know nothing and need to acquire basic skills before they can understand more complex topics. It's used in everything from martial arts to music to even basic math and reading skills.

This book instructs you in Python by slowly building and establishing skills through techniques such as practice and memorization, then applying them to increasingly difficult problems. By the end of the book you will have the tools needed to begin learning more complex programming topics. I like to tell people that my book gives you your "programming black belt." What this means is that you know the basics well enough to now start learning programming.

If you work hard, take your time, and build these skills, you will learn to code.

Improvements in the Fifth Edition

This latest edition of *Learn Python the Hard Way* features many innovations from over a decade of teaching absolute beginners (aka pre-beginners) how to code. The following improvements are just a few that should help almost anyone learn to code:

1. A focus on getting started quickly using Jupyter notebooks and Anaconda, rather than the traditional Python tools from the previous books.

2. Though starting with Jupyter and Anaconda, students later "graduate" to a more traditional environment found in professional Python development.

3. Less repetition of the same concepts but more combination and interaction with previous concepts to reinforce learning.

4. A whole new Exercise 24 that teaches the basic concepts of a Turing machine by teaching students how to use dis() to inspect Python's byte codes. I've found this solves a major problem where students feel they don't "really know how Python works" by giving them a looking glass into how Python actually works.

5. A completely rewritten Object-Oriented Programming section that teaches Python's objects and classes by having students create their own toy OOP system.

6. A whole new set of nine modules that teach the "Data part of Data Science," from covering introductory topics of processing CSV files to interacting with SQL databases.

xx LEARN PYTHON THE HARD WAY

7. New typographic conventions that make clear exactly what kind of code is being discussed. For example, I'll say, "look at the `talk()` function," when I want you to review the function named "talk" in the code. Traditionally, programming textbooks would leave off the `()` characters since it's seen as redundant because they also used the word "function." I've found adding the `()` helps students find the functions in their code and eliminates any confusion about what `talk!` refers to.

8. Lots of brand new subtle humor and programmer "dad jokes" to make the topic unserious and a bit more fun.

I hope you enjoy my latest work, and if you ever find any mistakes or have any questions you can email me at help@learncodethehardway.com. You can also find quick fixes, updated install instructions, and additional advice at https://learncodethehardway.com/setup/python/. I recommend visiting this link first if you have any weird errors while installing software as there may be updates that are not in your printed copy.

Register your copy of *Learn Python the Hard Way, Fifth Edition*, on the InformIT site for convenient access to updates and corrections as they become available. To start the registration process, go to informit.com/register and log in or create an account. Enter the product ISBN (9780138270575) and click Submit. If you would like to be notified of exclusive offers on new editions and updates, please check the box to receive email from us.

Acknowledgments

I'd like to thank Nick Cohron for reviewing the book and finding all the errors for me. I'd also like to thank my editor Debra Williams Cauley for putting up with my constant lateness and the late-night insomniac phone calls, as well as Julie Nahil and the whole crew at Pearson for their hard work producing the book.

I'd also like to give a special thanks to all the past students who supported my work over the years. My courses would not be as polished if it weren't for your feedback, criticism, and praise. I truly do thank you for helping me create something precious over the years, and I wish you all great success.

MODULE 1

Getting Started in Python

Gearing Up

This exercise has no code. It is simply the exercise you complete to get your computer to run Python. You should follow these instructions as exactly as possible. If you have problems following the written instructions, then visit https://learncodethehardway.com/setup/python/ for possible corrections, updated instructions, and additional help.

General Instructions

Your general task is to get a "programming environment" with tools you can use to write code. Nearly every programmer has their own specialized environment, but at first you'll want something simple that can get you through this course. After the course you'll know enough about programming to then waste the rest of your life trying every tool you can imagine. It's a lot of fun.

What you'll need is the following:

- Jupyter, which will be used in the first part of the book to get you started easily. Jupyter is a programming and data analysis environment that uses many languages, but we'll use Python.

- Python. The version of Python you install mostly doesn't matter so long as it's newer than version 3.10. Versions of Python (and other software) use numbers to indicate their age, and the position of the numbers determines how much changed between versions. The general rule is the first number means "major change," the second number means "compatible changes," and a third number means only bug or security fixes. That means if you have version 3.8 and version 3.10, then they should be compatible. If you have versions 3.10.1 and 3.10.2, then there are only minor fixes.

- A *basic* programmer's editor. Programmers use very complicated text editors, but you should start with something simple that still works as a programmer's editor.

- A Terminal emulator. This is a text-based command interface to your computer. If you've ever seen a movie with hacking and programming in it, you've seen people furiously typing green text into a black screen so they can take down an entire alien race with their "unix exe 32 pipe attack." At first you won't need this, but later you'll "graduate" to using the Terminal as it's incredibly powerful and not too hard to learn.

You should have most of the other things you'll need on your computer already, so let's install each of these requirements for your operating system (OS).

Minimalist Start

The instructions in this exercise are designed to install most of the things you need for the rest of the course, but if you want to get going quickly with the least amount of work, then install:

1. Anaconda to get your Python

2. Jupyter to write and run some code

    a. On Windows the best way to run Jupyter is to hit the Windows key (Start menu) and type `jupyter-lab`. This will start it in a way that makes sense.

    b. On Linux it should be the same command in your Terminal.

    c. On macOS you can either type that command in the Terminal or start the app like normal.

This will give you enough to get started, but eventually you'll hit exercises that need the Terminal and Python from the "command line." Come back to this exercise when you reach that point in the course.

Complete Instructions

Eventually you'll need to install more software to complete the course. The problem with installation instructions in books is they become outdated quickly. To solve this problem, I have a web page you need to visit with all of the instructions for your OS with videos showing you the installations. These instructions are updated whenever things change, and the web page includes any errata needed for your book.

To view these instructions, visit the following link:

*   https://learncodethehardway.com/setup/python/

If you're not able to visit this link for some reason, then here's what you'll have to install:

1. Anaconda to get your Python

2. Jupyter to write and run some code

3. Geany for editing text later

4. On Windows use the full install of Cmder as your shell

5. On macOS you have Terminal, and Linux has whatever you want

Testing Your Setup

Once you have everything installed, go through these steps to confirm that everything is working:

1. Start your Terminal and type this command exactly, spaces and all: `mkdir lpthw`

2. Once that works, you have a directory `lpthw` where you can place your work.

3. Go into that directory with the command cd lpthw. This command "moves" your Terminal into that directory so your work is saved there.

4. A "directory" is also called a "folder" on Windows and macOS. You can make the connection between the "directory" in your Terminal and the "folder" you normally see by typing start. on Windows or open. on macOS. This opens the current directory into a graphical folder window you're used to normally seeing. If you're ever lost, type that.

5. The start command (open on macOS) works like double-clicking that thing with your mouse. If you are in the Terminal and want to "open" something, just use this command. Let's say there's a text file named test.txt and you want to open it in your editor. Type start test.txt on Windows or open test.txt on macOS.

6. Now that you can open your Terminal and open things while in your Terminal, you'll want to start your editor. This is Geany if you've been following instructions. Start it and create a file named test.txt and then save it in the lpthw directory you made. If you can't find it, remember you can open it from the Terminal with start (open on macOS) and then use that folder window to find it.

7. Once you've saved the file in the lpthw directory, you should be able to type ls test.txt in your Terminal to see that it's there. If you get an error, then either you're not in the lpthw directory and need to type cd ~/lpthw *or* you saved it in the wrong place. Try again until you can do this.

8. Finally, in the Terminal, type jupyter-lab to start Jupyter and make sure it works. It should open your web browser, and then you'll see the Jupyter app inside your browser. It's kind of like a little website on your personal computer.

Think of these tasks as a kind of puzzle to solve. If you get stuck, then visit https://learncodethehardway .com/setup/python/ for possible updates and video install guides.

Learning the Command Line

You don't need to do this right now, but if you're struggling with the previous tasks, you might need to go through the Command Line Crash Course (https://learncodethehardway.com/command-line-crash-course/) to learn the basics of the Terminal (also called the "command line"). You won't need these skills for a while, but the command line is a very good introduction to controlling your computer with words. It will also help you with many other tasks in programming later, so learning it now can only help.

Next Steps

Once you have everything working, you can continue with the rest of the course. If you ever run into trouble, you can email me at help@learncodethehardway.com, and I'll help you. When you email me for help, take the time to describe your problem in as much detail as possible, and include screenshots.

A Good First Program

WARNING! If you skipped Exercise 0, then you are not doing this book right. Are you trying to use IDLE or an IDE? I said not to use one in Exercise 0, so you should not use one. If you skipped Exercise 0, please go back to it and read it.

You should have spent a good amount of time in Exercise 0 learning how to install Jupyter, run Jupyter, run the Terminal, and work with both of them. If you haven't done that, then do not proceed. You will not have a good time. This is the only time I'll start an exercise with a warning that you should not skip or get ahead of yourself.

Type the following text into a Jupyter cell:

Listing 1.1: ex1.py

```
1    print("Hello World!")
2    print("Hello Again")
3    print("I like typing this.")
4    print("This is fun.")
5    print('Yay! Printing.')
6    print("I'd much rather you 'not'.")
7    print('I "said" do not touch this.')
```

Your Jupyter cell should look something like this:

```
Untitled.ipynb            ×   +

 🖫   +   ✂   🗐   🗂   ▶   ■   ⟳   ⏩   Code        ∨              ⚙   Python 3 (ipykernel)  ○

    [1]:   print("Hello World!")
           print("Hello Again")
           print("I like typing this.")
           print("This is fun.")
           print('Yay! Printing.')
           print("I'd much rather you 'not'.")
           print('I "said" do not touch this.')
```

Don't worry if your Jupyter window doesn't look exactly the same; it should be close though. You may have a slightly different window header, maybe slightly different colors, and the left side of your Jupyter window won't be the same, but will instead show the directory you used for saving your files. All of those differences are fine.

When you create this cell, keep in mind these points:

1. I did not type the line numbers on the left. Those are printed in the book so I can talk about specific lines by saying, "See line 5..." You do not type line numbers into Python scripts.

2. I have the print at the beginning of the line, and it looks exactly the same as what I have in the cell. Exactly means exactly, not kind of sort of the same. Every single character has to match for it to work. Color doesn't matter, only the characters you type.

Once it is *exactly* the same, you can hit SHIFT-ENTER to run the code. If you did it right, then you should see the same output as I in the *What You Should See* section of this exercise. If not, you have done something wrong. No, the computer is not wrong.

What You Should See

The Jupyter output will look like this after you hold SHIFT and hit ENTER (which I'll write as SHIFT-ENTER):

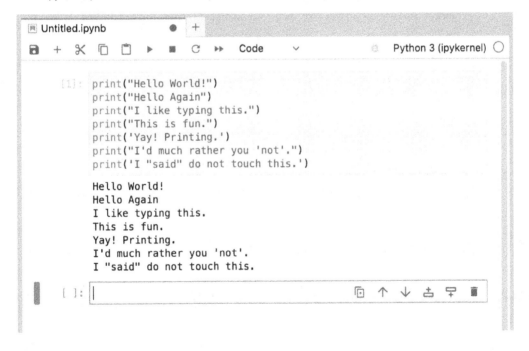

You may see different window appearance and layout, but the important part is that you type the command and see the output is the same as mine.

If you have an error, it will look like this:

```
1   Cell In[1], line 3
2     print("I like typing this.
3          ^
4   SyntaxError: unterminated string literal (detected at line 1)
```

It's important that you can read these error messages because you will be making many of these mistakes. Even I make many of these mistakes. Let's look at this line by line.

1. We ran our command in the Jupyter cell with SHIFT-ENTER.

2. Python tells us that the cell has an error on line 3.

3. It prints this line of code for us to see it.

4. Then it puts a ^ (caret) character to point at where the problem is. Notice the missing " (double-quote) character at the end though?

5. Finally, it prints out a "SyntaxError" and tells us something about what might be the error. Usually these errors are very cryptic, but if you copy that text into a search engine, you will find someone else who's had that error, and you can probably figure out how to fix it.

Study Drills

The Study Drills contain things you should *try* to do. If you can't, skip it and come back later.

For this exercise, try these things:

1. Make your script print another line.

2. Make your script print only one of the lines.

3. Put a # (octothorpe) character at the beginning of a line. What did it do? Try to find out what this character does.

From now on, I won't explain how each exercise works unless an exercise is different.

INFO An "octothorpe" is also called a "pound," "hash," "mesh," or any number of names. Pick the one that makes you chill out.

Common Student Questions

These are *actual* questions that real students have asked when doing this exercise:

Can I use IDLE?   No, for now just use Jupyter and later we'll use a regular text editor for extra superpowers.

Editing the code in Jupyter is annoying. Can I use a text editor?   Totally, you can also create a Python file in Jupyter and get a "good enough" editor. In the left panel where you see all your files, click the blue + (plus) button on the top left. That will bring you to the first screen you saw when you started Jupyter. Down at the bottom under `$_ Other` you'll see a button for `Python File` with the Python logo. Click that and you'll get an editor to work on your file.

My code doesn't run; I just get the prompt back with no output.   You most likely took the code in my cell literally and thought that `print("Hello World!")` meant to type only `"Hello World!"` into the cell, without the `print`. Your cell has to be *exactly* like mine.

The Blue Plus

If you ever want to create a file with Jupyter and use its editor you can use the "blue plus" as shown in this image which I've placed a giant red circle around:

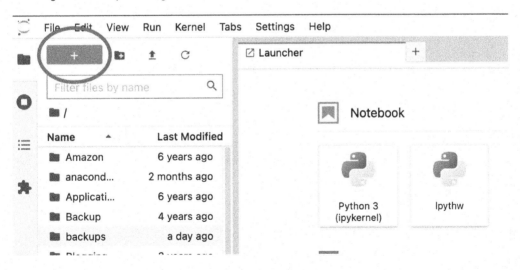

If you don't see this then you most likely started Jupyter wrong by accidentally starting the *Jupyter Notebook* in your start menu instead of typing `jupyter-lab`.

Comments and Pound Characters

C omments are very important in your programs. They are used to tell you what something does in English, and they are used to disable parts of your program if you need to remove them temporarily. Here's how you use comments in Python:

Listing 2.1: ex2.py

```
1    # A comment, this is so you can read your program later.
2    # Anything after the # is ignored by python.
3
4    print("I could have code like this.") # and the comment after is ignored
5
6    # You can also use a comment to "disable" or comment out code:
7    # print("This won't run.")
8
9    print("This will run.")
```

From now on, I'm going to write code like this. It is important for you to understand that everything does not have to be literal. If my Jupyter looks a little different from yours or if I'm using a text editor, the results will be the same. Focus more on the textual output and less on the visual display such as fonts and colors.

What You Should See

```
1    I could have code like this.
2    This will run.
```

Again, I'm not going to show you screenshots of all the Terminals possible. You should understand that the preceding is not a literal translation of what your output should look like visually, but the text is what you focus on.

Study Drills

1. Find out if you were right about what the # character does and make sure you know what it's called (octothorpe or pound character).

2. Take your code and review each line going backward. Start at the last line, and check each word in reverse against what you should have typed.

3. Did you find more mistakes? Fix them.

4. Read what you typed out loud, including saying each character by its name. Did you find more mistakes? Fix them.

Common Student Questions

Are you sure # is called the pound character?   I call it the octothorpe because that is the only name that no one country uses and that works in every country. Every country thinks its name for this one character is both the most important way to do it and the only way it's done. To me this is simply arrogance and, really, y'all should just chill out and focus on more important things like learning to code.

Why does the # in `print("Hi # there.")` **not get ignored?**   The # in that code is inside a string, so it will be put into the string until the ending " character is hit. Pound characters in strings are just considered characters, not comments.

How do I comment out multiple lines?   Put a # in front of each one.

I can't figure out how to type a # character on my country's keyboard. How do I do that?   Some countries use the ALT key and combinations of other keys to print characters foreign to their language. You'll have to search online to see how to type it.

Why do I have to read code backward?   It's a trick to make your brain not attach meaning to each part of the code, and doing that makes you process each piece exactly. This catches errors and is a handy error-checking technique.

Numbers and Math

Every programming language has some kind of way of doing numbers and math. Do not worry: programmers frequently lie about being math geniuses when they really aren't. If they were math geniuses, they would be doing math, not writing buggy web frameworks so they can drive race cars.

This exercise has lots of math symbols. Let's name them right away so you know what they are called. As you type this one in, say the name. When saying them feels boring, you can stop saying them. Here are the names:

- + plus
- − minus
- / slash
- * asterisk
- % percent
- < less-than
- > greater-than
- <= less-than-equal
- >= greater-than-equal

Notice how the operations are missing? After you type in the code for this exercise, go back and figure out what each of these does and complete the table. For example, + does addition.

Listing 3.1: ex3.py

```
 1   print("I will now count my chickens:")
 2
 3   print("Hens", 25 + 30 / 6)
 4   print("Roosters", 100 − 25 * 3 % 4)
 5
 6   print("Now I will count the eggs:")
 7
 8   print(3 + 2 + 1 − 5 + 4 % 2 − 1 / 4 + 6)
 9
10   print("Is it true that 3 + 2 < 5 − 7?")
11
12   print(3 + 2 < 5 − 7)
13
14   print("What is 3 + 2?", 3 + 2)
15   print("What is 5 - 7?", 5 − 7)
```

```
16
17   print("Oh, that's why it's False.")
18
19   print("How about some more.")
20
21   print("Is it greater?", 5 > -2)
22   print("Is it greater or equal?", 5 >= -2)
23   print("Is it less or equal?", 5 <= -2)
```

Make sure you type this exactly before you run it. Compare each line of your file to my file.

What You Should See

```
1    I will now count my chickens:
2    Hens 30.0
3    Roosters 97
4    Now I will count the eggs:
5    6.75
6    Is it true that 3 + 2 < 5 - 7?
7    False
8    What is 3 + 2? 5
9    What is 5 - 7? -2
10   Oh, that's why it's False.
11   How about some more.
12   Is it greater? True
13   Is it greater or equal? True
14   Is it less or equal? False
```

Study Drills

1. Above each line, use the # to write a comment to yourself explaining what the line does.

2. You can type most math directly into a Jupyter cell and get results. Try using it to do some basic calculations like 1+2 and hit SHIFT-ENTER.

3. Find something you need to calculate and write a new .py file that does it.

4. Rewrite this exercise to use floating point numbers so it's more accurate. 20.0 is floating point.

Common Student Questions

Why is the % character a "modulus" and not a "percent"?   Mostly that's just how the designers chose to use that symbol. In normal writing you are correct to read it as a "percent." In programming this calculation is typically done with simple division and the / operator. The % modulus is a different operation that just happens to use the % symbol.

How does % work?   Another way to say it is, "X divided by Y with J remaining." For example, "100 divided by 16 with 4 remaining." The result of % is the J part, or the remaining part.

What is the order of operations?   In the United States, we use an acronym called PEMDAS which stands for Parentheses Exponents Multiplication Division Addition Subtraction. That's the order Python follows as well. The mistake people make with PEMDAS is to think this is a strict order, as in "Do P, then E, then M, then D, then A, then S." The actual order is you do the multiplication *and* division (M&D) in one step, from left to right, and *then* you do the addition and subtraction in one step from left to right. So, you could rewrite PEMDAS as PE(M&D)(A&S).

Variables and Names

Now you can print things with print, and you can do math. The next step is to learn about variables. In programming, a variable is nothing more than a name for something, similar to how my name "Zed" is a name for "the human who wrote this book." Programmers use these variable names to make their code read more like English and because they have lousy memories. If they didn't use good names for things in their software, they'd get lost when they tried to read their code again.

If you get stuck with this exercise, remember the tricks you have been taught so far for finding differences and focusing on details:

1. Write a comment above each line explaining to yourself what it does in English

2. Read your Python code backward

3. Read your Python code out loud, saying even the characters

Listing 4.1: ex4.py

```
1    cars = 100
2    space_in_a_car = 4.0
3    drivers = 30
4    passengers = 90
5    cars_not_driven = cars - drivers
6    cars_driven = drivers
7    carpool_capacity = cars_driven * space_in_a_car
8    average_passengers_per_car = passengers / cars_driven
9
10
11   print("There are", cars, "cars available.")
12   print("There are only", drivers, "drivers available.")
13   print("There will be", cars_not_driven, "empty cars today.")
14   print("We can transport", carpool_capacity, "people today.")
15   print("We have", passengers, "to carpool today.")
16   print("We need to put about", average_passengers_per_car,
17           "in each car.")
```

INFO The _ in space_in_a_car is called an underscore character. Find out how to type it if you do not already know. We use this character a lot to put an imaginary space between words in variable names.

What You Should See

```
1    There are 100 cars available.
2    There are only 30 drivers available.
3    There will be 70 empty cars today.
4    We can transport 120.0 people today.
5    We have 90 to carpool today.
6    We need to put about 3.0 in each car.
```

Study Drills

When I wrote this program the first time, I had a mistake, and Python told me about it like this:

```
1    Traceback (most recent call last):
2      Cell In[1], line 8, in <module>
3        average_passengers_per_car = car_pool_capacity / passenger
4    NameError: name 'car_pool_capacity' is not defined
```

Explain this error in your own words. Make sure you use line numbers and explain why.

Here are more drills:

1. I used 4.0 for space_in_a_car, but is that necessary? What happens if it's just 4?

2. Remember that 4.0 is a floating point number. It's just a number with a decimal point, and you need 4.0 instead of just 4 so that it is floating point.

3. Write comments above each of the variable assignments.

4. Make sure you know what = is called (equals) and that its purpose is to give data (numbers, strings, etc.) names (cars_driven, passengers).

5. Remember that _ is an underscore character.

Common Student Questions

What is the difference between = (single-equal) and == (double-equal)?   The = (single-equal) assigns the value on the right to a variable on the left. The == (double-equal) tests whether two things have the same value. You'll learn about this later.

Can we write x=100 **instead of** x = 100?   You can, but it's bad form. You should add space around operators like this so that it's easier to read.

What do you mean by "read the file (code) backward"?   Very simple. Imagine you have a file with 16 lines of code in it. Start at line 16, and compare it to my code at line 16. Then do it again for 15, and so on until you've read all of the code backward.

Why did you use 4.0 **for** space_in_a_car?   It is mostly so you can then find out what a floating point number is and ask this question. See the *Study Drills* section.

More Variables and Printing

N ow we'll do even more typing of variables and printing them out. This time we'll use something called a "format string." Every time you put " (double-quotes) around a piece of text you have been making a *string*. A string is how you make something that your program might give to a human. You print strings, save strings to files, send strings to web servers, and many other things.

Strings are really handy, so in this exercise you will learn how to make strings that have variables embedded in them. You embed variables inside a string by using a special {} sequence and then put the variable you want inside the {} characters. You also must start the string with the letter f for "format," as in f"Hello {somevar}". This little f before the " (double-quote) and the {} characters tell Python 3, "Hey, this string needs to be formatted. Put these variables in there."

As usual, just type this in even if you do not understand it, and make it exactly the same.

Listing 5.1: ex5.py

```
1    my_name = 'Zed A. Shaw'
2    my_age = 35 # not a lie
3    my_height = 74 # inches
4    my_weight = 180 # lbs
5    my_eyes = 'Blue'
6    my_teeth = 'White'
7    my_hair = 'Brown'
8
9    print(f"Let's talk about {my_name}.")
10   print(f"He's {my_height} inches tall.")
11   print(f"He's {my_weight} pounds heavy.")
12   print("Actually that's not too heavy.")
13   print(f"He's got {my_eyes} eyes and {my_hair} hair.")
14   print(f"His teeth are usually {my_teeth} depending on the coffee.")
15
16   # this line is tricky; try to get it exactly right
17   total = my_age + my_height + my_weight
18   print(f"If I add {my_age}, {my_height}, and {my_weight} I get {total}.")
```

What You Should See

```
1    Let's talk about Zed A. Shaw.
2    He's 74 inches tall.
3    He's 180 pounds heavy.
4    Actually that's not too heavy.
5    He's got Blue eyes and Brown hair.
```

```
6    His teeth are usually white depending on the coffee.
7    If I add 35, 74, and 180 I get 289.
```

Study Drills

1. Change all the variables so there is no my_ in front of each one. Make sure you change the name everywhere, not just where you used = to set them.

2. Try to write some variables that convert the inches and pounds to centimeters and kilograms. Do not just type in the measurements. Work out the math in Python.

Common Student Questions

Can I make a variable like this: `1 = 'Zed Shaw'`**?**   No, 1 is not a valid variable name. They need to start with a character, so a1 would work, but 1 will not.

How can I round a floating point number?   You can use the `round()` function like this: `round(1.7333)`.

Why does this not make sense to me?   Try making the numbers in this script your measurements. It's weird, but talking about yourself will make it seem more real. Also, you're just starting out, so it won't make too much sense. Keep going and more exercises will explain it more.

Strings and Text

While you have been writing strings, you still do not know what they do. In this exercise we create a bunch of variables with complex strings so you can see what they are for. First an explanation of strings.

A string is usually a bit of text you want to display to someone or "export" out of the program you are writing. Python knows you want something to be a string when you put either " (double-quotes) or ' (single-quotes) around the text. You saw this many times with your use of print when you put the text you want to go inside the string inside " or ' after the print to print the string.

Strings can contain any number of variables that are in your Python script. Remember that a variable is any line of code where you set a name = (equal) to a value. In the code for this exercise, types_of_people = 10 creates a variable named types_of_people and sets it = (equal) to 10. You can put that in any string with {types_of_people}. You also see that I have to use a special type of string to "format"; it's called an "f-string" and looks like this:

```
1  f"some stuff here {avariable}"
2  f"some other stuff {anothervar}"
```

Python *also* has another kind of formatting using the .format() syntax, which you see on line 17. You'll see me use that sometimes when I want to apply a format to an already created string, such as in a loop. We'll cover that more later.

We will now type in a whole bunch of strings, variables, and formats, and print them. You will also practice using short abbreviated variable names. Programmers love saving time at your expense by using annoyingly short and cryptic variable names, so let's get you started reading and writing them early on.

Listing 6.1: ex6.py

```
1  types_of_people = 10
2  x = f"There are {types_of_people} types of people."
3
4  binary = "binary"
5  do_not = "don't"
6  y = f"Those who know {binary} and those who {do_not}."
7
8  print(x)
9  print(y)
```

```
10
11    print(f"I said: {x}")
12    print(f"I also said: '{y}'")
13
14    hilarious = False
15    joke_evaluation = "Isn't that joke so funny?! {}"
16
17    print(joke_evaluation.format(hilarious))
18
19    w = "This is the left side of..."
20    e = "a string with a right side."
21
22    print(w + e)
```

What You Should See

```
1    There are 10 types of people.
2    Those who know binary and those who don't.
3    I said: There are 10 types of people.
4    I also said: 'Those who know binary and those who don't.'
5    Isn't that joke so funny?! False
6    This is the left side of...a string with a right side.
```

Study Drills

1. Go through this program and write a comment above each line explaining it.

2. Find all the places where a string is put inside a string.

3. Are you sure there are only four places? How do you know? Maybe I like lying.

4. Explain why adding the two strings w and e with + makes a longer string.

Break It

You are now at a point where you can try to break your code to see what happens. Think of this as a game to devise the most clever way to break the code. You can also find the simplest way to break it. Once you break the code, you then need to fix it. If you have a friend, then the two of you can try to break each other's code and fix it. Give your friend your code in a file named ex6.py so they can break something. Then you try to find their error and fix it. Have fun with this, and remember that if you wrote this code once, you can do it again. If you take your damage too far, you can always type it in again for extra practice.

Common Student Questions

Why do you put ' (single-quotes) around some strings and not others?   Mostly it's because of style, but I'll use a single-quote inside a string that has double-quotes. Look at lines 6 and 15 to see how I'm doing that.

If you thought the joke was funny, could you write `hilarious = True`**?**   Yes, and you'll learn more about these boolean values later.

Combining Strings

Now we are going to do a bunch of exercises where you just type code in and make it run. I won't be explaining this exercise because it is more of the same. The purpose is to build up your chops. See you in a few exercises, and *do not skip!* Do not *paste!*

Listing 7.1: ex7.py

```
1    print("Mary had a little lamb.")
2    print("Its fleece was white as {}.".format('snow'))
3    print("And everywhere that Mary went.")
4    print("." * 10)   # what'd that do?
5
6    end1 = "C"
7    end2 = "h"
8    end3 = "e"
9    end4 = "e"
10   end5 = "s"
11   end6 = "e"
12   end7 = "B"
13   end8 = "u"
14   end9 = "r"
15   end10 = "g"
16   end11 = "e"
17   end12 = "r"
18
19   # watch end = ' ' at the end.  try removing it to see what happens
20   print(end1 + end2 + end3 + end4 + end5 + end6, end=' ')
21   print(end7 + end8 + end9 + end10 + end11 + end12)
```

What You Should See

```
1    Mary had a little lamb.
2    Its fleece was white as snow.
3    And everywhere that Mary went.
4    ..........
5    Cheese Burger
```

Study Drills

For these next few exercises, you will have the exact same Study Drills.

1. Go back through and write a comment on what each line does.

2. Read each one backward or out loud to find your errors.

3. From now on, when you make mistakes, write down on a piece of paper what kind of mistake you made.

4. When you go to the next exercise, look at the mistakes you have made and try not to make them in this new one.

5. Remember that everyone makes mistakes. Programmers are like magicians who fool everyone into thinking they are perfect and never wrong, but it's all an act. They make mistakes all the time.

Break It

Did you have fun breaking the code in Exercise 6? From now on you're going to break all the code you write or a friend's code. I won't have a Break It section explicitly in every exercise, but your goal is to find as many different ways to break your code until you get tired or exhaust all possibilities. In some exercises, I might point out a specific common way people break that exercise's code, but otherwise consider this a standing order to always break it.

Common Student Questions

Why are you using the variable named 'snow'?   That's actually not a variable: it is just a string with the word snow in it. A variable wouldn't have the single-quotes around it.

Is it normal to write an English comment for every line of code like you say to do in Study Drill 1?   No, you write comments only to explain difficult to understand code or why you did something. Why is usually much more important, and then you try to write the code so that it explains how something is being done on its own. However, sometimes you have to write such nasty code to solve a problem that it does need a comment on every line. In this case, it's strictly for you to practice translating code to English.

Can I use single-quotes or double-quotes to make a string or do they do different things?   In Python, either way to make a string is acceptable, although typically you'll use single-quotes for any short strings like `'a'` or `'snow'`.

Formatting Strings Manually

We will now see how to do a more complicated formatting of a string. This code looks complex, but if you do your comments above each line and break each thing down to its parts, you'll understand it.

Listing 8.1: ex8.py

```
1   formatter = "{} {} {} {}"
2
3   print(formatter.format(1, 2, 3, 4))
4   print(formatter.format("one", "two", "three", "four"))
5   print(formatter.format(True, False, False, True))
6   print(formatter.format(formatter, formatter, formatter, formatter))
7   print(formatter.format(
8       "Try your",
9       "Own text here",
10      "Maybe a poem",
11      "Or a song about fear"
12  ))
```

What You Should See

```
1   1 2 3 4
2   one two three four
3   True False False True
4   {} {} {} {} {} {} {} {} {} {} {} {} {} {} {} {}
5   Try your Own text here Maybe a poem Or a song about fear
```

In this exercise, I'm using something called a "function" to turn the formatter variable into other strings. When you see me write formatter.format(...), I'm telling Python to do the following:

1. Take the formatter string defined on line 1.

2. Call its format() function, which is similar to telling it to do a command line command named format

3. Pass to format four arguments, which match up with the four {} in the formatter variable. This is like passing arguments to the command line command format

4. The result of calling format on formatter is a new string that has the {} replaced with the four variables. This is what print is now printing out.

That's a lot for the eighth exercise, so what I want you to do is consider this a brainteaser. It's alright if you don't *really* understand what's going on because the rest of the book will slowly make this clear. At this point, try to study this and see what's going on, and then move on to the next exercise.

Study Drills

Repeat the Study Drills from Exercise 7.

Common Student Questions

Why do I have to put quotes around "one" but not around `True` **or** `False`?   Python recognizes `True` and `False` as keywords representing the concept of true and false. If you put quotes around them, then they are turned into strings and won't work. You'll learn more about how these work later.

Can I use IDLE to run this?   No, you should use Jupyter or the command line if you know how. It is essential to learning programming and is a good place to start if you want to learn about programming. Jupyter is a far superior tool than IDLE.

Multi-Line Strings

B y now you should realize the pattern for this book is to use more than one exercise to teach you something new. I start with code that you might not understand, and then more exercises explain the concept. If you don't understand something now, you will later as you complete more exercises. Write down what you don't understand, and keep going.

Listing 9.1: ex9.py

```
1    # Here's some new strange stuff, remember type it exactly.
2
3    days = "Mon Tue Wed Thu Fri Sat Sun"
4    months = "Jan\nFeb\nMar\nApr\nMay\nJun\nJul\nAug"
5
6    print("Here are the days: ", days)
7    print("Here are the months: ", months)
8
9    print("""
10   There's something going on here.
11   With the three double-quotes.
12   We'll be able to type as much as we like.
13   Even 4 lines if we want, or 5, or 6.
14   """)
```

What You Should See

```
1    Here are the days:  Mon Tue Wed Thu Fri Sat Sun
2    Here are the months:  Jan
3    Feb
4    Mar
5    Apr
6    May
7    Jun
8    Jul
9    Aug
10
11   There's something going on here.
12   With the three double-quotes.
13   We'll be able to type as much as we like.
14   Even 4 lines if we want, or 5, or 6.
```

Study Drills

Repeat the Study Drills from Exercise 7.

Common Student Questions

Why do I get an error when I put spaces between the three double-quotes? You have to type them like
`"""` and not `"  "  "`, meaning with *no* spaces between each one.

What if I wanted to start the months on a new line? You simply start the string with \n like this:
`"\nJan\nFeb\nMar\nApr\nMay\nJun\nJul\nAug"`.

Is it bad that my errors are always spelling mistakes? Most programming errors in the beginning
(and even later) are simple spelling mistakes, typos, or getting simple things out of order.

Escape Codes in Strings

In Exercise 9, I threw you some new stuff just to keep you on your toes. I showed you two ways to make a string that goes across multiple lines. In the first way, I put the characters \n (backslash n) between the names of the months. These two characters put a new line character into the string at that point.

This \ (backslash) character encodes difficult-to-type characters into a string. There are various "escape sequences" available for different characters you might want to use. We'll try a few of these sequences so you can see what I mean.

An important escape sequence is to escape a single-quote ' or double-quote ". Imagine you have a string that uses double-quotes and you want to put a double-quote inside the string. If you write "I "understand" joe." then Python will get confused because it will think the " around "understand" actually *ends* the string. You need a way to tell Python that the " inside the string isn't a *real* double-quote.

To solve this problem you *escape* double-quotes and single-quotes so Python knows to include them in the string. Here's an example:

```
1  "I am 6'2\" tall."  # escape double-quote inside string
2  'I am 6\'2" tall.'  # escape single-quote inside string
```

The second way to solve this problem is to use triple-quotes, which is just """ and works like a string, but you also can put as many lines of text as you want until you type """ again. We'll also play with these.

Listing 10.1: ex10.py

```
1   tabby_cat = "\tI'm tabbed in."
2   persian_cat = "I'm split\non a line."
3   backslash_cat = "I'm \\ a \\ cat."
4
5   fat_cat = """
6   I'll do a list:
7   \t* Cat food
8   \t* Fishies
9   \t* Catnip\n\t* Grass
10  """
11
12  print(tabby_cat)
13  print(persian_cat)
14  print(backslash_cat)
15  print(fat_cat)
```

What You Should See

Look for the tab characters that you made. In this exercise, the spacing is important to get right.

```
1                 I'm tabbed in.
2    I'm split
3    on a line.
4    I'm \ a \ cat.
5
6    I'll do a list:
7             * Cat food
8             * Fishies
9             * Catnip
10            * Grass
```

Escape Sequences

This is all of the escape sequences Python supports. You may not use many of these, but memorize their format and what they do anyway. Try them out in some strings to see if you can make them work.

Escape	What it does.
\\	Backslash (\)
\'	Single-quote (')
\"	Double-quote (")
\a	ASCII bell (BEL)
\b	ASCII backspace (BS)
\f	ASCII formfeed (FF)
\n	ASCII linefeed (LF)
\N{name}	Character named name in the Unicode database (Unicode only)
\r	Carriage return (CR)
\t	Horizontal tab (TAB)
\uxxxx	Character with 16-bit hex value xxxx
\Uxxxxxxxx	Character with 32-bit hex value xxxxxxxx
\v	ASCII vertical tab (VT)
\000	Character with octal value 000
\xhh	Character with hex value hh

Study Drills

1. Memorize all the escape sequences by putting them on flash cards.

2. Use ' ' ' (triple-single-quote) instead. Can you see why you might use that instead of """?

3. Combine escape sequences and format strings to create a more complex format.

Common Student Questions

I still haven't completely figured out the last exercise. Should I continue?   Yes, keep going. Instead of stopping, take notes listing things you don't understand for each exercise. Periodically, go through your notes and see if you can figure these things out after you've completed more exercises. Sometimes, though, you may need to go back a few exercises and do them again.

What makes \\ special compared to the other ones?   It's simply the way you would write out one backslash (\) character. Think about why you would need this.

When I write // or /n it doesn't work.   That's because you are using a forward-slash / and not a backslash \. They are different characters that do very different things.

I don't get Study Drill 3. What do you mean by "combine" escape sequences and formats?   One con-cept I need you to understand is that each of these exercises can be combined to solve problems. Take what you know about format strings and write some new code that uses format strings *and* the escape sequences from this exercise.

What's better, ' ' ' or """?   It's entirely based on style. Go with the ' ' ' (triple-single-quote) style for now, but be ready to use either depending on what feels best or what everyone else is doing.

Asking People Questions

Now it is time to pick up the pace. You are doing a lot of printing to get you familiar with typing simple things, but those simple things are fairly boring. What we want to do now is get data into your programs. This is a little tricky because you have to learn to do two things that may not make sense right away, but trust me and do it anyway. It will make sense in a few exercises.

Most of what software does is the following:

1.   Take some kind of input from a person

2.   Change it

3.   Print out something to show how it changed

So far you have been printing strings, but you haven't been able to get any input from a person. You may not even know what "input" means, but type this code in anyway and make it exactly the same. In the next exercise we'll do more to explain input.

Listing 11.1: ex11.py

```
1    print("How old are you?", end=' ')
2    age = input()
3    print("How tall are you?", end=' ')
4    height = input()
5    print("How much do you weigh?", end=' ')
6    weight = input()
7
8    print(f"So, you're {age} old, {height} tall and {weight} heavy.")
```

INFO We put an end=' ' at the end of each print line. This tells print to not end the line with a newline character and go to the next line.

What You Should See

```
1    How old are you? 38
2    How tall are you? 6'2"
3    How much do you weigh? 180lbs
4    So, you're 38 old, 6'2" tall and 180lbs heavy.
```

Study Drills

1.   Go online and find out what Python's input does.

2.   Can you find other ways to use it? Try some of the samples you find.

3.   Write another "form" like this to ask some other questions.

Common Student Questions

How do I get a number from someone so I can do math?   That's a little advanced, but try `x = int(input())`, which gets the number as a string from `input()` and then converts it to an integer using `int()`.

I put my height into raw input using `input("6'2")` but it doesn't work.   You don't put your height in there; you type it directly into your Terminal. First thing is, go back and make the code exactly like mine. Next, run the script, and when it pauses, type your height in at your keyboard. That's all there is to it.

An Easier Way to Prompt

When you typed input(), you were typing the (and) characters, which are parenthesis characters. For input you can also put in a prompt to show to a person so they know what to type. Put a string that you want for the prompt inside the ( ) so that it looks like this:

```
1  y = input("Name? ")
```

This prompts the user with "Name?" and puts the result into the variable y. This is how you ask someone a question and get the answer.

This means we can completely rewrite our previous exercise using just input to do all the prompting.

Listing 12.1: ex12.py

```
1   age = input("How old are you? ")
2   height = input("How tall are you? ")
3   weight = input("How much do you weigh? ")
4
5   print(f"So, you're {age} old, {height} tall and {weight} heavy.")
```

What You Should See

```
1   How old are you?  38
2   How tall are you?  6'2"
3   How much do you weigh?  180lbs
4   So, you're 38 old, 6'2" tall and 180lbs heavy.
```

Study Drills

1. In your Jupyter cell, right-click on any print and select Show Contextual Help. This will give you quick documentation for print.

2. If you do this and the panel says "Click on a function to see documentation." then you need to run the code with SHIFT-ENTER and then click on the print() function again.

3. Next, go to Google and search for python print site:python.org to get official documentation for the Python print() function.

Common Student Questions

Why does the Contextual Help disappear?   I'm not sure, but I suspect it can't figure out what function you want documentation for while you're editing the code. Run the code and then suddenly it'll work. You can also click on any other functions in any other cell you work on.

Where does this documentation come from?   These are documentation comments added to the code itself, which is why it might be different from the online documentation. Get in the habit of studying both when you can.

Parameters, Unpacking, Variables

We're now going to take a quick detour into the world of the Terminal (aka PowerShell) version of Python. If you did Exercise 0, "Getting Started," correctly, you should have learned how to start your Terminal. If not, then simply find the program named PowerShell on Windows or Terminal on macOS. Later in this course you'll learn how to use the Terminal more extensively, but in this exercise we'll just do a tiny test.

First, I want you to create a file named ex13.py using Jupyter's new Python file:

1. On the left there's a list of the files in your directory

2. Above that list is a blue [+] button

3. Click that button, and scroll to the very bottom where there should be a button for Python File with the Python "blue and yellow snakes" logo

4. Click that button to open a new panel you can type code into

5. Right away, use your mouse to select File > Save Python File or hold CTRL and hit s (normally shown as Ctrl-S but you don't use SHIFT to get that S)

6. This will open a modal prompt that says "Rename File." Type "ex13" and it should keep the .py, but be sure that this input says ex13.py

7. Hit the blue [Rename] button to save the file in that directory

Once that file is saved, you can then type this code into the file:

Listing 13.1: ex13.py

```
1    from sys import argv
2    # read the WYSS section for how to run this
3    script, first, second, third = argv
4
5    print("The script is called:", script)
6    print("Your first variable is:", first)
7    print("Your second variable is:", second)
8    print("Your third variable is:", third)
```

I recommend you type only one or two lines of code and then do the following:

1. Save your file again. CTRL-s is the easiest way, but use the menu if you can't remember it. This time it shouldn't ask you to "rename" the file but instead should just save it.

2. Your file is now saved to your projects directory. If you remember from Exercise 0, "Getting Started," you created a directory in ~/Projects/lpythw, and when you run jupyter-lab, you first cd ~/Projects/lpythw

3.　Now start a new Terminal (aka PowerShell on Windows) and `cd ~/Projects/lpythw/` again to get a terminal there.

4.　Finally, type `python ex13.py first 2nd 3rd`. (Type this without the terminal period.) When you do, you should see *absolutely nothing*! Yes, this is *very important*. You only typed one or two lines, so there are no `print` lines in your code. That means it does not print anything, but that's good. If you get errors, then stop and figure out what you're doing wrong. Did you type that line wrong? Did you run `python ex13.py`? That is also wrong. You have to run `python ex13.py first 2nd 3rd`. (Again, type without the terminal period.)

If You Get Lost

If you're confused about where you are, use the `open` command on macOS and the `start` command on Windows. If you type this:

```
1    open .
```

on a macOS computer, it will open a window with the contents of where your Terminal is currently located. The same happens when you type:

```
1    start .
```

on Windows inside PowerShell. Doing this will help you connect your idea of "files are in folders in a window" to "files are in directories in the Terminal (PowerShell)."

If this is the first time you're seeing this advice, then go back to Exercise 0, "Getting Started," and review it as it seems you missed this important concept.

Code Description

On line 1, we have what's called an "import." This is how you add features to your script from the Python feature set. Rather than give you all the features at once, Python asks you to say what you plan to use. This keeps your programs small, but it also acts as documentation for other programmers who read your code later.

The `argv` is the "argument variable," a very standard name in programming that you will find used in many other languages. This variable *holds* the arguments you pass to your Python script when you run it. In the exercises you will get to play with this more and see what happens.

Line 3 "unpacks" `argv` so that, rather than holding all the arguments, it gets assigned to four variables you can work with: `script`, `first`, `second`, and `third`. This may look strange, but "unpack" is probably the best word to describe what it does. It just says, "Take whatever is in `argv`, unpack it, and assign it to all of these variables on the left in order."

After that we just print them out like normal.

Hold Up! Features Have Another Name

I call them "features" here (these little things you `import` to make your Python program do more), but nobody else calls them features. I just used that name because I needed to trick you into learning what they are without jargon. Before you can continue, you need to learn their real name: `modules`.

From now on we will be calling these "features" that we `import` *modules*. I'll say things like, "You want to import the sys module." They are also called "libraries" by other programmers, but let's just stick with modules.

What You Should See

WARNING! Pay attention! You have been running Python scripts without command line arguments. If you type only `python3 ex13.py`, you are doing it wrong! Pay close attention to how I run it. This applies any time you see argv being used.

When you are done typing in all of the code, it should finally run like this (and you *must* pass *three* command line arguments):

```
1    $ python ex13.py first 2nd 3rd
2    The script is called: ex13.py
3    Your first variable is: first
4    Your second variable is: 2nd
5    Your third variable is: 3rd
```

This is what you should see when you do a few different runs with different arguments:

```
1    $ python ex13.py stuff things that
2    The script is called: ex13.py
3    Your first variable is: stuff
4    Your second variable is: things
5    Your third variable is: that
```

Here's one more example showing it can be anything:

```
1    $ python ex13.py apple orange grapefruit
2    The script is called: ex13.py
3    Your first variable is: apple
4    Your second variable is: orange
5    Your third variable is: grapefruit
```

You can actually replace `first`, `second`, and `third` with any three things you want.

If you do not run it correctly, then you will get an error like this:

```
Command failed: python ex13.py first 2nd Traceback (most recent call last):
File "/Users/zedshaw/Projects/learncodethehardway.com/private/db/mod
ules/learn-python-the-hard-way-5e-section-1/code/ex13.py", line 3, in
script, first, second, third = argv ValueError: not enough values to unpack
(expected 4, got 3)
```

This happens when you do not put enough arguments on the command when you run it (in this case, just `first 2nd`). Notice that when I run it, I give it `first 2nd`, which caused it to give an error about "need more than 3 values to unpack" telling you that you didn't give it enough parameters.

Study Drills

1. Try giving fewer than three arguments to your script. See that error you get? See if you can explain it.

2. Write a script that has fewer arguments and one that has more. Make sure you give the unpacked variables good names.

3. Combine `input` with `argv` to make a script that gets more input from a user. Don't overthink it. Just use `argv` to get something, and use `input` to get something else from the user.

4. Remember that modules give you features. Modules. Modules. Remember this because we'll need it later.

Common Student Questions

When I run it, I get `ValueError: need more than 1 value to unpack`.   Remember that an important skill is paying attention to details. If you look at the *What You Should See* section, you see that I run the script with parameters on the command line. You should replicate how I ran it exactly. There's also a giant warning right there explaining the mistake you just made, so again, please pay attention.

What's the difference between `argv` **and** `input()`?   The difference has to do with where the user is required to give input. If they give your script inputs on the command line, then you use `argv`. If you want them to input using the keyboard while the script is running, then use `input()`.

Are the command line arguments strings?   Yes, they come in as strings, even if you typed numbers on the command line. Use `int()` to convert them just like with `int(input())`.

How do you use the command line?   If you want to learn it now rather than waiting, you can jump to Module 3, Exercise 38 for Windows and Exercise 39 for macOS and Linux.

I can't combine `argv` **with** `input()`.   Don't overthink it. Just slap two lines at the end of this script that uses `input()` to get something and then print it. From that, start playing with more ways to use both in the same script.

Why can't I do this `input('? ') = x`**?**   Because that's backward to how it should work. Do it the way I do it and it'll work.

Why do you want me to type one line at a time?   The biggest mistake beginners make—and professionals too—is they type a massive block of code, run it once, and then cry because of all the errors they have to fix. Errors in programming languages are awful and frequently point at the wrong locations in your source. If you're typing only a few lines at a time, you will run your code more often, and when you get an error, you know it's probably a problem with the line(s) you just typed. When you type 100 lines of code, you'll spend the next 5 days trying to find all the errors and just give up. Save yourself the trouble and just type a little at a time. It's what I—and most capable programmers—do in real life.

Prompting and Passing

Let's do an exercise that uses `argv` and `input` together to ask the user something specific. You will need this for the next exercise where you learn to read and write files. In this exercise, we'll use `input` slightly differently by having it print a simple > prompt.

Listing 14.1: ex14.py

```
1    from sys import argv
2
3    script, user_name = argv
4    prompt = '> '
5
6    print(f"Hi {user_name}, I'm the {script} script.")
7    print("I'd like to ask you a few questions.")
8    print(f"Do you like me {user_name}?")
9    likes = input(prompt)
10
11   print(f"Where do you live {user_name}?")
12   lives = input(prompt)
13
14   print("What kind of computer do you have?")
15   computer = input(prompt)
16
17   print(f"""
18   Alright, so you said {likes} about liking me.
19   You live in {lives}.  Not sure where that is.
20   And you have a {computer} computer.  Nice.
21   """)
```

We make a variable `prompt` that is set to the prompt we want, and we give that to `input` instead of typing it over and over. Now if we want to make the prompt something else, we just change it in this one spot and rerun the script. Very handy.

WARNING! Remember that you have to do the same thing you did in Exercise 13 and use the Terminal to make this work. It's important to know how to run code from the Terminal since that's a very common way to run Python code.

What You Should See

When you run this, remember that you have to give the script your name for the `argv` arguments.

```
1    $ python ex14.py zed
2    Hi zed, I'm the ex14.py script.
3    I'd like to ask you a few questions.
4    Do you like me zed?
5    > Yes
6    Where do you live zed?
7    > San Francisco
8    What kind of computer do you have?
9    > Tandy 1000
10
11   Alright, so you said Yes about liking me.
12   You live in San Francisco.  Not sure where that is.
13   And you have a Tandy 1000 computer.  Nice.
```

Study Drills

1. Find out what the games Zork and Adventure were. Try to find a copy and play them.

2. Change the `prompt` variable to something else entirely.

3. Add another argument and use it in your script, the same way you did in the previous exercise with `first, second = ARGV`.

4. Make sure you understand how I combined a `"""` style multi-line string with the `{}` format activator as the last print.

5. Try to find a way to run this in Jupyter. You will probably have to replace the code that uses `argv` with something else, like some variables.

Common Student Questions

I get `SyntaxError: invalid syntax` **when I run this script.**   Again, you have to run it right on the command line, not inside Python. If you type `python3` and then try to type `python3 ex14.py Zed`, it will fail because you are running *Python inside Python*. Close your window and then just type `python3 ex14.py Zed`.

I don't understand what you mean by changing the prompt.   See the variable `prompt = '> '`. Change that to have a different value. You know this; it's just a string and you've done 13 exercises making them, so take the time to figure it out.

I get the error `ValueError: need more than 1 value to unpack`.   Remember when I said you need to look at the *What You Should See* (WYSS) section and replicate what I did? You need to do the same thing here and focus on how I type the command in and why I have a command line argument.

How can I run this from IDLE?   Don't use IDLE. It's garbage.

Can I use double-quotes for the `prompt` **variable?**   You totally can. Go ahead and try that.

You have a Tandy computer?   I did when I was little.

I get `NameError: name 'prompt' is not defined` **when I run it.**   You either spelled the name of the `prompt` variable wrong or forgot that line. Go back and compare each line of code to mine, from at the bottom of the script to the top. Any time you see this error, it means you spelled something wrong or forgot to create the variable.

Reading Files

You know how to get input from a user with input or argv. Now you will learn about reading from a file. You may have to play with this exercise the most to understand what's going on, so do the exercise carefully and remember your checks. Working with files is an easy way to *erase your work* if you are not careful.

This exercise involves writing two files. One is the usual ex15.py file that you will run, but the *other* is named ex15_sample.txt. This second file isn't a script but a plain-text file we'll be reading in our script. Here are the contents of that file:

```
1    This is stuff I typed into a file.
2    It is really cool stuff.
3    Lots and lots of fun to have in here.
```

What we want to do is "open" that file in our script and print it out. However, we do not want to just "hard-code" the name ex15_sample.txt into our script. "Hard-coding" means putting some bit of information that should come from the user as a string directly in our source code. That's bad because we want it to load other files later. The solution is to use argv or input to ask the user what file to open instead of "hard-coding" the file's name.

Listing 15.1: ex15.py

```
1    from sys import argv
2
3    script, filename = argv
4
5    txt = open(filename)
6
7    print(f"Here's your file {filename}:")
8    print(txt.read())
9
10   print("Type the filename again:")
11   file_again = input("> ")
12
13   txt_again = open(file_again)
14
15   print(txt_again.read())
```

A few fancy things are going on in this file, so let's break it down really quickly.

Lines 1–3 uses argv to get a filename. Next we have line 5, where we use a new command: open. Right now, run pydoc open and read the instructions. Notice how, like your own scripts and input, it takes a parameter and returns a value you can set to your own variable. You just opened a file.

Line 7 prints a little message, but on line 8 we have something very new and exciting. We call a function on `txt` named `read`. What you get back from open is a `file`, and it also has commands you can give it. You give a file a command by using the . (dot or period), the name of the command, and parameters, just like with `open` and `input`. The difference is that `txt.read()` says, "Hey `txt`! Do your read command with no parameters!"

The remainder of the file is more of the same, but we'll leave the analysis to you in the *Study Drills* section.

What You Should See

WARNING! Pay attention! I said pay attention! You have been running scripts with just the name of the script, but now that you are using `argv` you have to add arguments. Look at the very first line of the following example, and you will see I do `python ex15.py ex15_sample.txt` to run it. See the extra argument `ex15_sample.txt` after the `ex15.py` script name. If you do not type that, you will get an error, so pay attention!

I made a file called `ex15_sample.txt` and ran my script.

```
1    Here's your file ex15_sample.txt:
2    This is stuff I typed into a file.
3    It is really cool stuff.
4    Lots and lots of fun to have in here.
5
6
7    Type the filename again:
8    > ex15_sample.txt
9    This is stuff I typed into a file.
10   It is really cool stuff.
11   Lots and lots of fun to have in here.
```

Study Drills

This is a big jump, so be sure you do these Study Drills as best you can before moving on.

1. Above each line, write out in English what that line does.

2. If you are not sure, ask someone for help or search online. Many times searching for "python3 THING" will find answers to what that THING does in Python. Try searching for "python3 open."

3. I used the word "commands" here, but commands are also called "functions" and "methods." You will learn about functions and methods later in the book.

4.   Get rid of the lines 10–15 where you use `input` and run the script again.

5.   Use only `input` and try the script that way. Why is one way of getting the filename better than another?

6.   Start `python3` to start the `python3` shell, and use `open` from the prompt just like in this program. Notice how you can open files and run `read` on them from within `python3`?

7.   Have your script also call `close()` on the `txt` and `txt_again` variables. It's important to close files when you are done with them.

Common Student Questions

Does `txt = open(filename)` return the contents of the file?   No, it doesn't. It actually makes something called a "file object." You can think of a file like an old tape drive that you saw on mainframe computers in the 1950s or even like a DVD player from today. You can move around inside them and then "read" them, but the DVD player is not the DVD the same way the file object is not the file's contents.

I can't type code into Terminal/PowerShell like you say in Study Drill 7.   First thing, from the command line just type `python3` and press Enter. Now you are in `python3` as we've done a few other times. Then you can type in code and Python will run it in little pieces. Play with that. To get out of it type `quit()` and hit Enter.

Why is there no error when we open the file twice?   Python will not restrict you from opening a file more than once, and sometimes this is necessary.

What does `from sys import argv` mean?   For now just understand that `sys` is a package, and this phrase just says to get the `argv` feature from that package. You'll learn more about this later.

I put the name of the file in as `script, ex15_sample.txt = argv`, but it doesn't work.   No, that's not how you do it. Make the code exactly like mine, and then run it from the command line the exact same way I do. You don't put the names of files in; you let Python put the name in.

Reading and Writing Files

If you did the Study Drills from the previous exercise, you should have seen all sorts of commands (methods/functions) you can give to files. Here's the list of commands I want you to remember:

- `close`—Closes the file. Like `File->Save` in a text editor or word processor.
- `read`—Reads the contents of the file. You can assign the result to a variable.
- `readline`—Reads just one line of a text file.
- `truncate`—Empties the file. Watch out if you care about the file.
- `write('stuff')`—Writes "stuff" to the file.
- `seek(0)`—Move the read/write location to the beginning of the file.

One way to remember what each of these does is to think of a vinyl record, cassette tape, VHS tape, DVD, or CD player. In the early days of computers data was stored on each of these kinds of media, so many of the file operations still resemble a storage system that is linear. Tape and DVD drives need to "seek" a specific spot, and then you can read or write at that spot. Today, we have operating systems and storage media that blur the lines between random access memory and disk drives, but we still use the older idea of a linear tape with a read/write head that must be moved.

For now, these are the important commands you need to know. Some of them take parameters, but we do not really care about that. You only need to remember that `write` takes a parameter of a string you want to write to the file.

Let's use some of this to make a simple little text editor:

Listing 16.1: ex16.py

```
1   filename = "test.txt"
2
3   print(f"We're going to erase {filename}.")
4   print("If you don't want that, hit CTRL-C (^C).")
5   print("If you do want that, hit RETURN.")
6
7   input("?")
8
9   print("Opening the file...")
10  target = open(filename, 'w')
11
12  print("Truncating the file.  Goodbye!")
13  target.truncate()
14
```

```
15    print("Now I'm going to ask you for three lines.")
16
17    line1 = input("line 1: ")
18    line2 = input("line 2: ")
19    line3 = input("line 3: ")
20
21    print("I'm going to write these to the file.")
22
23    target.write(line1)
24    target.write("\n")
25    target.write(line2)
26    target.write("\n")
27    target.write(line3)
28    target.write("\n")
29
30    print("And finally, we close it.")
31    target.close()
```

That's a large file, probably the largest you have typed in. So go slow, do your checks, *run it frequently,* and take it slowly. One trick is to get bits of it running at a time. Get lines 1–2 running, then two more, then a few more, until it's all done and running.

What You Should See

There are actually two things you will see. First the output of your new script:

```
1     We're going to erase test.txt.
2     If you don't want that, hit CTRL-C (^C).
3     If you do want that, hit RETURN.
4     ?
5     Opening the file...
6     Truncating the file.  Goodbye!
7     Now I'm going to ask you for three lines.
8     line 1:  Mary had a little lamb
9     line 2:  Its fleece was white as snow
10    line 3:  It was also tasty
11    I'm going to write these to the file.
12    And finally, we close it.
```

Now, open up the file you made (in my case test.txt) using the left panel of Jupyter and check it out. Neat, right?

Study Drills

1.   If you do not understand this, go back through and use the comment trick to get it squared away in your mind. One simple English comment above each line will help you understand or at least let you know what you need to research more.

2. Write a `.py` script similar to the last Exercise 14 that uses `read` (Exercise 15) and `argv` (Exercise 13) to read the file you just created. Be sure you run this in Terminal/PowerShell instead of Jupyter.

3. There's too much repetition in this file. Use strings, formats, and escapes to print out `line1`, `line2`, and `line3` with just one `target.write()` command instead of six.

4. Find out why we had to pass a `'w'` as an extra parameter to open. Hint: open tries to be safe by making you explicitly say you want to write a file.

5. If you open the file with `'w'` mode, then do you really need the `target.truncate()`? Read the documentation for Python's `open()` function and see if that's true.

Common Student Questions

Is the `truncate()` necessary with the `'w'` parameter?   See Study Drill 5.

What does `'w'` mean?   It's really just a string with a character in it for the kind of mode for the file. If you use `'w'`, then you're saying "open this file in 'write' mode," which is the reason for the `'w'` character. There's also `'r'` for "read," `'a'` for append, and modifiers on these.

What modifiers to the file modes can I use?   The most important one to know for now is the + modifier, so you can do `'w+'`, `'r+'`, and `'a+'`. This will open the file in both read and write mode and, depending on the character use, position the file in different ways.

Does just doing `open(filename)` open it in `'r'` (read) mode?   Yes, that's the default for the `open()` function.

More Files

N ow let's do a few more things with files. We'll write a Python script to copy one file to another. It'll be very short but will give you ideas about other things you can do with files.

Listing 17.1: ex17.py

```
1    from sys import argv
2    from os.path import exists
3
4    from_file = "test.txt"
5    to_file = "new_test.txt"
6
7    print(f"Copying from {from_file} to {to_file}")
8
9    # we could do these two on one line, how?
10   in_file = open(from_file)
11   indata = in_file.read()
12
13   print(f"The input file is {len(indata)} bytes long")
14
15   print(f"Does the output file exist? {exists(to_file)}")
16   print("Ready, hit RETURN to continue, CTRL-C to abort.")
17   input()
18
19   out_file = open(to_file, 'w')
20   out_file.write(indata)
21
22   print("Alright, all done.")
23
24   out_file.close()
25   in_file.close()
```

You should immediately notice that we import another handy command named exists. This returns True if a file exists, based on its name in a string as an argument. It returns False if not. We'll be using this function in the second half of this book to do lots of things, but right now you should see how you can import it.

Using import is a way to get a ton of free code other better (well, usually) programmers have written so you do not have to write it.

What You Should See

Just like your other scripts, run this one with two arguments: the file to copy from and the file to copy it to. I'm going to use a simple test file named test.txt:

```
1   Copying from test.txt to new_test.txt
2   The input file is 70 bytes long
3   Does the output file exist? True
4   Ready, hit RETURN to continue, CTRL-C to abort.
5
6   Alright, all done.
```

It should work with any file. Try a bunch more and see what happens. Just be careful you do not blast an important file.

Study Drills

1. This script is *really* annoying. There's no need to ask you before doing the copy, and it prints too much out to the screen. Try to make the script friendlier to use by removing features.

2. See how short you can make the script. I could make this one line long.

3. Find out why you had to write out_file.close() in the code.

4. Go read up on Python's import statement, and start python3 to try it out. Try importing some things and see if you can get it right. It's alright if you do not.

5. Try converting this code to an ex17.py script you can run from Terminal/PowerShell again. If you're getting tired of Jupyter's text editor, then check out one of the editors mentioned in Exercise 0, "Getting Started." You can also try any of the editors mentioned in Exercise 0 or found on the Complete Setup Page (https://learncodethehardway.com/setup/python/).

Common Student Questions

Why is the 'w' in quotes?   That's a string. You've been using strings for a while now. Make sure you know what a string is.

No way you can make this one line!   That ; depends ; on ; how ; you ; define ; one ; line ; of ; code.

Is it normal to feel like this exercise was really hard?   Yes, it is totally normal. Programming may not "click" for you until maybe even Exercise 36, or it might not until you finish the book and then make something with Python. Everyone is different, so just keep going and keep reviewing exercises that you had trouble with until it clicks. Be patient.

What does the `len()` **function do?**   It gets the length of the string that you pass to it and then returns that as a number. Play with it.

When I try to make this script shorter, I get an error when I close the files at the end.   You probably did something like this, `indata = open(from_file).read()`, which means you don't need to then do `in_file.close()` when you reach the end of the script. It should already be closed by Python once that one line runs.

I get a `Syntax:EOL while scanning string literal` **error.**   You forgot to end a string properly with a quote. Go look at that line again.

MODULE 2

The Basics of Programming

Names, Variables, Code, Functions

Big title, right? I am about to introduce you to *the function*! Dum dum dah! Every programmer will go on and on about functions and all the different ideas about how they work and what they do, but I will give you the simplest explanation you can use right now.

Functions do three things:

1. They name pieces of code the way variables name strings and numbers

2. They take arguments the way Python scripts take `argv` in Exercise 13

3. Using 1 and 2, they let you make your own "mini-scripts" or "tiny commands"

You can create an *empty* function by using the word `def` in Python like this:

Listing 18.1: ex18_demo.py

```
1    def do_nothing():
2        pass
```

This creates the function, but the `pass` keyword tells Python this function is empty. To make the function do something, you add the code for the function *under* the `def` line, but indent it four spaces:

Listing 18.2: ex18_demo.py

```
1    def do_something():
2        print("I did something!")
```

This effectively assigns the code `print("I did something!")` to the name `do_something` so you can then use it again later in your code, similar to other variables. Using a function you've defined is how you "run" it, or "call" it:

Listing 18.3: ex18_demo.py

```
1    def do_something():
2        print("I did something!")
3
4    # now we can call it by its name
5    do_something()
```

When the do_something( ) at the bottom runs, Python does the following:

1. Finds the do_something( ) function in Python's memory

2. Sees you're calling it with ( )

3. Jumps to where the def do_something( ) line is

4. Runs the lines of code *under* the def, which in this case is one line: print("I did ↳ something!")

5. When the code under the def is finished, Python exits the function and jumps back to where you called it

6. Then it continues, which in this case is the end of the code

For this exercise you need only one more concept, which is "arguments" to functions:

Listing 18.4: ex18_demo.py

```
1   def do_more_things(a, b):
2       print("A IS", a, "B IS", b)
3
4   do_more_things("hello", 1)
```

In this case, I have two arguments (also called "parameters") to the do_more_things( ) function: a and b. When I call this function using do_more_things("hello", 1), Python *temporarily* assigns a="hello" and b=1 and then calls the function. That means, inside the function a and b will have those values, and they'll disappear when the function exits. It's kind of like doing this:

Listing 18.5: ex18_demo.py

```
1   def do_more_things(a, b):
2       a = "hello"
3       b = 1
4       print("A IS", a, "B IS", b)
```

Keep in mind this is not entirely accurate, since if you called do_more_things with different arguments, the a and b would be different. It's only an example of this *one* time you call it with do_more_things ("hello", 1).

Exercise Code

Take some time right now to play around in Jupyter by making your own functions and calling them before attempting this code. Be sure you understand how your code jumps to functions and then jumps back. Then I'm going to have you make four different functions, and I'll then show you how each one is related:

Listing 18.6: ex18.py

```
1    # this one is like your scripts with argv
2    def print_two(*args):
3        arg1, arg2 = args
4        print(f"arg1: {arg1}, arg2: {arg2}")
5
6    # ok, that *args is actually pointless, we can just do this
7    def print_two_again(arg1, arg2):
8        print(f"arg1: {arg1}, arg2: {arg2}")
9
10   # this just takes one argument
11   def print_one(arg1):
12       print(f"arg1: {arg1}")
13
14   # this one takes no arguments
15   def print_none():
16       print("I got nothin'.")
17
18
19   print_two("Zed","Shaw")
20   print_two_again("Zed","Shaw")
21   print_one("First!")
22   print_none()
```

Let's break down the first function, print_two, which is the most similar to what you already know from making scripts:

1. First we tell Python we want to make a function using def for "define."

2. On the same line as def we give the function a name. In this case, we just called it "print_two", but it could also be "peanuts". It doesn't matter, except that your function should have a short name that says what it does.

3. Then we tell it we want *args (asterisk args), which is a lot like your argv parameter but for functions. This *has* to go inside ( ) parentheses to work.

4. Then we end this line with a : (colon) and start indenting.

5. After the colon all the lines that are indented four spaces will become attached to this name, print_two. Our first indented line is one that unpacks the arguments, the same as with your scripts.

6. To demonstrate how it works we print these arguments out, just like we would in a script.

The problem with print_two is that it's not the easiest way to make a function. In Python, we can skip the whole unpacking arguments and just use the names we want right inside ( ). That's what print_two_again does.

After that you have an example of how you make a function that takes one argument in print_one.

Finally you have a function that has no arguments in `print_none`.

WARNING! This is very important. Do not get discouraged right now if this doesn't quite make sense. We're going to do a few exercises linking functions to your scripts and show you how to make more. For now, just keep thinking "mini-script" when I say "function" and keep playing with them.

What You Should See

If you run `ex18.py`, you should see:

```
1    arg1: Zed, arg2: Shaw
2    arg1: Zed, arg2: Shaw
3    arg1: First!
4    I got nothin'.
```

Right away you can see how a function works. Notice that you used your functions the way you use things like `exists`, `open`, and other "commands." In fact, I've been tricking you because in Python those "commands" are just functions. This means you can make your own commands and use them in your scripts too.

Study Drills

Create a *function checklist* for later exercises. Write these checks on an index card and keep it by you while you complete the rest of these exercises or until you feel you do not need the index card anymore:

1. Did you start your function definition with `def`?

2. Does your function name have only characters and _ (underscore) characters?

3. Did you put ((an open parenthesis) right after the function name?

4. Did you put your arguments after ((the open parenthesis) separated by commas?

5. Did you make each argument unique (meaning no duplicated names)?

6. Did you put): (a close parenthesis and a colon) after the arguments?

7. Did you indent all lines of code you want in the function four spaces? No more, no less

8. Did you "end" your function by going back to writing with no indent ("dedenting" we call it)?

When you run ("use" or "call") a function, check these things:

1. Did you call/use/run this function by typing its name?

2.   Did you put the (character after the name to run it?

3.   Did you put the values you want into the parentheses separated by commas?

4.   Did you end the function call with a) character?

Use these two checklists on the remaining lessons until you do not need them anymore.

Finally, repeat this a few times to yourself:

```
1    "To 'run,' 'call,' or 'use' a function all mean the same thing."
```

Common Student Questions

What's allowed for a function name?   The same as variable names. Anything that doesn't start with a number and is letters, numbers, and underscores will work.

What does the * in *args do?   That tells Python to take all the arguments to the function and then put them in args as a list. It's like argv that you've been using but for functions. It's not normally used too often unless specifically needed.

This feels really boring and monotonous.   That's good. It means you're starting to get better at typing in the code and understanding what it does. To make it less boring, take everything I tell you to type in, and then break it on purpose.

Functions and Variables

You're now going to combine functions with what you know of variables from previous exercises. As you know, a variable gives a piece of data a name so you can use it in your program. If you have this code:

```
1    x = 10
```

then you created a piece of data named x that is equal to the number 10.

You also know that you can define (create) functions with parameters like this:

```
1    def print_one(arg1):
2        print(f"arg1: {arg1}")
```

The parameter arg1 is a variable similar to the x before, except it's created for you when you *call* the function like this:

```
1    print_one("First!")
```

In Exercise 18, you learned how Python runs functions when you call them, but what happens if you did this:

```
1    y = "First!"
2    print_one(y)
```

Instead of calling print_one directly with "First!" you're assigning "First!" to y and *then* passing y to print_one. Does this work? Here's a small sample code you can use to test this out in Jupyter:

```
1    def print_one(arg1):
2        print(f"arg1: {arg1}")
3
4    y = "First!"
5    print_one(y)
```

This shows how you can combine the concept of variables y = "First!" with calling functions that use the variables. Study this and try your own variations before working on this longer exercise, but first a bit of advice:

1. This one is long, so if you find it difficult to manage in Jupyter, then try typing it into an ex19.py file to run in Terminal.

2. As usual, you should type only a few lines at a time, but you'll have problems if you type only the first line of a function. You can solve this by using the pass keyword like this:

> `def some_func(some_arg): pass`. The `pass` word is how you make an empty function without causing an error.

3. If you want to see what each function is doing, you can use "debug printing" like this: `print (">>>> I'm here", something)`. That will print out a message to help you "trace" through the code and see what `something` is in each function.

Listing 19.1: ex19.py

```
 1  def cheese_and_crackers(cheese_count, boxes_of_crackers):
 2      print(f"You have {cheese_count} cheeses!")
 3      print(f"You have {boxes_of_crackers} boxes of crackers!")
 4      print("Man that's enough for a party!")
 5      print("Get a blanket.\n")
 6
 7
 8  print("We can just give the function numbers directly:")
 9  cheese_and_crackers(20, 30)
10
11
12  print("OR, we can use variables from our script:")
13  amount_of_cheese = 10
14  amount_of_crackers = 50
15
16  cheese_and_crackers(amount_of_cheese, amount_of_crackers)
17
18
19  print("We can even do math inside too:")
20  cheese_and_crackers(10 + 20, 5 + 6)
21
22
23  print("And we can combine the two, variables and math:")
24  cheese_and_crackers(amount_of_cheese + 100, amount_of_crackers + 1000)
```

What You Should See

```
 1  We can just give the function numbers directly:
 2  You have 20 cheeses!
 3  You have 30 boxes of crackers!
 4  Man that's enough for a party!
 5  Get a blanket.
 6
 7  OR, we can use variables from our script:
 8  You have 10 cheeses!
 9  You have 50 boxes of crackers!
10  Man that's enough for a party!
11  Get a blanket.
12
```

```
13    We can even do math inside too:
14    You have 30 cheeses!
15    You have 11 boxes of crackers!
16    Man that's enough for a party!
17    Get a blanket.
18
19    And we can combine the two, variables and math:
20    You have 110 cheeses!
21    You have 1050 boxes of crackers!
22    Man that's enough for a party!
23    Get a blanket.
```

Study Drills

1. Did you remember to type only a few lines at a time? Did you use pass to make an empty function before filling it? If not, delete your code and do it again.

2. Change the name of cheese_and_crackers to have a spelling mistake and view the error message. Now fix it.

3. Delete one of the + symbols in the math to see what error you get.

4. Make changes to the math and then try to predict what output you'll get.

5. Change the variables and try to guess the output with those changes.

Common Student Questions

This exercise has no questions yet, but you can ask me at help@learncodethehardway.org to get help. Maybe your question will show up here.

Functions and Files

R emember your checklist for functions, and then do this exercise paying close attention to how functions and files can work together to make useful stuff. You should also continue to type only a few lines before running your code. If you catch yourself typing too many lines, then delete them and do it again. Doing this uses python to train your understanding of Python.

Here's the code for this exercise. Once again, it's long, so if you find Jupyter is difficult to use, then write a ex20.py file and run it that way.

Listing 20.1: ex20.py

```
1   from sys import argv
2
3   input_file = "ex20_test.txt"
4
5   def print_all(f):
6       print(f.read())
7
8   def rewind(f):
9       f.seek(0)
10
11  def print_a_line(line_count, f):
12      print(line_count, f.readline())
13
14  current_file = open(input_file)
15
16  print("First let's print the whole file:\n")
17
18  print_all(current_file)
19
20  print("Now let's rewind, kind of like a tape.")
21
22  rewind(current_file)
23
24  print("Let's print three lines:")
25
26  current_line = 1
27  print_a_line(current_line, current_file)
28
29  current_line = current_line + 1
30  print_a_line(current_line, current_file)
31
32  current_line = current_line + 1
33  print_a_line(current_line, current_file)
```

Pay close attention to how we pass in the current line number each time we run `print_a_line`. There's nothing new in this exercise. It has functions, and you know those. It has files and you know those too. Just take your time with it and you'll get it.

You'll also need a file named `ex20_test.txt` with the following contents:

```
1    This is line 1
2    This is line 2
3    This is line 3
```

You can use Jupyter to create this file so that it's in the same directory where you're working and then your Python code should load it.

What You Should See

```
1    First let's print the whole file:
2
3    This is line 1
4    This is line 2
5    This is line 3
6
7    Now let's rewind, kind of like a tape.
8    Let's print three lines:
9    1 This is line 1
10
11   2 This is line 2
12
13   3 This is line 3
```

Study Drills

1. Write English comments for each line to understand what that line does.

2. Each time `print_a_line` is run, you are passing in a variable `current_line`. Write out what `current_line` is equal to on each function call, and trace how it becomes `line_count` in `print_a_line`.

3. Find each place a function is used, and check its `def` to make sure that you are giving it the right arguments.

4. Research online what the `seek()` function for `file` does. Try `pydoc file`, and see if you can figure it out from there. Then try `pydoc file.seek` to see what `seek` does.

5. Research the shorthand notation `+=`, and rewrite the script to use `+=` instead.

6. Can you convert this to a Terminal (command line) script that uses `argv` like in Exercise 14?

Common Student Questions

What is f **in the** `print_all` **and other functions?** The f is a variable just like you had in other functions in Exercise 18, except this time it's a file. A file in Python is kind of like an old tape drive on a mainframe or maybe a DVD player. It has a "read head," and you can "seek" this read head around the file to a position and then work with it there. Each time you do `f.seek(0)` you're moving to the start of the file. Each time you do `f.readline()` you're reading a line from the file and moving the read head to the right after the \n that ends that line. This will be explained more as you go on.

Why does `seek(0)` **not set the** `current_line` **to 0?** First, the `seek()` function is dealing in *bytes*, not lines. The code `seek(0)` moves the file to the 0 byte (first byte) in the file. Second, `current_line` is just a variable and has no real connection to the file at all. We are manually incrementing it.

What is +=? You know how in English I can rewrite "it is" as "it's"? Or I can rewrite "you are" as "you're"? In English this is called a "contraction," and this is kind of like a contraction for the two operations = and +. That means x = x + y is the same as x += y.

How does `readline()` **know where each line is?** Inside `readline()` is code that scans each byte of the file until it finds a \n character and then stops reading the file to return what it found so far. The file f is responsible for maintaining the current position in the file after each `readline()` call so that it will keep reading each line.

Why are there empty lines between the lines in the file? The `readline()` function returns the \n that's in the file at the end of that line. Add an end = "" at the end of your `print()` function calls to avoid adding double \n to every line.

Functions Can Return Something

Y ou have been using the = character to name variables and set them to numbers or strings. We're now going to blow your mind again by showing you how to use = and a new Python word `return` to set variables to be a *value from a function*. There will be one thing to pay close attention to, but first type this in:

Listing 21.1: ex21.py

```python
1   def add(a, b):
2       print(f"ADDING {a} + {b}")
3       return a + b
4
5   def subtract(a, b):
6       print(f"SUBTRACTING {a} - {b}")
7       return a - b
8
9   def multiply(a, b):
10      print(f"MULTIPLYING {a} * {b}")
11      return a * b
12
13  def divide(a, b):
14      print(f"DIVIDING {a} / {b}")
15      return a / b
16
17
18  print("Let's do some math with just functions!")
19
20  age = add(30, 5)
21  height = subtract(78, 4)
22  weight = multiply(90, 2)
23  iq = divide(100, 2)
24
25  print(f"Age: {age}, Height: {height}, Weight: {weight}, IQ: {iq}")
26
27
28  # A puzzle for the extra credit, type it in anyway.
29  print("Here is a puzzle.")
30
31  what = add(age, subtract(height, multiply(weight, divide(iq, 2))))
32
33  print("That becomes: ", what, "Can you do it by hand?")
```

We are now doing our own math functions for add, subtract, multiply, and divide. The important thing to notice is the last line where we say return a + b (in add). What this does is the following:

1. Our function is called with two arguments: a and b

2. We print out what our function is doing, in this case "ADDING."

3. Then we tell Python to do something kind of backward: we return the addition of a + b. You might say this as, "I add a and b and then return them."

4. Python adds the two numbers. Then when the function ends, any line that runs it will be able to assign this a + b result to a variable.

As with many other things in this book, you should take this really slowly, break it down, and try to trace what's going on. To help there is extra credit to solve a puzzle and learn something cool.

What You Should See

```
1    Let's do some math with just functions!
2    ADDING 30 + 5
3    SUBTRACTING 78 − 4
4    MULTIPLYING 90 * 2
5    DIVIDING 100 / 2
6    Age: 35, Height: 74, Weight: 180, IQ: 50.0
7    Here is a puzzle.
8    DIVIDING 50.0 / 2
9    MULTIPLYING 180 * 25.0
10   SUBTRACTING 74 − 4500.0
11   ADDING 35 + −4426.0
12   That becomes: −4391.0 Can you do it by hand?
```

Study Drills

1. If you aren't really sure what return does, try writing a few of your own functions and have them return some values. You can return anything that you can put to the right of an =.

2. At the end of the script is a puzzle. I'm taking the return value of one function and *using* it as the argument of another function. I'm doing this in a chain so that I'm kind of creating a formula using the functions. It looks really weird, but if you run the script, you can see the results. What you should do is try to figure out the normal formula that would re-create this same set of operations.

3. Once you have the formula worked out for the puzzle, get in there and see what happens when you modify the parts of the functions. Try to change it on purpose to make another value.

4. Do the inverse. Write a simple formula and use the functions in the same way to calculate it.

This exercise might really wreck your brain, but take it slow and and treat it like a little game. Figuring out puzzles like this is what makes programming fun, so I'll be giving you more little problems like this as we go.

Common Student Questions

Why does Python print the formula or the functions "backward"? It's not really backward, it's "inside out." You'll see how it works when you start breaking down the function into separate formulas and functions. Try to understand what I mean by "inside out" rather than "backward."

How can I use `input()` **to enter my own values?** Remember `int(input())`? The problem with that is then you can't enter floating point, so also try using `float(input())` instead.

What do you mean by "write out a formula"? Try `24 + 34 / 100 — 1023` as a start. Convert that to use the functions. Now come up with your own similar math equation, and use variables so it's more like a formula.

Strings, Bytes, and Character Encodings

To do this exercise you'll need to *download* a text file that I've written named languages.txt. This file was created with a list of human languages to demonstrate a few interesting concepts:

- How modern computers store human languages for display and processing and how Python 3 calls these strings

- How you must "encode" and "decode" Python's strings into a type called bytes

- How to handle errors in your string and byte handling

- How to read code and find out what it means even if you've never seen it before

You can get this file by doing a right click with your mouse and selecting "Download" to download the file reliably. Use the link https://learnpythonthehardway.org/python3/languages.txt to download the file.

In addition, you'll get a brief glimpse of the Python 3 if-statement and lists for processing a list of things. You don't have to master this code or understand these concepts right away. You'll get plenty of practice in later exercises. For now your job is to get a taste of the future and learn the four topics in the preceding list.

WARNING! This exercise is hard! There's a lot of information in it that you need to understand, and it's information that goes deep into computers. This exercise is complex because Python's strings are complex and difficult to use. I recommend you take this exercise painfully slow. Write down every word you don't understand, and look it up or research it. Take a paragraph at a time if you must. You can continue with other exercises while you study this one, so don't get stuck here. Just chip away at it for as long as it takes.

Initial Research

You will create a file named ex22.py and run it in the shell for this exercise. Be sure you know how to do that, and if not, revisit Exercise 0 where you learned how to run Python code from the Terminal.

I'm going to teach you how to research a piece of code to expose its secrets. You'll need the languages.↳ txt file for this code to work, so make sure you download it first. The languages.txt file simply contains a list of human language names that are encoded in UTF-8.

Listing 22.1: ex22.py

```
1    import sys
2    script, input_encoding, error = sys.argv
3
4
5    def main(language_file, encoding, errors):
6        line = language_file.readline()
7
8        if line:
9            print_line(line, encoding, errors)
10           return main(language_file, encoding, errors)
11
12
13   def print_line(line, encoding, errors):
14       next_lang = line.strip()
15       raw_bytes = next_lang.encode(encoding, errors=errors)
16       cooked_string = raw_bytes.decode(encoding, errors=errors)
17
18       print(raw_bytes, "<===>", cooked_string)
19
20
21   languages = open("languages.txt", encoding="utf-8")
22
23   main(languages, input_encoding, error)
```

Try to study this code by writing down each thing you don't recognize, and then search for it with the usual python THING site:python.org. For example, if you don't know what encode( ) does, then search for python encode site:python.org. Once you've read the documentation for everything you don't know, continue with this exercise.

Once you have that you'll want to run this Python script in your shell to play with it. Here are some example commands I used to test it:

```
1    python ex22.py "utf-8" "strict"
2    python ex22.py "utf-8" "ignore"
3    python ex22.py "utf-8" "replace"
```

See the documentation for the str.encode( ) function for more options.

WARNING! You'll notice I'm using images here to show you what you should see. After extensive testing it turns out that so many people have their computers configured to not display utf-8 that I had to use images so you'll know what to expect. Even my own typesetting system (LaTeX) couldn't handle these encodings, forcing me to use images instead. If you don't see this, then your Terminal is most likely not able to display utf-8, and you should try to fix that.

These examples use the `utf-8`, `utf-16`, and `big5` encodings to demonstrate the conversion and the types of errors you can get. Each of these names are called a "codec" in Python 3, but you use the parameter "encoding". At the end of this exercise, there's a list of the available encodings if you want to try more. I'll cover what all of this output means shortly. You're only trying to get an idea of how this works so we can talk about it.

After you've run it a few times, go through your list of symbols and make a guess as to what they do. When you've written down your guesses, try looking the symbols up online to see if you can confirm your hypothesis. Don't worry if you have no idea how to search for them. Just give it a try.

Switches, Conventions, and Encodings

Before I can get into what this code means, you need to learn some basics about how data is stored in a computer. Modern computers are incredibly complex, but at their core they are like a huge array of light switches. Computers use electricity to flip switches on or off. These switches can represent 1 for on, and 0 for off. In the old days there were all kinds of weird computers that did more than just 1 or 0, but these days it's just 1s and 0s. One represents energy, electricity, on, power, substance. Zero represents off, done, gone, power down, the lack of energy. We call these 1s and 0s "bits."

Now, a computer that lets you work only with 1 and 0 would be both horribly inefficient and incredibly annoying. Computers take these 1s and 0s and use them to encode larger numbers. At the small end a computer will use 8 of these 1s and 0s to encode 256 numbers (0–255). What does "encode" mean though? It's nothing more than an agreed upon standard for how a sequence of bits should represent a number. It's a convention humans picked or stumbled on that says that `00000000` would be 0, `11111111` would be 255, and `00001111` would be 15. There were even huge wars in the early history of computers on nothing more than the order of these bits because they were simply conventions we all had to agree on.

Today we call a "byte" a sequence of 8 bits (1s and 0s). In the old days everyone had their own convention for a byte, so you'll still run into people who think that this term should be flexible and handle sequences of 9 bits, 7 bits, 6 bits, but now we just say it's 8 bits. That's our convention, and that convention defines our encoding for a byte. There are further conventions for encoding large numbers using 16, 32, 64, and even more bits if you get into really big math. There are entire standards groups who do nothing but argue about these conventions and then implement them as encodings that eventually turn switches on and off.

Once you have bytes, you can start to store and display text by deciding on another convention for how a number maps to a letter. In the early days of computing there were many conventions that mapped 8 or 7 bits (or less or more) onto lists of characters kept inside a computer. The most popular convention ended up being American Standard Code for Information Interchange, or ASCII. This standard maps a number to a letter. The number 90 is Z, which in bits is `1011010`, which gets mapped to the ASCII table inside the computer.

You can try this out in Python right now:

```
1    >>> 0b1011010
2    90
3    >>> ord('Z')
4    90
5    >>> chr(90)
6    'Z'
7    >>>
```

First, I write the number 90 in binary, then I get the number based on the letter Z, then I convert the number to the letter Z. Don't worry about needing to remember this though. I think I've had to do it twice the entire time I've used Python.

Once we have the ASCII convention for encoding a character using 8 bits (a byte), we can then "string" them together to make a word. If I want to write my name "Zed A. Shaw," I just use a sequence of bytes that is [90, 101, 100, 32, 65, 46, 32, 83, 104, 97, 119]. Most of the early text in computers was nothing more than sequences of bytes, stored in memory, that a computer used to display text to a person. Again, this is just a sequence of conventions that turned switches on and off.

The problem with ASCII is that it only encodes English and maybe a few other similar languages. Remember that a byte can hold 256 numbers (0–255, or 00000000–11111111). Turns out, there are *many* more characters than 256 used throughout the world's languages. Different countries created their own encoding conventions for their languages, and that mostly worked, but many encodings could handle only one language. That meant if you want to put the title of an American English book in the middle of a Thai sentence, you were kind of in trouble. You'd need one encoding for Thai and another for English.

To solve this problem a group of people created Unicode. It sounds like "encode," and it is meant to be a "universal encoding" of all human languages. The solution Unicode provides is like the ASCII table, but it's huge by comparison. You can use 32 bits to encode a Unicode character, and that is more characters than we could possibly find. A 32-bit number means we can store 4,294,967,295 characters (2^32), which is enough space for every possible human language and probably a lot of alien ones too. Right now we use the extra space for important things like poop and smile emojis.

We now have a convention for encoding any character we want, but 32 bits is 4 bytes (32/8 == 4), which means there is so much wasted space in most text we want to encode. We can also use 16 bits (2 bytes), but still there's going to be wasted space in most text. The solution is to use a clever convention to encode most common characters using 8 bits and then "escape" into larger numbers when we need to encode more characters. That means we have one more convention that is nothing more than a compression encoding, making it possible for most common characters to use 8 bits and then escape out into 16 or 32 bits as needed.

The convention for encoding text in Python is called "utf-8", which means "Unicode Transformation Format 8 Bits." It is a convention for encoding Unicode characters into sequences of bytes (which are sequences of bits (which turn sequences of switches on and off)). You can also use other conventions (encodings), but utf-8 is the current standard.

Dissecting the Output

We can now look at the output of the previous commands. Let's take just that first command and the first few lines of output:

```
$ python ex22.py "utf-8" "strict"
b'Afrikaans' <===> Afrikaans
b'\xe1\x8a\xa0\xe1\x88\x9b\xe1\x88\xad\xe1\x8a\x9b' <===> ኦሮሟ
b'\xd0\x90\xd2\xa7\xd1\x81\xd1\x88\xd3\x99\xd0\xb0' <===> Аҧсшәа
b'\xd8\xa7\xd9\x84\xd8\xb9\xd8\xb1\xd8\xa8\xd9\x8a\xd8\xa9' <===> العربية
b'Aragon\xc3\xa9s' <===> Aragonés
b'Arpetan' <===> Arpetan
b'Az\xc9\x99rbaycanca' <===> Azərbaycanca
b'Bamanankan' <===> Bamanankan
b'\xe0\xa6\xac\xe0\xa6\xbe\xe0\xa6\x82\xe0\xa6\xb2\xe0\xa6\xbe' <===> বাংলা
b'B\xc3\xa2n-l\xc3\xa2m-g\xc3\xba' <===> Bân-lâm-gú
b'\xd0\x91\xd0\xb5\xd0\xbb\xd0\xb0\xd1\x80\xd1\x83\xd1\x81\xd0\xba\xd0\xb0\xd1\x8f' <===> Беларуская
b'\xd0\x91\xd1\x8a\xd0\xbb\xd0\xb3\xd0\xb0\xd1\x80\xd1\x81\xd0\xba\xd0\xb8' <===> Български
b'Boarisch' <===> Boarisch
b'Bosanski' <===> Bosanski
b'\xd0\x91\xd1\x83\xd1\x80\xd1\x8f\xd0\xb0\xd0\xb4' <===> Буряад
```

The ex22.py script is taking bytes written inside the b'' (byte string) and converting them to the UTF-8 (or other) encoding you specified. On the left are the numbers for each byte of the utf-8 (shown in hexadecimal), and the right has the character output as actual utf-8. The way to think of this is on the left side of <===> are the Python numerical bytes, or the "raw" bytes Python uses to store the string. You specify this with b'' to tell Python this is "bytes". These raw bytes are then displayed "cooked" on the right so you can see the real characters in your Terminal.

Dissecting the Code

We have an understanding of strings and byte sequences. In Python, a string is a UTF-8 encoded sequence of characters for displaying or working with text. The bytes are then the "raw" sequence of bytes that Python uses to store this UTF-8 string and start with a b' to tell Python you are working with raw bytes. This is all based on conventions for how Python wants to work with text. Here's a Python session showing me encoding strings and decoding bytes:

```
[2]: raw_bytes = b'\xe6\x96\x87\xe8\xa8\x80'
     raw_bytes.decode()

[2]: '文言'

[3]: utf_string = '文言'
     utf_string.encode()

[3]: b'\xe6\x96\x87\xe8\xa8\x80'

[4]: raw_bytes == utf_string.encode()

[4]: True

[6]: utf_string == raw_bytes.decode()

[6]: True
```

All you need to remember is if you have raw bytes, then you must use `.decode()` to get the `string`. Raw `bytes` have no convention to them. They are just sequences of bytes with no meaning other than numbers, so you must tell Python to "decode this into a utf string." If you have a string and want to send it, store it, share it, or do some other operation, then usually it'll work, but sometimes Python will throw up an error saying it doesn't know how to "encode" it. Again, Python knows its internal convention, but it has no idea what convention you need. In that case, you must use `.encode()` to get the bytes you need.

The way to remember this (even though I look it up almost every time) is to remember the mnemonic "DBES," which stands for "Decode Bytes Encode Strings." I say "dee bess" in my head when I have to convert bytes and strings. When you have `bytes` and need a `string`, "Decode Bytes." When you have a string and need bytes, "Encode Strings."

With that in mind, let's break down the code in `ex22.py` line by line:

1-2   I start with your usual command line argument handling that you already know.

5   I start the main meat of this code in a function conveniently called `main`. This will be called at the end of this script to get things going.

6   The first thing this function does is read one line from the languages file it is given. You have done this before, so there's nothing new here. Just `readline` as before when dealing with text files.

8   Now I use something *new*. You will learn about this in the second half of the book, so consider this a teaser of interesting things to come. This is an `if-statement`, and it lets you make decisions in your Python code. You can "test" the truth of a variable and, based on that truth, run a piece of code or not run it. In this case, I'm testing whether `line` has something in it. The `readline()` function will return an empty string when it reaches the end of the file and `if line` simply tests for this empty string. As long as `readline` gives us something, this will be true, and the code *under* (indented in, lines 9–10) will run. When this is false, Python will skip lines 9–10.

9   I then call a separate function to do the actual printing of this line. This simplifies my code and makes it easier for me to understand it. If I want to learn what this function does, I can jump to it and study. Once I know what `print_line` does, I can attach my memory to the name `print_line` and forget about the details.

10   I have written a tiny yet powerful piece of magic here. I am calling `main` again inside `main`. Actually, it's not magic since nothing really is magical in programming. All the information you need is there. This looks like I am calling the function *inside* itself, which seems like it should be illegal to do. Ask yourself, why should that be illegal? There's no technical reason why I can't call any function I want right there, even this `main()` function. If a function is simply a jump to the top where I've named it `main`, then calling this function at the end of itself would ... jump back to the top and run it again. That would make it loop. Now look back at line 8, and you'll see the `if-statement` keeps this function from looping forever. Carefully study this because it is a significant concept, but don't worry if you can't grasp it right away.

13   I now start the definition for the `print_line()` function, which does the actual encoding of each line from the `languages.txt` file.

14   This is a simple stripping of the trailing `\n` on the `line` string.

15   Now I *finally* take the language I've received from the `languages.txt` file and "encode" it into the raw bytes. Remember the "DBES" mnemonic. "Decode Bytes, Encode Strings." The `next_lang` variable is a string, so to get the raw bytes I must call `.encode()` on it to "Encode Strings." I pass to `encode()` the encoding I want and how to handle errors.

16   I then do the extra step of showing the inverse of line 15 by creating a `cooked_string` variable from the `raw_bytes`. Remember, "DBES" says I "Decode Bytes," and `raw_bytes` is `bytes`, so I call `.decode()` on it to get a Python `string`. This string should be the same as the `next_lang` variable.

18   Then I simply print them both out to show you what they look like.

21   I'm done defining functions, so now I want to open the `languages.txt` file.

23   The end of the script simply runs the `main()` function with all the correct parameters to get everything going and kick-start the loop. Remember that this then jumps to where the `main()` function is defined on line 5, and on line 10 `main` is called again, causing this to keep looping. The `if line:` on line 8 will prevent our loop from going forever.

Encodings Deep Dive

We can now use our little script to explore other encodings. Here's me playing with different encodings and seeing how to break them:

```
$ python ex22.py "utf-16" "strict"
b'\xff\xfeA\x00f\x00r\x00i\x00k\x00a\x00a\x00n\x00s\x00' <===> Afrikaans
b'\xff\xfe\xa0\x12\x1b\x12-\x12\x9b\x12' <===> አማርኛ
b'\xff\xfe\x10\x04\xa7\x04A\x04H\x04\xd9\x04@\x04' <===> Аҧсшәа
b"\xff\xfe'\x06D\x069\x061\x06(\x06J\x06)\x06" <===> العربية
...

$ python ex22.py "big5" "strict"
b'Afrikaans' <===> Afrikaans
Traceback (most recent call last):
  # cut the stack trace
UnicodeEncodeError: 'big5' codec can't encode character '\u12a0' in position 0: illegal multibyte sequence
$
```

First, I'm doing a simple UTF-16 encoding so you can see how it changes compared to UTF-8. You can also use "utf-32" to see how that's even bigger and get an idea of the space saved with UTF-8. After that I try Big5, and you'll see that Python does *not* like that at all. It throws up an error that "big5" can't encode some of the characters at position 0 (which is super helpful). One solution is to tell Python to "replace" any bad characters for the Big5 encoding. Try that and you'll see it puts a ? character wherever it finds a character that doesn't match the Big5 encoding system.

Breaking It

Rough ideas include the following:

1. Find strings of text encoded in other encodings and place them in the ex22.py file to see how it breaks.

2. Find out what happens when you give an encoding that doesn't exist.

3. Extra challenging: Rewrite this using the b'' bytes instead of the UTF-8 strings, effectively reversing the script.

4. If you can do that, then you can also *break* these bytes by removing some to see what happens. How much do you need to remove to cause Python to break? How much can you remove to damage the string output but pass Python's decoding system?

5. Use what you learned from #4 to see if you can mangle the files. What errors do you get? How much damage can you cause and get the file past Python's decoding system?

Introductory Lists

Most programming languages have some way to store data inside the computer. Some languages only have raw memory locations, but programmers easily make mistakes when that's the case. In modern languages you're provided with some core ways to store data called "data structures." A data structure takes pieces of data (integers, strings, and even other data structures) and organizes them in some useful way. In this exercise we'll learn about the sequence style of data structures called a "list" or "Array" depending on the language.

Python's simplest sequence data structure is the list, which is an ordered list of things. You can access the elements of a list randomly, in order, extend it, shrink it, and do most anything else you could do to a sequence of things in real life.

You make a list like this:

```
1    fruit = ["apples", "oranges", "grapes"];
```

That's all. Just put [(left-square-bracket) and] (right-square-bracket) around the list of things and separate them with commas. You can also put anything you want into a list, even other lists:

```
1    inventory = [ ["Buick", 10], ["Corvette", 1], ["Toyota", 4]];
```

In this code I have a list, and that list has three lists inside it. Each of those lists then has a name of a car type and the count of inventory. Study this and make sure you can take it apart when you read it. Storing lists inside lists inside other data structures is very common.

Accessing Elements of a List

What if you want the first element of the inventory list? How about the number of Buick cars you have on inventory? You do this:

```
1    # get the buick record
2    buicks = inventory[0]
3    buick_count = buicks[1]
4    # or in one move
5    count_of_buicks = inventory[0][1]
```

In the first two lines of code (after the comment), I do a two-step process. I use the inventory[0] code to get the *first* element. If you're not familiar with programming languages, most start at 0, not 1, as that makes math work better in most situations. The use of [ ] right after a variable name tells Python that this is a "container thing" and says we want to "index into this thing with this value," in this case 0. In the next line, I take the buicks[1] element and get the count 10 from it.

You don't have to do that though as you can chain the uses of [ ] in a sequence so that you dive deeper into a list as you go. In the last line of code, I do that with inventory[0][1], which says "get the 0 element and then get the 1 element of *that*."

Here's where you're going to make a mistake. The second [1] does not mean to get the entire ["Buick", ↳ 10]. It's not linear, it's "recursive," meaning it dives into the structure. You are getting 10 in ["Buick", ↳ 10]. It is more accurately just a combination of the first two lines of code.

Practicing Lists

Lists are simple enough, but you need practice accessing different parts of very complicated lists. It's important that you can *correctly* understand how an index into a nested list will work. The best way to do that is to drill using such a list in Jupyter.

How this works is I have a series of lists in the following code. You are to type this code in like normal, and then you have to use Python to access the elements so you get the same answers as I do.

The Code

To complete this challenge you need this code:

Listing 23.1: ex23.py

```
1    fruit = [
2        ['Apples', 12, 'AAA'], ['Oranges', 1, 'B'],
3        ['Pears', 2, 'A'], ['Grapes', 14, 'UR']]
4
5    cars = [
6        ['Cadillac', ['Black', 'Big', 34500]],
7        ['Corvette', ['Red', 'Little', 1000000]],
8        ['Ford', ['Blue', 'Medium', 1234]],
9        ['BMW', ['White', 'Baby', 7890]]
10   ]
11
12   languages = [
13       ['Python', ['Slow', ['Terrible', 'Mush']]],
14       ['JavaScript', ['Moderate', ['Alright', 'Bizarre']]],
15       ['Perl6', ['Moderate', ['Fun', 'Weird']]],
16       ['C', ['Fast', ['Annoying', 'Dangerous']]],
17       ['Forth', ['Fast', ['Fun', 'Difficult']]],
18   ]
```

It's fine to copy-paste this code since the point of this exercise is learning how to access data, but if you want extra practice typing Python, then enter it in manually.

The Challenge

I will give you a `list` name and a piece of data in the `list`. Your job is to figure out what indexes you need to get that information. For example, if I tell you `fruit 'AAA'`, then your answer is `fruit[0][2]`. You should attempt to do this in your head by looking at the code and then test your guess in the Jupyter.

Fruit Challenge

You need to get all of these elements out of the `fruit` variable:

- 12
- 'AAA'
- 2
- 'Oranges'
- 'Grapes'
- 14
- 'Apples'

Cars Challenge

You need to get all of these elements out of the `cars` variable:

- 'Big'
- 'Red'
- 1234
- 'White'
- 7890
- 'Black'
- 34500
- 'Blue'

Languages Challenge

You need to get all of these elements out of the `languages` variable:

- 'Slow'

- 'Alright'

- 'Dangerous'

- 'Fast'

- 'Difficult'

- 'Fun'

- 'Annoying'

- 'Weird'

- 'Moderate'

Final Challenge

You now have to figure out what this code spells out:

```
1    cars[1][1][1]
2    cars[1][1][0]
3    cars[1][0]
4    cars[3][1][1]
5    fruit[3][2]
6    languages[0][1][1][1]
7    fruit[2][1]
8    languages[3][1][0]
```

Don't attempt to run this in Jupyter first. Instead, try to work out manually what each line will spell out, and then test it in Jupyter.

Introductory Dictionaries

I n this exercise, we'll use the same data from the previous exercise on lists and use it to learn about Dictionaries or dicts.

Key/Value Structures

You use key=value data all the time without realizing it. When you read an email, you might have:

```
1    From: j.smith@example.com
2    To: zed.shaw@example.com
3    Subject: I HAVE AN AMAZING INVESTMENT FOR YOU!!!
```

On the left are the keys (From, To, Subject), which are *mapped* to the contents on the right of the :. Programmers say the key is "mapped" to the value, but they could also say "set to" as in, "I set From to j.smith@example.com." In Python, I might write this same email using a data object like this:

```
1    email = {
2        "From": "j.smith@example.com",
3        "To": "zed.shaw@example.com",
4        "Subject": "I HAVE AN AMAZING INVESTMENT FOR YOU!!!"
5    };
```

You create a data object by:

1. Opening it with a { (curly-brace)

2. Writing the key, which is a string here, but can be numbers, or almost anything

3. Writing a : (colon)

4. Writing the value, which can be anything that's valid in Python

Once you do that, you can access this Python email like this:

```
1    email["From"]
2    'j.smith@example.com'
3
4    email["To"]
5    'zed.shaw@example.com'
6
7    email["Subject"]
8    'I HAVE AN AMAZING INVESTMENT FOR YOU!!!'
```

The only difference from `list` indexes is that you use a string (`'From'`) instead of an integer. However, you could use an integer as a key if you want (more on that soon).

Combining Lists with Data Objects

A common theme in programming is combining components for surprising results. Sometimes the surprise is a crash or a bug. Other times the surprise is a novel new way to accomplish some task. Either way, what happens when you make novel combinations isn't really a surprise or a secret. To *you* it may be surprising, but there is usually an explanation somewhere in the language specification (even if that reason is absolutely stupid). There is no magic in your computer, just complexity you don't understand.

A good example of combining Python components is putting data Objects inside `lists`. You can do this:

```
1   messages = [
2     {"to": 'Sun', "from": 'Moon', "message": 'Hi!'},
3     {"to": 'Moon', "from": 'Sun', "message": 'What do you want Sun?'},
4     {"to": 'Sun', "from": 'Moon', "message": "I'm awake!"},
5     {"to": 'Moon', "from": 'Sun', "message": 'I can see that Sun.'}
6   ];
```

Once I do that I can now use `list` syntax to access the data objects like this:

```
1   messages[0]['to']
2   'Sun'
3
4   messages[0]['from']
5   'Moon'
6   messages[0]['message']
7   'Hi!'
8
9   messages[1]['to']
10  'Moon'
11
12  messages[1]['from']
13  'Sun'
14
15  messages[1]['message']
16  'What do you want Sun?'
```

Notice how I can also use the [] (index) syntax on the data object right after doing `messages[0]`? Again, you can try combining features to see if they work, and if they do, go find out why because there's always a reason (even if it's stupid).

The Code

You are now going to repeat the exercise you did with `lists` and write out three data objects I've crafted. Then you'll type them into Python and attempt to access the data I give you. Remember to try to do this in your head and then check your work with Python. You should also practice doing this to `list` and `dict` structures until you're confident you can access the contents. You'll realize that the data is the same, it's simply been restructured.

Listing 24.1: ex24.py

```
1    fruit = [
2        {'kind': 'Apples',   'count': 12, 'rating': 'AAA'},
3        {'kind': 'Oranges',  'count': 1,  'rating': 'B'},
4        {'kind': 'Pears',    'count': 2,  'rating': 'A'},
5        {'kind': 'Grapes',   'count': 14, 'rating': 'UR'}
6    ];
7
8    cars = [
9        {'type': 'Cadillac', 'color': 'Black',
10       'size': 'Big', 'miles': 34500},
11       {'type': 'Corvette', 'color': 'Red',
12       'size': 'Little', 'miles': 1000000},
13       {'type': 'Ford', 'color': 'Blue',
14       'size': 'Medium', 'miles': 1234},
15       {'type': 'BMW', 'color': 'White',
16       'size': 'Baby', 'miles': 7890}
17   ];
18
19   languages = [
20       {'name': 'Python', 'speed': 'Slow',
21       'opinion': ['Terrible', 'Mush']},
22       {'name': 'JavaScript', 'speed': 'Moderate',
23       'opinion': ['Alright', 'Bizarre']},
24       {'name': 'Perl6', 'speed': 'Moderate',
25       'opinion': ['Fun', 'Weird']},
26       {'name': 'C', 'speed': 'Fast',
27       'opinion': ['Annoying', 'Dangerous']},
28       {'name': 'Forth', 'speed': 'Fast',
29       'opinion': ['Fun', 'Difficult']},
30   ];
```

What You Should See

Keep in mind that you're doing some complicated data access moves here, so take it slow. You have to go through the data variable you assign the module to, and then access lists, followed by data objects, and in some cases another list.

The Challenge

I will give you the exact same set of data elements for you to get. Your job is to figure out what indexing you need to get that information. For example, if I tell you fruit 'AAA', then your answer is fruit[0]['rating']. You should attempt to do this in your head by looking at the code and then test your guess in the python shell.

Fruit Challenge

You need to get all of these elements out of the fruit variable:

- 12
- 'AAA'
- 2
- 'Oranges'
- 'Grapes'
- 14
- 'Apples'

Cars Challenge

You need to get all of these elements out of the cars variable:

- 'Big'
- 'Red'
- 1234
- 'White'
- 7890
- 'Black'
- 34500
- 'Blue'

Languages Challenge

You need to get all of these elements out of the `languages` variable:

- 'Slow'
- 'Alright'
- 'Dangerous'
- 'Fast'
- 'Difficult'
- 'Fun'
- 'Annoying'
- 'Weird'
- 'Moderate'

Final Challenge

Your final challenge is to write out the Python code that writes out the same song lyric from Exercise 23. Again, take it slow and try to do it in your head before seeing whether you get it right. If you get it wrong, take the time to understand why you got it wrong. For comparison, I wrote out the lyrics in my head in one shot and didn't get it wrong. I am also *way* more experienced than you are, so you will probably make some mistakes and that is alright.

You didn't know those were song lyrics? It's a Prince song called "Little Red Corvette." You are now ordered to listen to 10 Prince songs before you continue with this book or we cannot be friends anymore. Anymore!

Dictionaries and Functions

I n this exercise, we're going to do something fun by combining functions with dicts. The purpose of this exercise is to confirm that you can combine different things in Python. Combination is a key aspect of programming, and you'll find that many "complex" concepts are nothing more than a combination of simpler concepts.

Step 1: Function Names Are Variables

To prepare we first have to confirm that a function's name is just like other variables. Take a look at this code:

```
1    def print_number(x):
2        print("NUMBER IS", x)
3
4    rename_print = print_number
5    rename_print(100)
6    print_number(100)
```

If you run this code, you'll see that rename_print does the exact same thing as print_number, and that's because they are the same. The name of a function is the same as a variable, and you can reassign the name to another variable. It's the same as doing this:

```
1    x = 10
2    y = x
```

Play around with this until you get the idea. Make your own functions and then assign them to new names until you get that idea.

Step 2: Dictionaries with Variables

It might be obvious, but just in case you haven't made the connection, you can put a variable into a dict:

```
1    color = "Red"
2
3    corvette = {
4      "color": color
5    }
6
7    print("LITTLE", corvette["color"], "CORVETTE")
```

This next piece of the puzzle makes sense, since you can put values into a `dict` like numbers and strings. You can also assign those same values to variables, so it makes sense you can combine both and put a variable into a `dict`.

Step 3: Dictionaries with Functions

You should be seeing where this is going, but now we can combine these concepts to put a function in a `dict`:

```
1    def run():
2      print("VROOM")
3
4    corvette = {
5      "color": "Red",
6      "run": run
7    }
8
9    print("My", corvette["color"], "can go")
10   corvette["run"]()
```

I've taken the `color` variable from before and simply put it right in the `dict` for the `corvette`. Then I made a function `run` and put that into the `corvette` as well. The tricky part is that last line `corvette ["run"]()`, but see if you can figure it out based on what you know. Take some time to write out a description of what this line is doing before continuing on.

Step 4: Deciphering the Last Line

The trick to deciphering that last line `corvette["run"]()` is to separate out each piece of it. What confuses people about lines like this is they see one single thing, "run the corvette." The truth is this line is composed of *many* things working together in combination. If we break this apart, we could have this code:

```
1    # get the run fuction out of the corvette dict
2    myrun = corvette["run"]
3    # run it
4    myrun()
```

Even those two lines isn't the entire story, but that shows you this is at *least* two operations on one line: get the function with `["run"]` and then run the function with `()`. To break this down further we can write:

1. `corvette` tells Python to load the `dict`

2. `[` tells Python to start an index into `corvette`

3. `"run"` tells Python to use `"run"` as the key to search the `dict`

4.   ] tells Python you are done and it should complete the index

5.   Python then *returns* the contents of `corvette` that match the key `"run"`, which is the previous `run()` function

6.   Python now has the `run()` function, so `()` tells Python to call it like you would any other function

Take some time to understand how this is working, and write your own functions on the `corvette` to make it do more things.

Study Drill

You now have a nice piece of code that's controlling a car. In this Study Drill you're going to create a new function that *creates any car*. Your *creator function* should meet these requirements:

1.   It should take parameters to set things like the color, speed, or anything else your cars can do.

2.   It should create a `dict` that has the correct settings and already contains all the functions you've created.

3.   It should return this `dict` so people can assign the results to anything they want and use later.

4.   It should be written so that someone can create any number of different cars and each one they make is independent.

5.   Your code should test #4 by changing settings in a few different cars and then confirming they didn't change in other cars.

This challenge is different because I'll show you the answer to the challenge in a later exercise. If you struggle with this challenge, then shelve it for a bit and move on. You'll see this again shortly.

Dictionaries and Modules

In this exercise, you're going to explore how the dict works with modules. You've been using modules any time you use import to add "features" to your own Python source. You did this the most in Exercise 17, so it might be good to go review that exercise before you begin this one.

Step 1: Review of import

The first step is review how import works and develop that knowledge further. Take some time to enter this code into a Python file named ex26.py. You can do this in Jupyter by creating a file (left side, blue [+] button) with that name:

Listing 26.1: ex26.py

```
1    name = "Zed"
2    height = 74
```

Once you've created this file you can import it with this:

Listing 26.2: ex26_code.py

```
1    import ex26
```

This will bring the contents of ex26.py into your Jupyter lab so you can access them like this:

Listing 26.3: ex26_code.py

```
1    print("name", ex26.name)
2    print("height", ex26.height)
```

Take some time to play with this as much as possible. Try adding new variables and doing the import again to see how that works.

Step 2: Find the __dict__

Once you understand that the import is the contents of ex26.py to your lab, you can start investigating the __dict__ variable like this:

Listing 26.4: ex26_code.py

```
1    from pprint import pprint
2
3    pprint(ex26.__dict__)
```

The pprint() function is a "pretty printer" that will print the __dict__ in a better format.

With pprint you suddenly see that ex26 has a "hidden" variable called __dict__, which is *literally* a dict that contains everything in the module. You'll find this __dict__ and many other secret variables all over Python. The contents of __dict__ contain quite a few things that aren't your code, but that's simply things Python needs to work with the module.

These variables are so hidden that even top professionals forget they exist. Many of these programmers believe that a module is *totally* different from a dict when internally a module uses a __dict__, which means it *is* the same as a dict. The only difference is Python has some syntax that lets you access a module using the . operator instead of the dict syntax, but you *can* still access the contents as a dict:

Listing 26.5: ex26_code.py

```
1    print("height is", ex26.height)
2    print("height is also", ex26.__dict__['height'])
```

You'll get the same output for both syntaxes, but the . module syntax is definitely easier.

Step 3: Change the __dict__

If a module is really a dict inside, then that means changing the contents of __dict__ should also change the variables in the module. Let's try it:

Listing 26.6: ex26_code.py

```
1    print(f"I am currently {ex26.height} inches tall.")
2
3    ex26.__dict__['height'] = 1000
4    print(f"I am now {ex26.height} inches tall.")
5
6    ex26.height = 12
7    print(f"Oops, now I'm {ex26.__dict__['height']} inches tall.")
```

As you can see, the variable ex26.height changes when you change ex26.__dict__['height'], which proves that the module is really the __dict__.

This means that the . operator is being translated into a __dict__[] access operation. I want you to remember this for later, because many times when beginning programmers see ex26.height, they think this is a single unit of code. It is actually three or four separate operations:

1. Find ex26

2. Find the ex26.__dict__

3. Index into __dict__ with "height"

4. Return that value

Once you make this connection you'll start to understand how the . works.

Study Drill: Find the "Dunders"

The __dict__ variables are typically called "double underscore" variables, but programmers are a lazy bunch so we just call them "dunder variables." For this final step in learning about dunder variables, you'll visit the Python documentation for the data model, which describes how many of these dunders are used.

This is a large document, and its writing style is very dry, so the best way to study it is search for __ (double underscore) and then find a way to access this variable based on its description. For example, you can try to access the __doc__ on almost anything:

Listing 26.7: ex26_code.py

```
1    from pprint import pprint
2    print(pprint.__doc__)
```

That will give you a little bit of documentation attached to the pprint() function. You can access the same information using the help() function:

Listing 26.8: ex26_code.py

```
1    help(pprint)
```

Try these experiments with all of the other dunders you can find. You most likely won't ever use them directly, but it's good to know how Python's internals work.

The Five Simple Rules to the Game of Code

INFO This exercise is intended to be studied periodically while you study the next exercises. You're expected to take this very slowly and to mix it with other explanations until you finally get it. If you get lost in this exercise, take a break and do the next ones. Then if you get confused in a later exercise, come back and study the details I describe here. Keep doing this until it "clicks." Remember, you can't fail, so just keep trying until you get it.

If you play a game like Go or Chess, you know the rules are fairly simple, yet the games they enable are extremely complex. Really good games have this unique quality of simple rules with complex interactions. Programming is also a game with a few simple rules that create complex interactions, and in this exercise we're going to learn what those rules are.

Before we do that, I need to stress that you most likely won't use these rules directly when you code. There are languages that do utilize these rules directly, and your CPU uses them too, but in daily programming you'll rarely use them. If that's the case, then why learn the rules?

Because these rules are everywhere, and understanding them will help you understand the code you write. It'll help you debug the code when it goes wrong. If you ever want to know how the code works, you'll be able to "disassemble" it down to its basic rules and really see how it works. These rules are a cheat *code*. Pun totally intended.

I'm also going to warn you that **you are not expected to totally understand this right away**. Think of this exercise as setting you up for the rest of the exercises in this module. You're expected to study this exercise deeply, and when you get stuck, move on to the next exercises as a break. You want to bounce between this one and the next ones until the concepts "click" and they start to make sense. You should also study these rules as deeply as you can, but don't get stuck here. Struggle for a few days, move on, come back, and keep trying. As long as you keep trying, you can't actually "fail."

Rule 1: Everything Is a Sequence of Instructions

All programs are a sequence of instructions that tell a computer to do something. You've seen Python doing this already when you type code like this:

```
1    x = 10
2    y = 20
3    z = x + y
```

This code starts at line 1, goes to line 2, and so on until the end. That's a sequence of instructions, but inside Python these three lines are converted into another sequence of instructions that look like this:

```
1   LOAD_CONST   0 (10) # load the number 10
2   STORE_NAME   0 (x)  # store that in x
3
4   LOAD_CONST   1 (20) # load the number 20
5   STORE_NAME   1 (y)  # store that in y
6
7   LOAD_NAME    0 (x)  # loads x (which is 10)
8   LOAD_NAME    1 (y)  # loads y (which is 20)
9   BINARY_ADD          # adds those
10  STORE_NAME   2 (z)  # store the result in z
```

That looks totally different from the Python version, but I *bet* you could probably figure out what this sequence of instructions is doing. I've added comments to explain each instruction, and you should be able to connect it back to the previous Python code.

I'm not joking. Take some time right now to connect each line of the Python code to the lines of this "byte code." Using the comments I provided I'm positive you can figure it out, and doing so might turn on a light in your head about the Python code.

It's not necessary to memorize this or even understand each of these instructions. What you should realize is your Python code is being translated into a sequence of simpler instructions that tell the computer to do something. This sequence of instructions is called "byte code" because it's usually stored in a file as a sequence of numbers a computer understands. The output you see is usually called an "assembly language" because it's a human "readable" (barely) version of those bytes.

These simpler instructions are processed starting at the top, do one small thing at a time, and go to the end when the program exits. That's just like your Python code but with a simpler syntax of INSTRUCTION OPTIONS. Another way to look at this is each part of x = 10 might become its own instructions in this "byte code."

That's the first rule of The Game of Code: Everything you write eventually becomes a sequence of bytes fed to a computer as instructions for what the computer should do.

How can I get this output?

To get this output yourself, you use a module called dis, which stands for "disassemble." This kind of code is traditionally called "byte code" or "assembly language," so dis means to "disassemble." To use dis you can import it and use the dis() function like this:

```
1   # import the dis function
2   from dis import dis
3
4   # pass code to dis() as a string
```

```
5   dis('''
6   x = 10
7   y = 20
8   z = x + y
9   ''')
```

In this Python code I'm doing the following:

1. I import the `dis()` function from the `dis` module

2. I run the `dis()` function, but I give it a multi-line string using `'''`

3. I then write the Python code I want to disassemble into this multi-line string

4. Finally, I end the multi-line string and the `dis()` function with `''')`

When you run this in Jupyter, you'll see it dump the byte code like I have, but maybe with some extras we'll cover in a minute.

Where are these bytes stored?

When you run Python (version 3), these bytes are stored in a directory named __pycache__. If you put this code into a `ex27.py` file and then run it with `python ex27.py`, you should see this directory.

Looking in this directory you should see a bunch of files ending in `.pyc` with names similar to the code that generated them. These `.pyc` files contain your compiled Python code as bytes.

When you run `dis()`, you're printing a human-readable version of the numbers in the `.pyc` file.

Rule 2: Jumps Make the Sequence Non-Linear

A sequence of simple instructions like LOAD_CONST 10 is not very useful. Yay! You can load the number 10! Amazing! Where code starts to become useful is when you add the concept of the "jump" to make this sequence *non-linear*. Let's look at a new piece of Python code:

```
1   while True:
2       x = 10
```

To understand this code we have to foreshadow a later exercise where you learn about the `while`-loop. The code `while True:` simply says "Keep running the code under me x = 10 while True is True." Since True will always be True, this will loop forever. If you run this in Jupyter, it will never end.

What happens when you `dis()` this code? You see the new instruction JUMP_ABSOLUTE:

```
1   dis("while True: x = 10")
2
3           0 LOAD_CONST           1 (10)
```

```
4          2 STORE_NAME          0 (x)
5          4 JUMP_ABSOLUTE       0 (to 0)
```

You saw the first two instructions when we covered the x = 10 code, but now at the end we have JUMP_ABSOLUTE 0. Notice there's numbers 0, 2, and 4 to the left of these instructions? In the previous code, I cut them out so you wouldn't be distracted, but here they're important because they represent locations in the sequence where each instruction lives. All JUMP_ABSOLUTE 0 does is tell Python to "jump to the instruction at position 0", which is LOAD_CONST 1 (10).

With this simple instruction we now have turned boring straight line code into a more complex loop that's not straight anymore. Later, we'll see how jumps combine with tests to allow even more complex movements through the sequence of bytes.

Why is this backward?

You may have noticed that the Python code reads as "while True is True set x equal to 10" but the dis( ) output reads more like "set x equal to 10, jump to do it again." That's because of Rule #1, which says we have to produce a *sequence of bytes only*. There are no nested structures, or any syntax more complex than INSTRUCTION OPTIONS, allowed.

To follow this rule Python has to figure out how to translate its code into a sequence of bytes that produces the desired output. That means moving the actual repetition part to the end of the sequence so it will be in a sequence. You'll find this "backward" nature comes up often when looking at byte codes and assembly language.

Can a JUMP go forward?

Yes, technically a JUMP instruction is simply telling the computer to process a different instruction in the sequence. It can be the next one, a previous one, or one in the future. The way this works is the computer keeps track of the "index" of the current instruction, and it simply increments that index.

When you JUMP, you're telling the computer to change this index to a new location in the code. In the code for our while loop (below) the JUMP_ABSOLUTE is at index 4 (see the 4 to the left). After it runs, the index changes to 0 where the LOAD_CONST is located, so the computer runs that instruction again. This loops forever.

```
1          0 LOAD_CONST          1 (10)
2          2 STORE_NAME          0 (x)
3          4 JUMP_ABSOLUTE       0 (to 0)
```

Rule 3: Tests Control Jumps

A JUMP is useful for looping, but what about making decisions? A common thing in programming is to ask questions like:

"If x is greater than 0 then set y to 10."

If we write this out in simple Python code, it might look like this:

```
1    if x > 0:
2        y = 10
```

Once again, this is foreshadowing something you'll learn later, but this is simple enough to figure out:

1.   Python will *test* if x is greater than > 0.

2.   If it is, then Python will run the line y = 10

3.   You see how that line is indented under the if x > 0:? That is called a "block" and Python uses indentation to say "this indented code is part of the code above it."

4.   If x is *NOT* greater than 0, then Python will *JUMP* over the y = 10 line to skip it.

To do this with our Python byte code we need a new instruction that implements the testing part. We have the JUMP. We have variables. We just need a way to *compare* two things and then a JUMP based on that comparison.

Let's take that code and dis() it to see how Python does this:

```
1    dis('''
2    x = 1
3    if x > 0:
4        y = 10
5    ''')
6
7        0 LOAD_CONST          0 (1)       # load 1
8        2 STORE_NAME          0 (x)       # x = 1
9
10       4 LOAD_NAME           0 (x)       # load x
11       6 LOAD_CONST          1 (0)       # load 0
12       8 COMPARE_OP          4 (>)       # compare x > 0
13      10 POP_JUMP_IF_FALSE  10 (to 20)   # jump if false
14
15      12 LOAD_CONST          2 (10)      # not false, load 10
16      14 STORE_NAME          1 (y)       # y = 10
17      16 LOAD_CONST          3 (None)    # done, load None
18      18 RETURN_VALUE                    # exit
19
20       # jump here if false
21      20 LOAD_CONST          3 (None)    # load none
22      22 RETURN_VALUE                    # exit
```

The key part of this code is the COMPARE_OP and POP_JUMP_IF_FALSE:

```
1       4 LOAD_NAME          0 (x)       # load x
2       6 LOAD_CONST         1 (0)       # load 0
3       8 COMPARE_OP         4 (>)       # compare x > 0
4      10 POP_JUMP_IF_FALSE 10 (to 20)   # jump if false
```

Here's what this code does:

1. Use LOAD_NAME to load the x variable.

2. Use LOAD_CONST to load the 0 constant.

3. Use COMPARE_OP, which does the > comparison and leaves a True or False result for later.

4. Finally, POP_JUMP_IF_FALSE makes the if x > 0 work. It "pops" the True or False value to get it, and if it reads False, it will JUMP to instruction 20.

5. Doing that will jump over the code that set y if the comparison is False, *but* if the comparison is True, then Python just runs the next instruction, which starts the y = 10 sequence.

Take some time walking through this to try to understand it. If you have a printer, try printing it out and set x to different values manually, and then trace through how the code works. What happens when you set x = –1?

What do you mean "pop"?

In the previous code, I'm skipping over exactly how Python "pops" the value to read it, but it's storing it in something called a "stack." For now just think of it as a temporary storage place that you "push" values into and then "pop" them off. You really don't need to go much deeper than that at this stage in your learning. Just understand the effect is to get the result of the last instruction.

Wait, aren't tests like *COMPARE_OP* used in loops too?

Yes, and you could probably figure out how that works right now based on what you know. Try to write a while-loop and see if you can get it to work with what you know now. Don't worry if you can't though as we'll be covering this in later exercises.

Rule 4: Storage Controls Tests

You need some way to keep track of changing data while the code operates, and this is done with "storage." Usually this storage is in the computer's memory and you create names for the data you're storing in memory. You've been doing this when you write code like this:

```
1    x = 10
```

```
2   y = 20
3   z = x + y
```

In each of the previous lines we're making a new piece of data and storing it in memory. We're also giving these pieces of memory the names x, y, and z. We can then use these names to "recall" those values from memory, which is what we do in z = x + y. We're just recalling the value of x and y from memory to add them together.

That's the majority of the story, but the important part of this little rule is that you almost always use memory to control tests.

Sure, you can write code like this:

```
1   if 1 < 2:
2       print("but...why?")
```

That's pointless though since it's just running the second line after a pointless test. 1 is always less than 2, so it's useless.

Where tests like COMPARE_OP shine is when you use variables to make the tests dynamic based on calculations. That's why I consider this a "rule of The Game of Code" because code without variables isn't really playing the game.

Take the time to go back through the previous examples and identify the places where LOAD instructions are used to load values, and STORE instructions are used to store values into memory.

Rule 5: Input/Output Controls Storage

The final rule of The Game of Code is how your code interacts with the outside world. Having variables is great, but a program that has only data you've typed into the source file isn't very useful. What you need is *input* and *output*.

Input is how you get data into your code from things like files, the keyboard, or the network. You've already used open() and input() to do that in the last module. You accessed input every time you opened a file, read the contents, and did something with them. You also used input when you used ... input() to ask the user a question.

Output is how you save or transmit the results of your program. Output can be to the screen with print(), to a file with file.write(), or even over a network.

Let's run dis() on a simple use of input('Yes? ') to see what it does:

```
1   from dis import dis
2   dis("input('Yes? ')")
3
```

```
4       0 LOAD_NAME           0 (input)
5       2 LOAD_CONST          0 ('Yes? ')
6       4 CALL_FUNCTION        1
7       6 RETURN_VALUE
```

You can see there's now a new instruction CALL_FUNCTION that implements the function calls you learned about in Exercise 18. When Python sees CALL_FUNCTION, it finds the function that's been loaded with LOAD_NAME and then jumps to it to run that function's code. There's a lot more behind how functions work, but you can think of CALL_FUNCTION as similar to JUMP_ABSOLUTE but to a named place in the instructions.

Putting It All Together

Taking the five rules, we have the following Game of Code:

1.   You read data as input to your program (Rule #5)

2.   You store this data in storage (variables) (Rule #4)

3.   You use these variables to perform tests... (Rule #3)

4.   ... so you can JUMP around... (Rule #2)

5.   ... the sequence of instructions... (Rule #1)

6.   ... transforming the data into new variables (Rule #4)...

7.   ... which you then write to output for storage or display (Rule #5)

While this seems simple, these little rules create very complicated software. Video games are a great example of *very* complicated software that does this. A video game reads your controller or keyboard as input, updates variables that control the models in the scene, and uses advanced instructions that render the scene to your screen as output.

Take the time now to go back through exercises you've completed and see if you understand them better. Does using dis() on code you didn't understand help, or is it more confusing? If it helps, then try it on everything to get new insights. If it doesn't help, then just remember it for later. This will be especially interesting when you do it to Exercise 26.

The List of Byte Codes

As you continue with the exercises, I'll have you run dis() on some code to analyze what it's doing. You'll need the full list of Python byte codes to study, which can be found at the end of the dis() documentation.

dis() Is a Side Quest

Later exercises will have short sections that ask you to run dis() on the code to study the byte codes. These sections are "side quests" in your education. That means they are *not* essential for understanding Python, but if you complete them, it may help you later. If they're too hard, then skip them and continue on with the rest of the course.

The most important thing about dis() is that it gives you direct access to what *Python* thinks your code does. That can help you if you're confused about how your code works or if you're just curious about what Python is actually doing.

Memorizing Logic

T oday is the day you start learning about logic. Up to this point you have done everything you possibly can reading and writing files, to the Terminal, and have learned quite a lot of the math capabilities of Python.

From now on, you will be learning *logic*. You won't learn complex theories that academics love to study but just the simple basic logic that makes real programs work and that real programmers need every day.

Learning logic has to come after you do some memorization. I want you to do this exercise for an entire week. Do not falter. Even if you are bored out of your mind, keep doing it. This exercise has a set of logic tables you must memorize to make it easier for you to do the later exercises.

I'm warning you this won't be fun at first. It will be downright boring and tedious, but this teaches you a very important skill you will need as a programmer. You *will* need to be able to memorize important concepts in your life. Most of these concepts will be exciting once you get them. You will struggle with them, like wrestling a squid, and then one day you will understand it. All that work memorizing the basics pays off big later.

Here's a tip on how to memorize something without going insane: Do a tiny bit at a time throughout the day and mark down what you need to work on most. Do not try to sit down for two hours straight and memorize these tables. This won't work. Your brain will retain only whatever you studied in the first 15 or 30 minutes anyway. Instead, create a bunch of index cards with each column on the left (True or False) on the front, and the column on the right on the back. You should then take them out, see the "True or False" and immediately say "True!" Keep practicing until you can do this.

Once you can do that, start writing out your own truth tables each night into a notebook. Do not just copy them. Try to do them from memory. When you get stuck, glance quickly at the ones I have here to refresh your memory. Doing this will train your brain to remember the whole table.

Do not spend more than one week on this, because you will be applying it as you go.

The Truth Terms

In Python, we have the following terms (characters and phrases) for determining if something is "True" or "False." Logic on a computer is all about seeing if some combination of these characters and some variables is True at that point in the program.

- and
- or
- not

- != (not equal)
- == (equal)
- >= (greater-than-equal)
- <= (less-than-equal)
- True
- False

You actually have run into these characters before but maybe not the terms. The terms (and, or, not) actually work the way you expect them to, just like in English.

The Truth Tables

We will now use these characters to make the truth tables you need to memorize. First is the table for not X:

NOT	True?
not False	True
not True	False

This is the table for X or Y:

OR	True?
True or False	True
True or True	True
False or True	True
False or False	False

Now the table for X and Y:

AND	True?
True and False	False
True and True	True
False and True	False
False and False	False

Then we have the table for not combined with or as not (X or Y):

NOT OR	True?
not (True or False)	False
not (True or True)	False
not (False or True)	False
not (False or False)	True

You should compare these tables to the or and and tables to see if you notice a pattern. Here's the table for not (X and Y). If you can figure out the pattern, you might not need to memorize them.

NOT AND	True?
not (True and False)	True
not (True and True)	False
not (False and True)	True
not (False and False)	True

Now we get into equalities, which is testing if one thing is equal to another in various ways. First is X != Y:

NOT AND	True?
1 != 0	True
1 != 1	False
0 != 1	True
0 != 0	False

Finally we have X == Y:

NOT AND	True?
1 == 0	False
1 == 1	True
0 == 1	False
0 == 0	True

Now use these tables to write up your own cards and spend the week memorizing them. Remember though, there is no failing in this book, just trying as hard as you can each day, and then a *little* bit more.

Common Student Questions

Can't I just learn the concepts behind Boolean algebra and not memorize this?   Sure, you can do that, but then you'll have to constantly go through the rules for Boolean algebra while you code. If you memorize these first, not only does it build your memorization skills, but it also makes these operations natural. After that, the concept of Boolean algebra is easy. But do whatever works for you.

Boolean Practice

The logic combinations you learned from the previous exercise are called "Boolean" logic expressions. Boolean logic is used *everywhere* in programming. It is a fundamental part of computation, and knowing these logic expressions very well is akin to knowing your scales in music.

In this exercise, you will take the logic exercises you memorized and start trying them out in Python. Take each of these logic problems and write what you think the answer will be. In each case, it will be either True or False. Once you have the answers written down, you will start Python in your Terminal and type each logic problem in to confirm your answers.

1.   `True and True`
2.   `False and True`
3.   `1 == 1 and 2 == 1`
4.   `"test" == "test"`
5.   `1 == 1 or 2 != 1`
6.   `True and 1 == 1`
7.   `False and 0 != 0`
8.   `True or 1 == 1`
9.   `"test" == "testing"`
10. `1 != 0 and 2 == 1`
11. `"test" != "testing"`
12. `"test" == 1`
13. `not (True and False)`
14. `not (1 == 1 and 0 != 1)`
15. `not (10 == 1 or 1000 == 1000)`
16. `not (1 != 10 or 3 == 4)`
17. `not ("testing" == "testing" and "Zed" == "Cool Guy")`
18. `1 == 1 and (not ("testing" == 1 or 1 == 0))`
19. `"chunky" == "bacon" and (not (3 == 4 or 3 == 3))`
20. `3 != 3 and (not ("testing" == "testing" or "Python" == "Fun"))`

I will also give you a trick to help you figure out the more complicated ones toward the end.

Whenever you see these Boolean logic statements, you can solve them easily by this simple process:

1. Find an equality test (== or !=) and replace it with its truth

2. Find each and/or inside parentheses and solve those first

3. Find each not and invert it

4. Find any remaining and/or and solve it

5. When you are done, you should have True or False

I will demonstrate with a *variation* on #20:

```
1    3 != 4 and not ("testing" != "test" or "Python" == "Python")
```

Here's me going through each of the steps and showing you the translation until I've boiled it down to a single result:

1. Solve each equality test:

    *   3 != 4 is True, so replace that with True to get True and not ("testing" != "test" or "Python" == "Python")

    *   "testing" != "test" is True, so replace *that* with True to get True and not (True or "Python" == "Python")

    *   "Python" == "Python" is True, so replace that with True, and we have True and not (True or True)

2. Find each and/or in parentheses ():

    *   (True or True) is True, so replace that to get True and not (True)

3. Find each not and invert it:

    *   not (True) is False, so replace that, and we have True and False

4. Find any remaining and/or and solve them:

    *   True and False is False, and you're done

With that we're done and know the result is False.

WARNING! The more complicated ones may seem very hard at first. You should be able to take a good first stab at solving them, but do not get discouraged. I'm just getting you primed for more of these "logic gymnastics" so that later cool stuff is much easier. Just stick with it, and keep track of what you get wrong, but do not worry that it's not getting in your head quite yet. It'll come.

What You Should See

After you have tried to guess at these, this is what your Jupyter cells might look like:

```
1   >>> True and True
2   True
3   >>> 1 == 1 and 2 == 2
4   True
```

Study Drills

1. There are a lot of operators in Python similar to != and ==. Try to find as many "equality operators" as you can. They should be like < or <=.

2. Write out the names of each of these equality operators. For example, I call != "not equal."

3. Play with Python by typing out new Boolean operators, and before you press Enter, try to shout out what it is. Do not think about it. Shout the first thing that comes to mind. Write it down, then press Enter, and keep track of how many you get right and wrong.

4. Throw away the piece of paper from Study Drill 3, so you do not accidentally try to use it later.

Common Student Questions

Why does `"test"` **and** `"test"` **return** `"test"` **or** `1` **and** `1` **return** `1` **instead of** `True`? Python and many languages like to return one of the operands to their Boolean expressions rather than just `True` or `False`. This means that if you did `False` and `1` you get the first operand (`False`), but if you do `True` and `1`, you get the second (`1`). Play with this a bit.

Is there any difference between `!=` **and** `<>`? Python has deprecated `<>` in favor of `!=`, so use `!=`. Other than that there should be no difference.

Isn't there a shortcut? Yes. Any and expression that has a `False` is immediately `False`, so you can stop there. Any or expression that has a `True` is immediately `True`, so you can stop there. But make sure that you can process the whole expression because later it becomes helpful.

What If

Here is the next script of Python you will enter, which introduces you to the `if-statement`. Type this in, make it run exactly right, and then we'll see if your practice has paid off.

Listing 30.1: ex30.py

```
1   people = 20
2   cats = 30
3   dogs = 15
4
5
6   if people < cats:
7       print("Too many cats! The world is doomed!")
8
9   if people > cats:
10      print("Not many cats! The world is saved!")
11
12  if people < dogs:
13      print("The world is drooled on!")
14
15  if people > dogs:
16      print("The world is dry!")
17
18
19  dogs += 5
20
21  if people >= dogs:
22      print("People are greater than or equal to dogs.")
23
24  if people <= dogs:
25      print("People are less than or equal to dogs.")
26
27
28  if people == dogs:
29      print("People are dogs.")
```

What You Should See

```
1   Too many cats! The world is doomed!
2   The world is dry!
3   People are greater than or equal to dogs.
4   People are less than or equal to dogs.
5   People are dogs.
```

dis( ) It

For the next few exercises I want you to run dis( ) on some of the code you're studying to get more insight into how it works:

```
1    from dis import dis
2
3    dis('''
4    if people < cats:
5        print("Too many cats! The world is doomed!")
6    ''')
```

This is *not* something you'd do normally when programming. I only want you to do it here to give you one more possible way to understand what's going on. If dis( ) doesn't really help you understand the code more, then feel free to do it and forget it.

To study this, simply put the Python code next to this dis( ) output and try to identify the lines of Python code that match the byte codes.

Study Drill

In this Study Drill, try to guess what you think the if-statement is and what it does. Try to answer these questions in your own words before moving on to the next exercise:

1. What do you think the if does to the code under it?

2. Why does the code under the if need to be indented four spaces?

3. What happens if it isn't indented?

4. Can you put other Boolean expressions from Exercise 28 in the if-statement? Try it

5. What happens if you change the initial values for people, cats, and dogs?

Common Student Questions

What does += mean?   The code x += 1 is the same as doing x = x + 1 but involves less typing. You can call this the "increment by" operator. The same goes for −= and many other expressions you'll learn later.

Else and If

In the previous exercise, you worked out some `if-statements` and then tried to guess what they are and how they work. Before you learn more, I'll explain what everything is by answering the questions you had from Study Drills. You did the Study Drills, right?

1. What do you think the `if` does to the code under it? An `if-statement` creates what is called a "branch" in the code. It's kind of like those choose-your-own-adventure books where you are asked to turn to one page if you make one choice and another if you go a different direction. The `if-statement` tells your script, "If this Boolean expression is True, then run the code under it; otherwise skip it."

2. Why does the code under the `if` need to be indented four spaces? A colon at the end of a line is how you tell Python you are going to create a new "block" of code, and then indenting four spaces tells Python what lines of code are in that block. This is *exactly* the same thing you did when you made functions in the first half of the book.

3. What happens if it isn't indented? If it isn't indented, you will most likely create a Python error. Python expects you to indent *something* after you end a line with a `:` (colon).

4. Can you put other Boolean expressions from Exercise 28 in the `if-statement`? Try it. Yes you can, and they can be as complex as you like, although really complex things generally are bad style.

5. What happens if you change the initial values for `people`, `cats`, and `dogs`? Because you are comparing numbers, if you change the numbers, different `if-statements` will evaluate to `True`, and the blocks of code under them will run. Go back and put different numbers in and see if you can figure out in your head which blocks of code will run.

Compare my answers to your answers, and make sure you *really* understand the concept of a "block" of code. This is important for when you do the next exercise where you write all the parts of `if-statements` that you can use.

Type this one in and make it work too.

Listing 31.1: ex31.py

```
1    people = 30
2    cars = 40
3    trucks = 15
4
5
6    if cars > people:
```

```
 7        print("We should take the cars.")
 8    elif cars < people:
 9        print("We should not take the cars.")
10    else:
11        print("We can't decide.")
12
13    if trucks > cars:
14        print("That's too many trucks.")
15    elif trucks < cars:
16        print("Maybe we could take the trucks.")
17    else:
18        print("We still can't decide.")
19
20    if people > trucks:
21        print("Alright, let's just take the trucks.")
22    else:
23        print("Fine, let's stay home then.")
```

What You Should See

```
1    We should take the cars.
2    Maybe we could take the trucks.
3    Alright, let's just take the trucks.
```

dis( ) It

We're now getting to a point where dis( ) is a bit too complicated to study. Let's just pick one of the code blocks to study:

```
 1    from dis import dis
 2
 3    dis('''
 4    if cars > people:
 5        print("We should take the cars.")
 6    elif cars < people:
 7        print("We should not take the cars.")
 8    else:
 9        print("We can't decide.")
10    ''')
```

I think the best way to study this is to put the Python code next to the dis( ) output and try to match the lines of Python to their byte codes. If you can do that, then you're going to be far ahead of many Python programmers who don't even know that Python has dis( ).

If you can't figure it out, don't worry. It's all about pushing your knowledge as far as possible to find new ways to understand Python.

Study Drills

1. Try to guess what `elif` and `else` are doing.

2. Change the numbers of `cars`, `people`, and `trucks`, and then trace through each `if-statement` to see what will be printed.

3. Try some more complex Boolean expressions like `cars > people or trucks < cars`.

4. Above each line write an English description of what the line does.

Common Student Questions

What happens if multiple `elif` blocks are `True`? Python starts at the top and runs the first block that is `True`, so it will run only the first one.

Making Decisions

In the first half of this book, you mostly just printed out things called "functions," but everything was basically in a straight line. Your scripts ran starting at the top and went to the bottom where they ended. If you made a function, you could run that function later, but it still didn't have the kind of branching you need to really make decisions. Now that you have if, else, and elif you can start to make scripts that decide things.

In the last script, you wrote out a simple set of tests asking some questions. In this script you will ask the user questions and make decisions based on their answers. Write this script, and then play with it quite a lot to figure it out.

Listing 32.1: ex32.py

```python
 1    print("""You enter a dark room with two doors.
 2    Do you go through door #1 or door #2?""")
 3
 4    door = input("> ")
 5
 6    if door == "1":
 7        print("There's a giant bear here eating a cheese cake.")
 8        print("What do you do?")
 9        print("1. Take the cake.")
10        print("2. Scream at the bear.")
11
12        bear = input("> ")
13
14        if bear == "1":
15            print("The bear eats your face off.  Good job!")
16        elif bear == "2":
17            print("The bear eats your legs off.  Good job!")
18        else:
19            print(f"Well, doing {bear} is probably better.")
20            print("Bear runs away.")
21
22    elif door == "2":
23        print("You stare into the endless abyss at Cthulhu's retina.")
24        print("1. Blueberries.")
25        print("2. Yellow jacket clothespins.")
26        print("3. Understanding revolvers yelling melodies.")
27
28        insanity = input("> ")
29
30        if insanity == "1" or insanity == "2":
31            print("Your body survives powered by a mind of jello.")
```

```
32              print("Good job!")
33          else:
34              print("The insanity rots your eyes into a pool of muck.")
35              print("Good job!")
36
37      else:
38          print("You stumble around and fall on a knife and die.  Good job!")
```

A key point here is that you are now putting the if-statements *inside* if-statements as code that can run. This is very powerful and can be used to create "nested" decisions, where one branch leads to another and another.

Make sure you understand this concept of if-statements inside if-statements. In fact, do the Study Drills to really nail it.

What You Should See

Here is me playing this little adventure game. I do not do so well.

```
1    You enter a dark room with two doors.
2    Do you go through door #1 or door #2?
3    > 1
4    There's a giant bear here eating a cheese cake.
5    What do you do?
6    1. Take the cake.
7    2. Scream at the bear.
8    > 2
9    The bear eats your legs off.  Good job!
```

dis() It

There is no *dis()* It section this time because this code is far too complicated to understand, but if you're feeling lucky, then try this:

```
1    from dis import dis
2
3    dis('''
4    if door == "1":
5        print("1")
6        bear = input("> ")
7        if bear == "1":
8            print("bear 1")
9        elif bear == "2":
10           print("bear 2")
11       else:
12           print("bear 3")
13   ''')
```

This will produce so much code to analyze, but do the best you can. It does get boring after a while, but it also helps you understand how Python works. Once again, if this is confusing, skip it and try it later.

Study Drills

1. Make new parts of the game and change what decisions people can make. Expand the game out as much as you can before it gets ridiculous.

2. Write a completely new game. Maybe you don't like this one, so make your own. This is your computer; do what you want.

Common Student Questions

Can you replace `elif` **with a sequence of** `if-else` **combinations?** You can in some situations, but it depends on how each `if/else` is written. It also means that Python will check *every* `if-else` combination, rather than just the first false ones like it would with `if-elif-else`. Try to make some of these to figure out the differences.

How do I tell whether a number is between a range of numbers? You have two options: Use $0 < x < 10$ or $1 <= x < 10$—which is classic notation—or use `x in range(1, 10)`.

What if I wanted more options in the `if-elif-else` **blocks?** Add more `elif` blocks for each possible choice.

Loops and Lists

You should now be able to do some programs that are much more interesting. If you have been keeping up, you should realize that now you can combine all the other things you have learned with if-statements and Boolean expressions to make your programs do smart things.

However, programs also need to do repetitive things very quickly. We are going to use a for-loop in this exercise to build and print various lists. When you do the exercise, you will start to figure out what they are. I won't tell you right now. You have to figure it out.

Before you can use a for-loop, you need a way to *store* the results of loops somewhere. The best way to do this is with lists. Lists are exactly what their name says: a container of things that are organized in order from first to last. It's not complicated; you just have to learn a new syntax. First, here's how you make lists:

```
1    hairs = ['brown', 'blond', 'red']
2    eyes = ['brown', 'blue', 'green']
3    weights = [1, 2, 3, 4]
```

You start the list with the [(left bracket), which "opens" the list. Then you put each item you want in the list separated by commas, similar to function arguments. Lastly, end the list with a] (right bracket) to indicate that it's over. Python then takes this list and all its contents and assigns them to the variable.

WARNING! This is where things get tricky for people who can't code. Your brain has been taught that the world is flat. Remember in the previous exercise where you put if-statements inside if-statements? That probably made your brain hurt because most people do not ponder how to "nest" things inside things. In programming nested structures are all over the place. You will find functions that call other functions that have if-statements that have lists with lists inside lists. If you see a structure like this that you can't figure out, take out a pencil and paper and break it down manually bit by bit until you understand it.

We now will build some lists using some for-loops and print them out:

Listing 33.1: ex33.py

```
1    the_count = [1, 2, 3, 4, 5]
2    fruits = ['apples', 'oranges', 'pears', 'apricots']
3    change = [1, 'pennies', 2, 'dimes', 3, 'quarters']
4
```

```
5    # this first kind of for-loop goes through a list
6    for number in the_count:
7        print(f"This is count {number}")
8
9    # same as above
10   for fruit in fruits:
11       print(f"A fruit of type: {fruit}")
12
13   # also we can go through mixed lists too
14   for i in change:
15       print(f"I got {i}")
16
17   # we can also build lists, first start with an empty one
18   elements = []
19
20   # then use the range function to do 0 to 5 counts
21   for i in range(0, 6):
22       print(f"Adding {i} to the list.")
23       # append is a function that lists understand
24       elements.append(i)
25
26   # now we can print them out too
27   for i in elements:
28       print(f"Element was: {i}")
```

What You Should See

```
1    This is count 1
2    This is count 2
3    This is count 3
4    This is count 4
5    This is count 5
6    A fruit of type: apples
7    A fruit of type: oranges
8    A fruit of type: pears
9    A fruit of type: apricots
10   I got 1
11   I got pennies
12   I got 2
13   I got dimes
14   I got 3
15   I got quarters
16   Adding 0 to the list.
17   Adding 1 to the list.
18   Adding 2 to the list.
19   Adding 3 to the list.
20   Adding 4 to the list.
21   Adding 5 to the list.
22   Element was: 0
```

```
23    Element was: 1
24    Element was: 2
25    Element was: 3
26    Element was: 4
27    Element was: 5
```

dis() It

This time let's keep it simple and just see how Python does the for-loop:

```
1   from dis import dis
2
3   dis('''
4   for number in the_count:
5       print(number)
6   ''')
```

This time I'm going to reproduce the output here so we can analyze it:

```
1     0 LOAD_NAME      0 (the_count) # get the count list
2     2 GET_ITER                     # start iteration
3     4 FOR_ITER       6 (to 18)     # for-loop jump to 18
4     6 STORE_NAME     1 (number)    # create number variable
5
6     8 LOAD_NAME      2 (print)     # load print()
7    10 LOAD_NAME      1 (number)    # load number
8    12 CALL_FUNCTION 1              # call print()
9    14 POP_TOP                      # clean stack
10   16 JUMP_ABSOLUTE 2 (to 4)       # jump back to FOR_ITER at 4
11
12   18 LOAD_CONST     0 (None)      # jump here when FOR_ITER done
13   20 RETURN_VALUE
```

Here we see a new thing in the FOR_ITER operation. This operation makes the for-loop work by doing these steps:

1.   Call the_count.__next__()

2.   If this says there are no more elements in the_count, jump to 18

3.   If there are still elements, then continue on

4.   The STORE_NAME then assigns the result of the_count.__next__() to the name number

That's all a for-loop actually does. It's mostly a single byte code FOR_ITER combined with a few others to iterate through a list.

Study Drills

1. Take a look at how you used `range()`. Look up the `range()` function to understand it.

2. Could you have avoided that `for-loop` entirely on line 22 and just assigned `range(0,6)` directly to `elements`?

3. Find the Python documentation on lists and read about them. What other operations can you do to lists besides append?

Common Student Questions

How do you make a two-dimensional (2D) list?   That's a list in a list like this: `[[1,2,3],[4,5,6]]`

Aren't lists and arrays the same thing?   Depends on the language and the implementation. In classic terms, a list is very different from an array because of how they're implemented. In Ruby though they call these "arrays." In Python they call them "lists." Just call these "lists" for now since that's what Python calls them.

Why is a for-loop able to use a variable that isn't defined yet?   The variable is defined by the `for-loop` when it starts, initializing it to the current element of the loop iteration each time through.

Why does `for i in range(1, 3):` **only loop two times instead of three times?**   The `range()` function only does numbers from the first to the last, *not including the last*. So it stops at two, not three in the preceding. This turns out to be the most common way to do this kind of loop.

What does `elements.append()` **do?**   It simply appends to the end of the list. Open up the Python shell and try a few examples with a list you make. Any time you run into things like this, always try to play with them interactively in the Python shell.

While Loops

N ow to totally blow your mind with a new loop, the while-loop. A while-loop will keep executing the code block under it as long as a Boolean expression is True.

Wait, you have been keeping up with the terminology, right? That if we write a line and end it with a : (colon), then that tells Python to start a new block of code? Then we indent, and that's the new code. This is all about structuring your programs so that Python knows what you mean. If you do not get that idea, then go back and do some more work with if-statements, functions, and the for-loop until you get it.

Later on, we'll have some exercises that will train your brain to read these structures, similar to how we burned Boolean expressions into your brain.

Back to while-loops. What they do is simply do a test like an if-statement, but instead of running the code block *once*, they jump back to the "top" where the while is, and repeat. A while-loop runs until the expression is False.

Here's the problem with while-loops: Sometimes they do not stop. This is great if your intention is to just keep looping until the end of the universe. Otherwise you almost always want your loops to end eventually.

To avoid these problems, there are some rules to follow:

1. Make sure that you use while-loops sparingly. Usually a for-loop is better.

2. Review your while-statements and make sure that the Boolean test will become False at some point.

3. When in doubt, print out your test variable at the top and bottom of the while-loop to see what it's doing.

In this exercise, you will learn the while-loop while doing these three checks:

Listing 34.1: ex34.py

```
1   i = 0
2   numbers = []
3
4   while i < 6:
5       print(f"At the top i is {i}")
6       numbers.append(i)
7
8       i = i + 1
```

```
 9          print("Numbers now: ", numbers)
10          print(f"At the bottom i is {i}")
11
12
13      print("The numbers: ")
14
15      for num in numbers:
16          print(num)
```

What You Should See

```
 1      At the top i is 0
 2      Numbers now:  [0]
 3      At the bottom i is 1
 4      At the top i is 1
 5      Numbers now:  [0, 1]
 6      At the bottom i is 2
 7      At the top i is 2
 8      Numbers now:  [0, 1, 2]
 9      At the bottom i is 3
10      At the top i is 3
11      Numbers now:  [0, 1, 2, 3]
12      At the bottom i is 4
13      At the top i is 4
14      Numbers now:  [0, 1, 2, 3, 4]
15      At the bottom i is 5
16      At the top i is 5
17      Numbers now:  [0, 1, 2, 3, 4, 5]
18      At the bottom i is 6
19      The numbers:
20      0
21      1
22      2
23      3
24      4
25      5
```

dis() It

For our final "side quest" in The Game of Code you'll use dis() to analyze how a while-loop works:

```
1      from dis import dis
2
3      dis('''
4      i = 0
5      while i < 6:
6          i = i + 1
7      ''')
```

You've already seen most of these byte codes, so it's up to you to figure out how this dis( ) output relates to the Python. Remember you can look up all of the byte codes at the end of the dis( ) documentation. Good luck!

Study Drills

1. Convert this while-loop to a function that you can call, and replace 6 in the test (i < 6) with a variable.

2. Use this function to rewrite the script to try different numbers.

3. Add another variable to the function arguments that you can pass in that lets you change the + 1 on line 8 so you can change how much it increments by.

4. Rewrite the script again to use this function to see what effect that has.

5. Write it to use for-loops and range. Do you need the incrementor in the middle anymore? What happens if you do not get rid of it?

If at any time that you are doing this it goes crazy (it probably will), just hold down CTRL and press c (CTRL-c) and the program will abort.

Common Student Questions

What's the difference between a for-loop and a while-loop?   A for-loop can only iterate (loop) "over" collections of things. A while-loop can do any kind of iteration (looping) you want. However, while-loops are harder to get right, and you normally can get many things done with for-loops.

Loops are hard. How do I figure them out?   The main reason people don't understand loops is because they can't follow the "jumping" that the code does. When a loop runs, it goes through its block of code, and at the end it jumps back to the top. To visualize this, put print statements all over the loop printing out where in the loop Python is running and what the variables are set to at those points. Write print lines before the loop, at the top of the loop, in the middle, and at the bottom. Study the output and try to understand the jumping that's going on.

Branches and Functions

You have learned if-statements, functions, and lists. Now it's time to bend your mind. Type this in, and see if you can figure out what it's doing:

Listing 35.1: ex35.py

```
1   from sys import exit
2
3   def gold_room():
4       print("This room is full of gold.  How much do you take?")
5
6       choice = input("> ")
7       if "0" in choice or "1" in choice:
8           how_much = int(choice)
9       else:
10          dead("Man, learn to type a number.")
11
12      if how_much < 50:
13          print("Nice, you're not greedy, you win!")
14          exit(0)
15      else:
16          dead("You greedy bastard!")
17
18
19  def bear_room():
20      print("There is a bear here.")
21      print("The bear has a bunch of honey.")
22      print("The fat bear is in front of another door.")
23      print("How are you going to move the bear?")
24      bear_moved = False
25
26      while True:
27          choice = input("> ")
28
29          if choice == "take honey":
30              dead("The bear looks at you then slaps your face off.")
31          elif choice == "taunt bear" and not bear_moved:
32              print("The bear has moved from the door.")
33              print("You can go through it now.")
34              bear_moved = True
35          elif choice == "taunt bear" and bear_moved:
36              dead("The bear gets pissed off and chews your leg off.")
37          elif choice == "open door" and bear_moved:
38              gold_room()
39          else:
```

```
40                    print("I got no idea what that means.")
41
42
43   def cthulhu_room():
44       print("Here you see the great evil Cthulhu.")
45       print("He, it, whatever stares at you and you go insane.")
46       print("Do you flee for your life or eat your head?")
47
48       choice = input("> ")
49
50       if "flee" in choice:
51           start()
52       elif "head" in choice:
53           dead("Well that was tasty!")
54       else:
55           cthulhu_room()
56
57
58   def dead(why):
59       print(why, "Good job!")
60       exit(0)
61
62   def start():
63       print("You are in a dark room.")
64       print("There is a door to your right and left.")
65       print("Which one do you take?")
66
67       choice = input("> ")
68
69       if choice == "left":
70           bear_room()
71       elif choice == "right":
72           cthulhu_room()
73       else:
74           dead("You stumble around the room until you starve.")
75
76
77   start()
```

What You Should See

Here's me playing the game:

```
1   You are in a dark room.
2   There is a door to your right and left.
3   Which one do you take?
4   > left
5   There is a bear here.
6   The bear has a bunch of honey.
```

```
7    The fat bear is in front of another door.
8    How are you going to move the bear?
9    >  taunt bear
10   The bear has moved from the door.
11   You can go through it now.
12   >  open door
13   This room is full of gold.  How much do you take?
14   >  1000
15   You greedy bastard! Good job!
```

Study Drills

1. Draw a map of the game and how you flow through it.

2. Fix all of your mistakes, including spelling mistakes.

3. Write comments for the functions you do not understand.

4. Add more to the game. What can you do to both simplify and expand it?

5. The gold_room has a weird way of getting you to type a number. What are all the bugs in this way of doing it? Can you make it better than what I've written? Look at how int() works for clues.

Common Student Questions

Help! How does this program work!?   When you get stuck understanding a piece of code, simply write an English comment above *every* line explaining what that line does. Keep your comments short and similar to the code. Then either diagram how the code works or write a paragraph describing it. If you do that, you'll get it.

Why did you write while True?   That makes an infinite loop.

What does exit(0) **do?**   On many operating systems a program can abort with exit(0), and the number passed in will indicate an error or not. If you do exit(1), then it will be an error, but exit(0) will be a good exit. The reason it's backward from normal Boolean logic (with 0==False) is that you can use different numbers to indicate different error results. You can do exit(100) for a different error result than exit(2) or exit(1).

Why is input() **sometimes written as** input('> ')**?**   The parameter to input is a string that it should print as a prompt before getting the user's input.

Designing and Debugging

N ow that you know if-statements, I'm going to give you some rules for for-loops and while-loops that will keep you out of trouble. I'm also going to give you some tips on debugging so that you can figure out problems with your program. Finally, you will design a little game similar to the previous exercise but with a slight twist.

From Idea to Working Code

There is a simple process anyone can follow to turn your idea into code. This isn't the *only* process, but it is one that works well for many people. Use this until you develop your own personal process.

1.   Get your idea out of your head in any form you understand. Are you a writer? Then write an essay about your idea. Are you an artist or designer? Then draw the user interface. Do you like charts and graphs? Check out the Sequence Diagram, which is one of the most useful diagrams in programming.

2.   Create a file for your code. Yes, believe it or not this is an important step that most people stumble over. If you can't come up with a name, just pick a random one for now.

3.   Write a description of your idea as comments, in plain English language (or whatever language is easiest for you).

4.   Start at the top, and convert the first comment into "pseudo-code," which is kind of Python but you don't care about syntax.

5.   Convert that "pseudo-code" into real Python code, and keep running your file until this code does what your comment says.

6.   Repeat this until you've converted all of the comments into Python.

7.   Step back, review your code, and then *delete it*. You don't have to do this all the time, but if you get in the habit of throwing away your first version, you'll receive two benefits:

     a.   Your second version is almost always better than the first.

     b.   You confirm to yourself that it wasn't just dumb luck. You actually can code. This helps with impostor syndrome and confidence.

Let's do an example with a simple problem of "create a simple Fahrenheit to Celsius converter." Step 1, I would write out what I know about the conversion:

C equals (F - 32) / 1.8. I should ask the user for the F and then print out the C.

A very basic math formula is an easy way to understand the problem. Step 2, I write comments describing what my code should do:

```
1    # ask the user for the F
2    # convert it to a float()
3    # C = (F − 32) / 1.8
4    # print C to the user
```

Once I have that, I "fill in the blanks" with pseudo-code. I'll do just the first line so you can finish this:

```
1    # ask the user for the F
2    F = input(?)
3
4    # convert it to a float()
5    # C = (F − 32) / 1.8
6    # print C to the user
```

Notice I'm being sloppy and not getting the syntax right, which is the point of pseudo-code. Once I have that, convert it to correct Python:

```
1    # ask the user for the F
2    F = input("C? ")
3
4    # convert it to a float()
5    # C = (F − 32) / 1.8
6    # print C to the user
```

Run it! You should be running your code constantly. If you type more than a few lines, just delete them and start over. It's so much easier.

Now that those lines work, I move on to the next comment and repeat the process until I have converted all of the comments into Python. When my script is finally working, I delete it and rewrite it using what I know. Maybe this time I just write the Python directly, or I just repeat the process again. Doing this will confirm to myself that I can actually do it. It was not just dumb luck.

Is This a Professional Process?

You may think that this process is not practical or unprofessional. I think when you're starting out, you need different tools than someone who's been coding for a really long time. I can sit down with an idea and just code, but I've been coding professionally for longer than you may have been alive. Yet, in my head this is essentially the process I follow. I'm just doing it inside my head rapidly, while you have to practice it externally until you internalize it.

I do use this process when I am stuck, or if I'm learning a new language. If I don't know a language but know what I want to do, then I can usually write comments and slowly convert them to code, which also teaches me that language. The only difference between me and you is that I do it faster because of years of training.

About the "X/Y" Non-Problem

Some professionals claim that this process gives students a strange disease called the "X/Y problem." They describe the X/Y problem as "Someone wants to do X, but only knows how to do Y, so they ask for help on how to do Y." The problem with the X/Y problem is it's critical of people who are simply learning how to code and presents no solution. To the "X/Y hater" the solution seems to be "know the answer already," since if they knew how to do X, they wouldn't bother with Y. The hypocrisy of this belief is that all of the people who hate these kinds of questions also went through a period of doing exactly this and asking these same exact kinds of "X/Y" questions.

The other problem is, they're blaming *you* for their terrible documentation. The classic example is from the original description of the X/Y problem:

```
1    <n00b> How can I echo the last three characters in a filename?
2
3    <feline> If they're in a variable:  echo ${foo: -3}
4    <feline> Why 3 characters?  What do you REALLY want?
5    <feline> Do you want the extension?
6
7    <n00b> Yes.
8
9    <feline> Then ASK FOR WHAT YOU WANT!
10   <feline> There's no guarantee that every filename will
11    have a three-letter extension,
12   <feline> so blindly grabbing three characters does not
13    solve the problem.
14   <feline> echo ${foo##*.}
```

First off, this feline person is literally yelling at someone for asking a question in an IRC channel devoted to answering questions. "ASK FOR WHAT YOU WANT!" The second problem is, their solution is something I—a multi-decade veteran bash and Linux professional—has to look up *every single time*. It is one of the worst documented, least usable features in bash. How is a beginner expected to know ahead of time that they should use some complicated "dollar brace name pound pound asterisk dot brace" operation? This person most likely would not have asked this question had there been simple documentation available online that explained how to do this. Even better would be if bash actually just *had* a basic feature for this incredibly common operation every human needs out of a shell.

When it comes to the "X/Y problem," it is really just an excuse to yell at beginners for being beginners. Every single person who claims to hate this either doesn't actually write code or has *definitely* done exactly this while they were learning to code. That's *how* you learn to code. You come up with problems and stumble through them learning how to implement solutions. So if you run into someone who acts like <feline>, just ignore them. They're just using you as an excuse to be angry at someone and feel superior.

Additionally, you'll notice that in the previous interaction not a single person *asked to see code*. If <n00b> had just shown their code, then <feline> could have recommended better ways to do that. Problem solved. I mean, assuming <feline> is actually able to code and is not just hanging out in IRC waiting to pounce on unsuspecting beginners asking questions.

Rules for If-Statements

1.   Every if-statement must have an else

2.   If this else should never run because it doesn't make sense, then you must use a die() function in the else that prints out an error message and dies, just like we did in the previous exercise. This will find *many* errors.

3.   The exception to rules #1 and #2 is in any for-loop or similar loop that is scanning for items in lists, or in list comprehensions. Add the else anyway, and if it doesn't make sense there then remove it.

4.   Try not to nest if-statements more than two deep and always try to do them one deep.

5.   Treat if-statements like paragraphs, where each if-elif-else grouping is like a set of sentences. Put blank lines before and after.

6.   Your Boolean tests should be simple. If they are complex, move their calculations to variables earlier in your function and use a good name for the variable.

If you follow these simple rules, you will start writing better code than most programmers. Go back to the previous exercise and see if I followed all of these rules. If not, fix my mistakes.

WARNING! Never be a slave to the rules in real life. For training purposes, you need to follow these rules to make your mind strong, but in real life sometimes these rules are just stupid. If you think a rule is stupid, try not using it.

Rules for Loops

1.   Use a while-loop only to loop forever, and that means probably never. This applies only to Python; other languages are different.

2.   Use a for-loop for all other kinds of looping, especially if there is a fixed or limited number of things to loop over.

Tips for Debugging

1.   Do not use a "debugger." A debugger is like doing a full-body scan on a sick person. You do not get any specific useful information, and you find a whole lot of information that doesn't help and is just confusing.

2.   The best way to debug a program is to use `print` to print out the values of variables at points in the program to see where they go wrong.

3.   Make sure parts of your programs work as you work on them. Do not write massive files of code before you try to run them. Code a little, run a little, fix a little.

Homework

Now write a game similar to the one that I created in the previous exercise. It can be any kind of game you want in the same flavor. Spend a week on it making it as interesting as possible. For Study Drills, use lists, functions, and modules (remember those from Exercise 13?) as much as possible, and find as many new pieces of Python as you can to make the game work.

Before you start coding you must draw a map for your game. Create the rooms, monsters, and traps that the player must go through on paper before you code.

Once you have your map, try to code it up. If you find problems with the map, then adjust it and make the code match.

The best way to work on a piece of software is in small chunks like this:

1.   On a sheet of paper or an index card, write a list of tasks you need to complete to finish the software. This is your to-do list

2.   Pick the easiest thing you can do from your list

3.   Write out English comments in your source file as a guide for how you would accomplish this task in your code

4.   Write some of the code under the English comments

5.   Quickly run your script so you can see if that code worked

6.   Keep working in a cycle of writing some code, running it to test it, and fixing it until it works

7.   Cross this task off your list, and then pick your next easiest task and repeat

This process will help you work on software in a methodical and consistent manner. As you work, update your list by removing tasks you don't really need and adding ones you do.

Symbol Review

It's time to review the symbols and Python words you know and to try to pick up a few more for the next few lessons. I have written out all the Python symbols and keywords that are important to know.

In this lesson, take each keyword and first try to write out what it does from memory. Next, search online for it and see what it really does. This may be difficult because some of these are difficult to search for, but try anyway.

If you get one of these wrong from memory, make an index card with the correct definition and try to "correct" your memory.

Finally, use each of these in a small Python program, or as many as you can get done. The goal is to find out what the symbol does, make sure you got it right, correct it if you did not, and then use it to lock it in.

Keywords

Keyword	Description	Example
and	Logical and	True and False == False
as	Part of the with-as statement	with X as Y: pass
assert	Assert (ensure) that something is true	assert False, "Error!"
break	Stop this loop right now	while True: break
class	Define a class	class Person(object)
continue	Don't process more of the loop; do it again	while True: continue
def	Define a function	def X(): pass
del	Delete from dictionary	del X[Y]
elif	Else if condition	if: X; elif: Y; else: J
else	Else condition	if: X; elif: Y; else: J
except	If an exception happens, do this	except ValueError as e: print(e)
exec	Run a string as Python	exec 'print("hello")'
finally	Exceptions or not, finally do this no matter what	finally: pass
for	Loop over a collection of things	for X in Y: pass
from	Used with import to bring in specific parts of a module	from x import Y

Keyword	Description	Example
global	Declare that you want a global variable	global X
if	If condition	if: X; elif: Y; else: J
import	Import a module into this one to use	import os
in	Part of for-loops. Also a test of X in Y	for X in Y: pass also 1 in [1] == True
is	Like == to test equality	1 is 1 == True
lambda	Create a short anonymous function	s = lambda y: y ** y; s(3)
not	Logical not	not True == False
or	Logical or	True or False == True
pass	This block is empty	def empty(): pass
print	Print this string	print('this string')
raise	Raise an exception when things go wrong	raise ValueError("No")
return	Exit the function with a return value	def X(): return Y
try	Try this block, and if exception, go to except	try: pass
while	While loop	while X: pass
with	With an expression as a variable do	with X as Y: pass
yield	Pause here and return to caller	def X(): yield Y; X().next()

Data Types

For data types, write out what makes up each one. For example, with strings, write out how you create a string. For numbers, write out a few numbers.

Type	Description	Example
True	True boolean value	True or False == True
False	False boolean value	False and True == False
None	Represents "nothing" or "no value"	x = None
bytes	Stores bytes, maybe of text, PNG, file, etc.	x = b"hello"
strings	Stores textual information	x = "hello"
numbers	Stores integers	i = 100
floats	Stores decimals	i = 10.389
lists	Stores a list of things	j = [1,2,3,4]
dicts	Stores a key=value mapping of things	e = {'x': 1, 'y': 2}

String Escape Sequences

For string escape sequences, use them in strings to make sure they do what you think they do.

Escape	Description
\\	Backslash
\'	Single-quote
\"	Double-quote
\a	Bell
\b	Backspace
\f	Formfeed
\n	Newline
\r	Carriage
\t	Tab
\v	Vertical tab

Old-Style String Formats

It's the same thing for string formats: use them in some strings to know what they do.

Escape	Description	Example
%d	Decimal integers (not floating point)	"%d" % 45 == '45'
%i	Same as %d	"%i" % 45 == '45'
%o	Octal number	"%o" % 1000 == '1750'
%u	Unsigned decimal	"%u" % -1000 == '-1000'
%x	Hexadecimal lowercase	"%x" % 1000 == '3e8'
%X	Hexadecimal uppercase	"%X" % 1000 == '3E8'
%e	Exponential notation, lowercase 'e'	"%e" % 1000 == '1.000000e+03'
%E	Exponential notation, uppercase 'E'	"%E" % 1000 == '1.000000E+03'
%f	Floating point real number	"%f" % 10.34 == '10.340000'
%F	Same as %f	"%F" % 10.34 == '10.340000'
%g	Either %f or %e, whichever is shorter	"%g" % 10.34 == '10.34'
%G	Same as %g but uppercase	"%G" % 10.34 == '10.34'
%c	Character format	"%c" % 34 == '"'

Escape	Description	Example
%r	Repr format (debugging format)	`"%r" % int == "<type 'int'>"`
%s	String format	`"%s there" % 'hi' == 'hi there'`
%%	A percent sign	`"%g%%" % 10.34 == '10.34%'`

Older Python 2 code uses these formatting characters to do what f-strings do. Try them out as an alternative.

Operators

Some of these may be unfamiliar to you, but look them up anyway. Find out what they do, and if you still can't figure it out, save it for later.

Operator	Description	Example
+	Addition	`2 + 4 == 6`
−	Subtraction	`2 - 4 == -2`
*	Multiplication	`2 * 4 == 8`
**	Power of	`2 ** 4 == 16`
/	Division	`2 / 4 == 0.5`
//	Floor division	`2 // 4 == 0`
%	String interpolate or modulus	`2 % 4 == 2`
<	Less than	`4 < 4 == False`
>	Greater than	`4 > 4 == False`
<=	Less than equal	`4 <= 4 == True`
>=	Greater than equal	`4 >= 4 == True`
==	Equal	`4 == 5 == False`
!=	Not equal	`4 != 5 == True`
( )	Parenthesis	`len('hi') == 2`
[ ]	List brackets	`[1,3,4]`
{ }	Dict curly braces	`{'x': 5, 'y': 10}`
@	At (decorators)	`@classmethod`
,	Comma	`range(0, 10)`
:	Colon	`def X():`
.	Dot	`self.x = 10`
=	Assign equal	`x = 10`

Operator	Description	Example
;	semi-colon	`print("hi"); print("there")`
+=	Add and assign	`x = 1; x += 2`
−=	Subtract and assign	`x = 1; x −= 2`
*=	Multiply and assign	`x = 1; x *= 2`
/=	Divide and assign	`x = 1; x /= 2`
//=	Floor divide and assign	`x = 1; x //= 2`
%=	Modulus assign	`x = 1; x %= 2`
**=	Power assign	`x = 1; x **= 2`

Spend about a week on this, but if you finish faster, that's great. The point is to try to get coverage on all these symbols and make sure they are locked in your head. What's also important is to find out what you *do not* know so you can fix it later.

Reading Code

Now find some Python code to read. You should be reading any Python code you can and trying to steal ideas that you find. You actually should have enough knowledge to be able to read but maybe not understand what the code does. What this lesson teaches is how to apply things you have learned to understand other people's code.

First, print out the code you want to understand. Yes, print it out, because your eyes and brain are more used to reading paper than computer screens. Make sure you print a few pages at a time.

Second, go through your printout and take notes on the following:

1. Functions and what they do.

2. Where each variable is first given a value.

3. Any variables with the same names in different parts of the program. These may be trouble later.

4. Any `if`-statements without else clauses. Are they right?

5. Any `while`-loops that might not end.

6. Any parts of code that you can't understand for whatever reason.

Third, once you have all of this marked up, try to explain it to yourself by writing comments as you go. Explain the functions, how they are used, what variables are involved and anything you can to figure this code out.

Lastly, on all of the difficult parts, trace the values of each variable line by line, function by function. In fact, do another printout, and write in the margin the value of each variable that you need to "trace."

Once you have a good idea of what the code does, go back to the computer and read it again to see if you find new things. Keep finding more code and doing this until you do not need the printouts anymore.

Study Drills

1. Find out what a "flow chart" is and draw a few.

2. If you find errors in code you are reading, try to fix them, and send the author your changes.

3. Another technique for when you are not using paper is to put # comments with your notes in the code. Sometimes, these could become the actual comments to help the next person.

Common Student Questions

How would I search for these things online?   Simply put "python3" before anything you want to find. For example, to find `yield` search for `python3 yield`.

Applying What You Know

Beyond Jupyter for Windows

J upyter is a great environment for interactive analysis. You can load your data, mess with it, refine it, generate graphs, add documentation, and even edit files. For most daily work an analyst does, that might be enough, but Jupyter has a few limitations:

1. It's difficult to share your analysis with other people in a way they can *reuse*. Sure, you can give them a notebook to look at or publish online in various ways, but there's no ability to *import* a Jupyter notebook the way you can easily `import` a Python module.

2. Jupyter notebooks tend to promote "copy-pasta code," which means you'll more often copy-paste the common code you need in every notebook or just keep a stock template notebook around with your usual setup. That works for a while, but eventually it degrades, especially if you find a bug and now have to go through every notebook fixing the bug in all your copy-paste code. It's far more efficient to take your common "boilerplate" code and place it in a module you import. This also makes something you can share with other people who might need to work with the same systems as you.

3. You can't run automated tests on a Jupyter notebook. Automated tests are an amazing resource for ensuring your code keeps working as you make changes and for helping other people who use your code confirm it's working. The primary area you'll find this useful is when you do data munging. Data tends to be gross and change often, so tests confirm your code keeps working when you have to update various data models.

4. Ninety-eight percent of other programmers do not use Jupyter. If you're working on any analysis that you plan on giving to a programmer, you'll need to "formalize" it into a Python project they can grab and use. If you can create a basic project, place in their favorite version control system, and write some documentation, then they can usually improve it for you. If you just throw them a `Untitled.ipynb` before going on vacation for a month, you will be hated with all the passion of a thousand dying suns. Or just ignored. It depends on where you work.

5. Another benefit of turning your `Untitled.ipynb` into a formal Python project is *perspective*. Many times something you thought was very good changes when you translate it to another language, platform, or medium. You might think your analysis is amazing and then you convert it to a Python module only to find that it's total junk or could be far more efficient. This is similar to how painters look at paintings upside down to find errors or musicians listen to their songs in cars. A change of perspective will almost always show ways you can improve the work.

6. The most important reason to learn how to code Python without Jupyter is *independence*. I don't indoctrinate people in my educational style because I feel it's wrong to create students who depend on specific products, companies, languages, or communities. I want you to be able to

migrate from one technology to another as the fashion of programming changes, because this really is a fashion industry. One day, Python and Jupyter are the best things ever, and the next day everyone is on some new hot technology an "influencer" raved about in a YouTube video. If you want a long career in this industry, you *do not* want to be dependent on anything, and the first step to this independence is learning how to use your computer like a programmer.

Does this mean you should *not* use Jupyter? No, Jupyter is awesome for doing your analysis and figuring out what to write. I want you to be able to use *both* Jupyter *and* other systems depending on what you need to do, and to accomplish this goal I will teach you the *basics of the command line.*

Why Learn PowerShell?

Did you know that Microsoft demoted the person who created PowerShell? From about 1990 to 2010 Microsoft was very against anything that didn't have a GUI. They spent a lot of money shaming and fear mongering anything that looked like text to control a computer in a weird attempt to get people to not use Linux. So when PowerShell came out, the people running Microsoft took it as an attempt at sabotage and demoted the poor fellow. This is one of the reasons so many people tend to avoid PowerShell even if it might be the right tool for the job.

Graphical systems are great for graphical things, but they tend to fall over when you have to do anything that requires a lot of repetition or pattern matching. Open an Explorer window now and try to list all of the files that start with ex but end with a number and .py. Doing this with PowerShell is trivial:

```
1  ls ex*[0-9].py
```

That seems complicated, but at the end of this exercise you'll understand it and be able to use PowerShell to control your computer. Should you use *only* PowerShell? No, of course not. Use the best tool for the job, and PowerShell is the best for many *programming* tasks.

What Is PowerShell?

Just in case you're not familiar with PowerShell, it's a mini programming language that allows you to control your computer with commands. These commands have a common form of:

```
1  command -option1 -option2 arg1,arg2
```

Command is usually something you need the computer to do:

- ls list files
- cp copy files
- rm remove files

In PowerShell you also have verbose versions of many commands:

- `ls` is also `Get-ChildItem`
- `cp` is also `Copy-Item`
- `rm` is also `Remove-Item`

Each of these commands takes options that start with a - (dash) character. For example, `ls` has the option `-Recurse` like this:

```
1  ls -Recurse
2  # or the verbose version
3  Get-ChildItem -Recurse
```

Finally, you can add arguments to a command, which is usually some resource to run the command against:

```
1  ls -Recurse ~/Desktop
```

If this spews a bunch of text to the screen, you can hold CTRL and hit c to abort it. You might have to hit it many times to make it abort. One caveat of PowerShell's arguments is it expects multiple items to be separated by a comma:

```
1  ls -Recurse ~/Desktop,"~/Photos/My Family Pics"
```

You'll learn this command more in this exercise, but let's break down this line so you understand it:

1. `ls` is the command we want. You can also use `Get-Item`
2. `-Recurse` means "recursively descend into all directories (folders)."
3. `~` (tilde) means "my home directory," which is the top folder that holds your user's files. Mine is `C:\Users\Zed`
4. You'll see me type / (slash) instead of \ (back-slash) because the / on my keyboard is easier to reach, and I'm an old Unix hacker, so my hands refuse to type the \ character. Luckily, PowerShell allows you to use either and will translate them, so use the one that's easiest to type.
5. `Desktop` is the first directory (folder) I want to list.
6. , (comma) separates the first directory to list from the second one.
7. `"~/Photos/My Family Pics"` is just like the first directory `~/Desktop`, but I have to put quotes around it because it has a space in the name `My Family Pics`. You have to do this because PowerShell would think `My`, `Family`, and `Pics` are all arguments to `ls`

Finally, any time you want to know about a command—or to learn more about PowerShell–you can consult the official Microsoft documentation at:
https://learn.microsoft.com/en-us/powershell/scripting/learn/ps101/00-introduction

Microsoft's documentation is top notch, and you could probably spend a week reading this introduction to learn nearly everything you need to learn about PowerShell. You can also get immediate help with the `help` command:

```
1  help ls
2
3  # it's also called
4  Get-Help ls
```

Keep in mind that `ls` is a handy alias for `Get-ChildItem`, so the `help` command lists documentation for `Get-ChildItem`.

PowerShell versus Cmder

In this lesson I'm going to cover the basic commands of PowerShell. Cmder is an improved "console emulator" for PowerShell. I recommend you install the full download of Cmder and use PowerShell through that rather than running the original PowerShell. Cmder comes with more developer-friendly settings and lets you use tabs, which are important when doing development.

> **INFO** As of 2022 there is a small bug in Cmder that will make it run cmd.exe instead of PowerShell. Before you do anything, hit your Windows key, and type PowerShell. You'll see PowerShell show in a list of available commands, and you should click on it to run it.

> **WARNING!** Do not, and I repeat NOT run the command named PowerShell ISE. This command is broken and will be missing all of your settings for some strange reason. Only run the PowerShell command. After you run this command once, your Cmder will use it.

If you can't run Cmder for some reason, then regular PowerShell still works for the entire course. Cmder doesn't actually replace PowerShell. All Cmder does is host PowerShell and display it for you in a nicer package. Everything else should work just fine.

Starting Jupyter

Since you're already using Jupyter, it helps to know how to start it while you're in PowerShell. The easiest way is with the `jupyter-lab` command:

```
1  jupyter-lab
```

In Cmder I like to hit CTRL-t to create a new "tab" and then on the far right check the box for "To bottom" so I can have the lab running on top and the code I'm typing on the bottom. You might just want a full new tab, so don't check that box.

You can run a specific notebook by adding it to the command:

```
1  jupyter-lab Untitled.ipynb
```

See the following instructions on using start to help you find your files with your mouse.

Getting Help

If you want to know the options to a command, you can easily search online for the documentation from Microsoft, but if you want to read the local documentation, then run this command:

```
1  Get-Help -Name Command
```

Replace "Command" with the command you are interested in, and it will print out the documentation. For example, if I want to get the help for the ls command, I do this:

```
1  Get-Help -Name ls
```

You don't have to use CamelCase and can simply type get-help -name ls.

When you run this command, it will show you the documentation for Get-ChildItem. In PowerShell the ls command is aliased to this core command, but otherwise the documentation should be correct.

Where Are You with start?

You've spent most of your time using the Explorer window to navigate your computer. If you don't know what "Explorer" is, it's just the GUI window that opens when you click on a folder. In fact, you'll usually call something a "folder," and in the Terminal you'll call it a "directory" when they're exactly the same thing. I've spent most of my computer life using the some kind of Terminal and shell to navigate computers, so I'm familiar with "seeing" the computer via the text outputs. You can use the command start to connect your view of the computer through graphics to my view of the computer through text like this:

```
1  start .
```

The . means "this current directory (folder)," and start opens this current directory in Explorer. The start command actually works like double-clicking on a file, so you can open any file with it to see it. Let's say you're in a folder with a PDF you want to open:

```
1  start taxes.pdf
```

That's just like double-clicking on `taxes.pdf`. You can also open any other directories:

```
1   start ~/Desktop/Games
```

That is just like double-clicking on the `Games` folder on your Desktop. I recommend you use `start` very frequently while you're learning PowerShell so you start to learn where you are using what you already know about the computer. Soon you won't need it unless you actually want to use your mouse on something and need to open the folder.

Going from Graphics to PowerShell

The `start` command is very useful, but you'll also need a way to go from a directory (folder) you have open in Explorer to a command in PowerShell. You can take any file that is open in your Explorer and drag it to your PowerShell window to "insert" that file's path into your PowerShell command. Test this by first opening your Desktop:

```
1   start ~/Desktop
```

Now start a new `ls` command, but *do not hit ENTER*:

```
1   ls  # stop here
```

Pick a random file in your Desktop window, grab it with your mouse, and drag it into the PowerShell window, and the full path should get inserted into your command. Here's what happens if I drag my `Games` folder to the window:

```
1   ls C:\Users\Zed\Desktop\Games
```

This is the other part of connecting your Explorer/Folder view of the computer to PowerShell's text view of the computer. This works on any file, so if you're ever lost trying to find where a file is, do this:

1.   Open the file in Explorer

2.   Grab the file you can't find with your mouse

3.   Drag it to any PowerShell window

4.   Now you have the full path to the file

Where Are You with pwd?

In Windows your home directory is located in `C:\Users\username` where `username` is whatever you use to log in. Mine is named `C:\Users\lcthw` because I use the login "lcthw" on my Windows computer.

When you start PowerShell, you start off in this directory. Try this command to see where that is:

```
1   pwd
```

This prints out your working directory (pwd means "print working directory"), which is where your Power Shell is located on your disk drive. You should then look to the left and see that PowerShell is printing out the same information for your command prompt. Here's mine:

```
1   Path
2   ----
3   C:\Users\lcthw\Projects\lpythw
```

The difference is pwd prints out the *entire path* to your current location, so in my case this is C:\Users ↳ \lcthw\Projects\lpythw. On the prompt, though, it prints only the name of the current directory, which is lpythw.

What's in Here?

When you save a file you're working on, it is written to the disk in your home directory. The problem is it's saved "somewhere" in your home directory and you have to go find it. To do that you need two commands: one to list a directory and one to change to a directory (which you learn later).

Each directory has a listing of its contents, which you can see with the ls command:

```
1   ls
2   ls Desktop
3   ls ~
```

In the previous examples I first list the contents of the current directory. The "current directory" is also the "working directory" from the pwd ("print working directory") command. It's simply wherever your Power-Shell says you are in the prompt or when you run pwd. Next, I list the contents of the Desktop directory, which should be files and "folders" sitting on your Desktop.

Finally, I use a special character ~ (tilde) to list the contents of my home directory. In PowerShell the ~ character is short for "my home directory." Look at this example to see how that works:

```
1   C:\Users\lcthw
2   > pwd
3
4   Path
5   ----
6   /Users/lcthw
7
8
9   C:\Users\lcthw
10  > ls /Users/lctw
```

```
11  # ... lots of output
12
13  C:\Users\lcthw
14  > ls ~
15  # ... the same output
```

You can see here that the pwd command says I'm in /Users/zed on my Windows computer, and if I use ls /Users/zed or ls ~, then I get the same output.

In PowerShell the # (octothorpe) character is used to make a comment or a block of text that PowerShell ignores. You can write a comment there like I did here. In this case I'm cutting all of the output, but I'm using a comment to tell you that it was a lot of output and then the same output. Because that line starts with #, it will be ignored by PowerShell.

Files, Folders, Directories, and Paths

Before I cover how to move around your directories, I need to explain three interconnected concepts. Files contain your data, and they will have names like mydiary.txt or ex1.py.

Those files are located inside directories, which you've seen such as /Users/zed. Directories can go "deeper," meaning I can put directories inside directories inside directories with files inside those. I could have a directory called /Users/zed/Projects/lpythw, and if I put my ex1.py file in there, it would live at /Users/zed/Projects/lpythw/ex1.py.

That last part is called the "path," and you can think of it like a path through a maze that leads to a special room. You can also combine the concept of ~ (tilde) to replace /Users/zed, and then the path becomes ~/Projects/lpythw/ex1.py.

If you have directories, files, and paths when you use PowerShell, then how do they map to "folders" when you're looking through Explorer?

There is no difference between "folder" and "directory." They are the same thing, so if you traverse a series of mouse clicks in Explorer to access "folders," then you can use that path of clicks to list the contents of that as a "directory." They are literally the same thing, and it's important for you to get this idea.

One way to learn that they are connected is to use your Explorer to create folders, place small files in them, and then use PowerShell to find these files and open them. Think of it like a treasure hunt in your Terminal. Before you can do that, you'll need the cd command for "changing directories."

Moving Around

You know how to list a directory from where you are in PowerShell:

```
1  ls ~/Projects/lpythw/
```

You can also *change* to that *directory* with the cd command:

```
1  cd ~/Projects/lpythw/
2  pwd
```

This exact command won't work for you since you never created the directory "Projects" and lpythw, but take the time now to make those in your Finder window (Create Folder is what you want) and then use cd like I demonstrate.

The idea with PowerShell and cd is you are moving around in the directories as if they're small rooms with connecting corridors. If you've ever played a video game, then you know what this is like. Your cd Projects/lpythw command is like moving your character into the room named Projects and then walking into the next room, lpythw.

Take the time right now to continue using ls, pwd, and cd to explore your computer. Make directories (folders) in your Finder window and then attempt to access them from inside PowerShell until your brain makes the connection. This might take a while since you're trying to map the graphical interface you've used for years to textual elements that are new.

Relative Paths

Imagine you did this:

```
1  cd ~/Projects/lpythw
```

Now you're stuck in this lpythw directory, so how you "go back"? You need the relative path operator:

```
1  cd ..
```

The .. (dot dot) says "the directory above my current directory," so in this case since Projects is "above" lpythw, it makes .. mean Projects. These two commands are the same then:

```
1  cd ..
2  cd ~/Projects
```

If Projects contained two directories named lpythw and mycode, you could do this:

```
1  cd ~/Projects/lpythw
2  # oops I meant mycode
3  cd ../mycode
```

If you're still thinking of cd like moving between rooms in a building, then .. is how you go back the way you came.

Creating and Destroying

You don't have to use any graphical interfaces to create directories. You can use commands, and for decades this was how you interacted with files. The commands for manipulating directories and files are:

- mkdir—Creates a new directory
- rmdir—Removes a directory, but only if it's empty
- rm—Removes (almost) anything
- new-item—Makes a new empty file or directory

I'm purposefully not fully explaining these commands because I want *you* to figure them out and learn them on your own. Figuring out these commands helps you *own* your own education and makes it stick. Use what you know so far to learn the commands, such as using get-help -name rm to read the manual.

Flags and Arguments

Commands have a structure that goes something (but not exactly) like this:

```
1  command flags arguments
```

The command is the word you type, like ls, cd, or cp. The "flags" are things you write to configure how the command should run, and they start with - in PowerShell.

> **INFO** Commands like python come from Unix, so they will use options flags that start with – as well. For example, python –help.

Then you have the "arguments," which are space-delimited (or comma-delimited) pieces of information you give to the command. With cp this is two arguments that give the source and destination of the files:

```
1  cp ex1.txt ex1.py
```

In this example the file ex1.txt is the first argument, and ex1.py is the second argument, so this would copy the first argument to the second argument.

Copy and Move

You can also copy a file and move a file, or directory. Continue with your self-education and attempt to learn about and use these new commands:

- cp—Copies files
- mv—Moves files

Remember that you can use `get-help cp` and `get-help mv` to study the commands. These commands are also the first ones to take multiple arguments, which you just learned about.

Environment Variables

The commands so far are clearly configured using the – (dash) options, but many of them are also configured using a slightly hidden thing called "environment variables," or "env vars" for short. These are settings that live in your shell and are not visible immediately but work to configure persistent options for all commands. To see your environment, type this:

```
1  get-childitem env:
```

You can also specify a single variable to view:

```
1  $env:path
```

That should print your PATH variable, which specifies the directories that PowerShell will search for programs you run, like `python.exe`.

Running Code

Finally! The entire point of this whole lesson! How do you run code? Imagine you have a Python file named `ex1.py` and you want to run it to see its output (and see if it works):

```
1  python ex1.py
```

As you can see, `python` is the Python "runner," and it simply loads the `ex1.py` file and runs it. Python also takes many options, so try this:

```
1  python --help
```

The other command you'll use often is the `conda` command, which installs Python libraries for your project:

```
1  conda install pytest
```

If you create a directory named `testproject`, cd into it, and run this command, you'll install the pytest testing framework. We'll use this command more later, but for now that's mostly what you need to know.

Common Key Sequences

There are three key sequences you'll need to know when you work with your software:

- CTRL-c—Aborts a program
- CTRL-z—Closes your input, usually exiting a program
- CTRL-d—In some Unix software ported to Windows, you have to use CTRL-d instead of CTRL-z

These aren't totally reliable ways to abort a program, since it's possible for programmers to catch them and prevent you from exiting. They should work most of the time, though.

Useful Developer Commands

Curl is useful when you're working on a website and you need to make sure you're getting the real output. You run it like this:

```
1  curl http://127.0.0.1:5000
```

We'll get into what all of that means later, but just remember curl is your tool for looking at the full text of a website.

Crash Landing

This is definitely not enough to be a master of the PowerShell, but it should be enough to understand what I'm doing in the rest of the course and to have enough to follow along. I highly recommend you constantly use start to figure out where you are and read the Microsoft Introductory Course to learn more than this.

Beyond Jupyter for macOS/Linux

Jupyter is a great environment for interactive analysis. You can load your data, mess with it, refine it, generate graphs, add documentation, and even edit files. For most daily work an analyst does, that might be enough, but Jupyter has a few limitations:

1. It's difficult to share your analysis with other people in a way they can *reuse*. Sure, you can give them a notebook to look at or publish online in various ways, but there's no ability to *import* a Jupyter notebook the way you can easily `import` a Python module.

2. Jupyter notebooks tend to promote "copy-pasta code," which means you'll more often copy-paste the common code you need in every notebook or just keep a stock template notebook around with your usual setup. That works for a while, but eventually it degrades, especially if you find a bug and now have to go through every notebook fixing the bug in all your copy-paste code. It's far more efficient to take your common "boilerplate" code and place it in a module you import. This also makes something you can share with other people who might need to work with the same systems as you.

3. You can't run automated tests on a Jupyter notebook. Automated tests are an amazing re-source for ensuring your code keeps working as you make changes and for helping other people who use your code confirm it's working. The primary area you'll find this useful is when you do data munging. Data tends to be gross and change often, so tests confirm your code keeps working when you have to update various data models.

4. Ninety-eight percent of other programmers do not use Jupyter. If you're working on any analysis that you plan on giving to a programmer, you'll need to "formalize" it into a Python project they can grab and use. If you can create a basic project, place in their favorite version control system, and write some documentation, then they can usually improve it for you. If you just throw them a `Untitled.ipynb` before going on vacation for a month, you will be hated with all the passion of a thousand dying suns. Or just ignored. It depends on where you work.

5. Another benefit of turning your `Untitled.ipynb` into a formal Python project is *perspective*. Many times something you thought was very good changes when you translate it to another language, platform, or medium. You might think your analysis is amazing and then you convert it to a Python module only to find that it's total junk or could be far more efficient. This is similar to how painters look at paintings upside down to find errors or musicians listen to their songs in cars. A change of perspective will almost always show ways you can improve the work.

6. The most important reason to learn how to code Python without Jupyter is *independence*. I don't indoctrinate people in my educational style because I feel it's wrong to create students who depend on specific products, companies, languages, or communities. I want you to be able

to migrate from one technology to another as the fashion of programming changes, because this really is a fashion industry. One day, Python and Jupyter are the best things ever, and the next day everyone is on some new hot technology an "influencer" raved about in a YouTube video. If you want a long career in this industry, you *do not* want to be dependent on anything, and the first step to this independence is learning how to use your computer like a programmer.

Does this mean you should *not* use Jupyter? No, Jupyter is awesome for doing your analysis and figuring out what to write. I want you to be able to use *both* Jupyter *and* other systems depending on what you need to do, and to accomplish this goal I will teach you the *basics of the command line*.

macOS Troubles

If you are using macOS, you may be forced to use a different shell called zsh. You should be able to use all of these commands with zsh, but if you want to use Bash, then you can force macOS to use Bash. Type this command in Terminal:

```
1   chsh -s /bin/bash
```

Then log out of your computer completely and log back in. If it worked, then you should be able to type:

```
1   echo $SHELL
```

That command should print out "/bin/bash" and you're done.

Why Learn Bash or ZSH?

Graphical systems are great for graphical things, but they tend to fall over when you have to do anything that requires a lot of repetition or pattern matching. Open an Finder window now and try to list all of the files that start with ex but end with a number and .py. Doing this with Bash is trivial:

```
1   ls ex*[0-9].py
```

That seems complicated, but at the end of this exercise you'll understand it and be able to use Bash to control your computer. Should use *only* Bash? No, of course not. Use the best tool for the job, and Bash is the best tool for many *programming* tasks.

What Is Bash?

Just in case you're not familiar with Bash, it's a mini programming language that allows you to control your computer with commands. These commands have a common form of:

```
1   command -o1 --option-number2 arg1 arg2
```

The -o1 is a "short option," which is usually a single character, but if those are hard to remember, most commands have a --two-word version you can use instead. A command is usually something you need the computer to do:

- ls – Lists files
- cp – Copies files
- rm – Removes files

Each of these commands takes options that start with a - (dash) character for single-letter options, and -- for one- or two-word options. For example, ls has the option -R like this:

```
1  ls -R
```

Finally, you can add arguments to a command, which is usually some resource to run the command against:

```
1  ls -R ~/Desktop
```

If this spews a bunch of text to the screen, you can hold CTRL and hit c to abort it. You might have to hit it many times to make it abort. One caveat of Bash's arguments is it expects multiple items to be separated by a space, and you may have to put quotes around anything with a space in the name:

```
1  ls -R ~/Desktop "~/Photos/My Family Pics"
```

You'll learn this command more in this exercise, but let's break down this line so you understand it:

1. ls is the command we want.
2. -R means "recursively descend into all directories (folders)."
3. ~ (tilde) means "my home directory," which is the top folder that holds your user's files. Mine is /Users/Zed
4. / separates directories (folders) in a path. A path is simply the chain of folders you click on to go from your home to some deeper folder you want to access.
5. Desktop is the first directory (folder) I want to list.
6. (space) separates the first directory to list from the second one.
7. "~/Photos/My Family Pics" is just like the first directory ~/Desktop, but I have to put quotes around it because it has a space in the name My Family Pics. You have to do this because Bash would think My, Family, and Pics are all arguments to ls

Now we can get into the commands you'll typically use the most. I think these commands make up 95% of my daily usage.

Starting Jupyter

Since you're already using Jupyter, it helps to know how to start it while you're in Bash. The easiest way is with the jupyter-lab command:

```
1  jupyter-lab
```

You can run a specific notebook by adding it to the command:

```
1  jupyter-lab Untitled.ipynb
```

See the following instructions on using open to help you find your files with your mouse.

Getting Help

Usually you can get help for a command by adding either -h or --help to the command like this:

```
1  man -h
```

This tends to fail with some commands, so the other way to get help is to use the man command to print out the "manual" for the command:

```
1  man ls
```

This will print out the entire documentation for the ls command. I usually try -h first, and if that doesn't work, then I use man.

Where Are You with open?

You've spent most of your time using the Finder window to navigate your computer. If you don't know what "Finder" is, it's just the GUI window that opens when you click on a folder. In fact, you'll usually call something a "folder" and in the Terminal you'll call it a "directory" when they're exactly the same thing. I've spent most of my computer life using some kind of Terminal and shell to navigate computers, so I'm familiar with "seeing" the computer via the text outputs. You can use the command open to connect your view of the computer through graphics to my view of the computer through text like this:

```
1  open .
```

The `.` means "this current directory (folder)," and open opens this current directory in Finder. The open command actually works like double-clicking on a file, so you can open any file with it to see it. Let's say you're in a folder with a PDF you want to open:

```
1   open taxes.pdf
```

That's just like double-clicking on `taxes.pdf`. You can also open directories that aren't just `.`:

```
1   open ~/Desktop/Games
```

That is just like double-clicking on the Games folder on your Desktop. I recommend you use open very frequently while you're learning Bash so you start to learn where you are using what you already know about the computer. Soon you won't need it unless you actually want to use your mouse on something and need to open the folder.

Going from Graphics to Bash

The open command is very useful, but you'll also need a way to go from a directory (folder) you have open in Finder to a command in Bash. You can take any file that is open in your Finder and drag it to your Bash window to "insert" that file's path into your bash command. Test this by first opening your Desktop:

```
1   open ~/Desktop
```

Now start a new `ls` command but *do not hit ENTER*:

```
1   ls  # stop here
```

Pick a random file in your Desktop window, grab it with your mouse, and drag it into the Bash window, and the full path should get inserted into your command. Here's what happens if I drag my Games folder to the window:

```
1   ls /Users/Zed/Desktop/Games
```

This is the other part of connecting your Finder/Folder view of the computer to Bash's text view of the computer. This works on any file, so if you're ever lost trying to find where a file is, do this:

1.   Open the file in Finder

2.   Grab the file you can't find with your mouse

3.   Drag it to any Bash window

Now you have the full path to the file.

Where Are You with pwd?

On macOS your real home directory is `/Users/username` where "username" is whatever you use to log in. Mine is therefore named `/Users/zed`, but on Linux they use `/home/username` instead. On Linux my home directory is `/home/zed`.

When you start a terminal, you start off in this home directory. Try this command to see where that is:

```
1    pwd
```

This prints out your working directory (pwd means "print working directory") and says you are in the disk drive. You should then look to the left and see that *Bash* is printing out the same information for your command prompt. Here's mine:

```
1    Zeds-iMac-Pro:lpythw zed$ pwd
2    /Users/zed/Projects/lpythw
```

The difference is pwd prints out the *entire path* to your current location, so in my case this is `/Users/zed` ↳ `/Projects/lpythw`. On the prompt, though, it prints only the name of the current directory, which is `lpythw`. Bash also prints out other useful information such as my computer name (`Zeds-iMac-Pro`) and my current username (`zed`).

What's in Here?

When you save a file you're working on, it is written to the disk in your home directory. The problem is it's saved "somewhere" in your home directory and you have to go find it. To do that, you need two commands: one to list a directory and one to change to a directory (which you learn later).

Each directory has a listing of its contents, which you can see with the `ls` command:

```
1    ls
2    ls Desktop
3    ls ~
```

In the previous examples I first list the contents of the current directory. The "current directory" is also the "working directory" from the pwd ("print working directory") command. It's simply wherever your Bash shell says you are in the prompt or when you run pwd. Next, I list the contents of the `Desktop` directory, which should be files and "folders" sitting on your Desktop.

Finally, I use a special character ~ (tilde) to list the contents of my home directory. On Unix systems (Linux and macOS) the ~ character is short for "my home directory." Look at this example to see how that works:

```
1    Zeds-iMac-Pro:~ zed$ pwd
2    /Users/zed
```

```
3    Zeds-iMac-Pro:~ zed$ ls /Users/zed
4    # ... lots of output
5    Zeds-iMac-Pro:~ zed$ ls ~
6    # ... the same output
```

You can see here that the pwd command says I'm in /Users/zed on my macOS computer, and if I use ls /Users/zed or ls ~, then I get the same output.

In Bash the # (octothorpe) character is used to make a comment or a block of text that Bash ignores. You can write a comment there like I did here. In this case I'm cutting all of the output, but I'm using a comment to tell you that it was a lot of output and then the same output. Because that line starts with #, it will be ignored by Bash.

Files, Folders, Directories, and Paths

Before I cover how to move around your directories, I need to explain three interconnected concepts. Files are what holds your data, and they will have names like mydiary.txt or ex1.py.

Those files are located inside directories that you've seen such as /Users/zed. Directories can go "deeper," meaning I can put directories inside directories inside directories with files inside those. I could have a directory called /Users/zed/Projects/lpythw, and if I put my ex1.py file in there, it would live at /Users/zed/Projects/lpythw/ex1.py.

That last part is called the "path," and you can think of it like a path through a maze that leads to a special room. You can also combine the concept of ~ (tilde) to replace /Users/zed, and then the path becomes ~/Projects/lpythw/ex1.py.

If you have directories, files, and paths when you use Bash, then how does that map to "folders" when you're looking through a graphical file browser? I say "graphical file browser" because Bash works on macOS and Linux, and how you view files graphically is different on both of them. On macOS this is the "Finder window" you get when you click on a *folder* on your computer.

There is no difference between "folder" and "directory." They are the same thing, so if you traverse a series of mouse clicks in Finder to access "folders," then you can use that path of clicks to list the contents of that as a "directory." They are literally the same thing, and it's important for you to get this idea.

One way to learn that they are connected is to use your Finder to create folders, place small files in them, and then use Bash to find these files and open them. Think of it like a treasure hunt in your Terminal. Before you can do that, you'll need the cd command for "changing directories."

Moving Around

You know how to list a directory from where you are in Bash:

```
1   ls ~/Projects/lpythw/
```

You can also *change* to that *directory* with the cd command:

```
1   cd ~/Projects/lpythw/
2   pwd
```

This won't magically work for you since you never created the directory "Projects" and "lpythw", but take the time now to make those in your Finder window (Create Folder is what you want) and then use cd like I demonstrate.

The idea with Bash and cd is you are moving around in the directories as if they're small rooms with connecting corridors. If you've ever played a video game, then you know what this is like. Your cd Projects/lpythw command is like moving your character into the room named Projects and then walking into the next room, lpythw.

Take the time right now to continue using ls, pwd, and cd to explore your computer. Make directories (folders) in your Finder window and then attempt to access them from inside Bash until your brain makes the connection. This might take a while since you're trying to map the graphical interface you've used for years to textual elements that are new.

Relative Paths

Imagine you did this:

```
1   cd ~/Projects/lpythw
```

Now you're stuck in this lpythw directory, so how you "go back"? You need the relative path operator:

```
1   cd ..
```

The .. (dot dot) says "the directory above my current directory," so in this case since Projects is "above" lpythw, it makes .. mean Projects. These two commands are the same then:

```
1   cd ..
2   cd ~/Projects
```

If Projects contained two directories named lpythw and mycode, you could do this:

```
1   cd ~/Projects/lpythw
2   # oops I meant mycode
3   cd ../mycode
```

If you're still thinking of cd like moving between rooms in a building, then .. is how you go back the way you came.

Creating and Destroying

You don't have to use any graphical interfaces to create directories. You can use commands, and for decades this was how you interacted with files. The commands for manipulating directories and files are:

- mkdir—Creates a new directory
- rmdir—Removes a directory, but only if it's empty
- rm—Removes anything. Use rm -rf to remove a directory no matter what
- touch—Makes a new empty file

I'm purposefully not fully explaining these commands because I want *you* to figure them out and learn them on your own. Figuring out these commands helps you *own* your own education and makes it stick. Use what you know so far to learn the commands, such as using man rm to read the manual.

Hidden Files

On Unix systems like macOS and Linux there's a slight "gotcha" when it comes to files. Imagine you attempt to delete a diretory:

```
1  Zeds-iMac-Pro:~ zed$ rmdir Projects
2  rmdir: Projects: Directory not empty
```

You get this error that Projects is not empty, and that's because the lpythw directory is in there, so you try this:

```
1  Zeds-iMac-Pro:~ zed$ rmdir Projects/lpythw
2  rmdir: Projects/lpythw: Directory not empty
```

What? You totally emptied that directory out, so how is "not empty"? Try this:

```
1  cd Projects/lpythw
2  ls -la
```

Now you see this weird new file, the dreaded .DS_Store. This would be only on the macOS system, because any Unix system considers a file starting with . (dot) to be a special file it won't show you normally. To see it, you have to use the ls -la command to list all of the files, even hidden ones.

Flags and Arguments

Commands have a structure that goes something (but not exactly) like this:

```
1   command flags arguments
```

The command is the word you type, like `ls`, `cd`, or `cp`. The "flags" are things you write to configure how the command should run, and they start with `-` or `--`. This is what you did with `ls -la`. You added the flags `-l` and `-a` to the `ls` command to tell it to "list all" files. You don't have to give each flag as an individual `-` when they are single letters. You can combine them as I did with `-la`.

The other kind of flag is the `--blah` style and is usually used only as an alternative that's more readable compared to the single-letter versions. Sometimes these flags are also written as `--var=value` style.

Then you have the "arguments," which are space-delimited pieces of information you give to the command. With `cp` this is two arguments that give the source and destination of the files:

```
1   cp ex1.txt ex1.py
```

In this example the file `ex1.txt` is the first argument, and `ex1.py` is the second argument, so this would copy the first argument to the second argument.

Finally, you can combine these, so if I want to copy an entire directory and its contents, I do:

```
1   cp -r lpythw backup
```

The `-r` option means "recursive," which is a fancy computer science way of saying "go down into the directory." Doing this will make a whole copy of `lpythw` to `backup`.

Copy and Move

You can also copy a file and move a file, or directory. Continue with your self-education and attempt to learn about and use these new commands:

- `cp`—Copies files
- `mv`—Moves files

Remember that you can use `man cp` and `man mv` to study the commands. These commands are also the first ones to take multiple arguments, which you just learned about.

Environment Variables

The commands so far are clearly configured using the - (dash) and - - (dash dash) style options, but many of them are also configured using a slightly hidden thing called "environment variables," or "env vars" for short. These are settings that live in your Shell and are not visible immediately but work to configure persistent options for all commands. To see your environment, type this:

```
1   env
```

There's also a handy command called grep, which takes the output of one command and filters it to show only what you want, so try this:

```
1   env | grep PATH
```

Now you should see only the PATH variable's settings. What's that | (pipe) character doing? It's called a "pipe," and you can think of it like a...pipe. Seriously, it's a pipe taking the output of one command and sending it to the input of another. They're very handy, and you'll see me use them a lot in the course, but they're also very simple. Output goes to input. That's it. Like a pipe.

Running Code

Finally! The entire point of this whole lesson! How do you run code? Imagine you have a Python file named ex1.py and you want to run it to see its output (and see if it works):

```
1   python ex1.py
```

As you can see, python is the Python "runner," and it simply loads the ex1.py file and runs it. Python also takes many options, so try this:

```
1   python --help
```

The other command you'll use often is the conda command, which installs Python libraries for your project:

```
1   conda install pytest
```

If you create a directory named testproject, cd into it, and run this command, you'll install the pytest web framework. We'll use this command more later, but for now that's mostly what you need to know.

Common Key Sequences

There's two key sequences you'll need to know when you work with your software:

- CTRL-c—Aborts a program
- CTRL-d—Closes your input, usually exiting a program

These aren't totally reliable ways to abort a program, since it's possible for programmers to catch them and prevent you from exiting. For example, here's the GNU bc command being very helpful (not):

```
1   Zeds-iMac-Pro:~ zed$ bc
2   bc 1.06
3   Copyright 1991-1994, 1997, 1998, 2000 Free Software Foundation, Inc.
4   This is free software with ABSOLUTELY NO WARRANTY.
5   For details type `warranty'.
6   2 + 5
7   7
8
9   (interrupt) use quit to exit.
10  quit
```

So helpful. Thank you for telling me that I can't use CTRL-c but have to use "quit" to quit. I'm sure someone spent many hours doing the work to catch the CTRL-c key sequence just to tell me to then type quit instead of just…quitting for me.

Despite this, usually these two key sequences will get you out of a program or print a message telling you how to do that.

Useful Developer Commands

There are three commands that come up as useful developer commands:

- curl—If you give this a URL from a browser, it will *usually* display the raw text. You might want to do curl -L URL to tell curl to follow redirects.
- ps—Lists all of the running processes on your computer.
- kill—Lets you kill a process. Use this if it's running and you can stop it: kill -KILL PID

Curl is useful when you're working on a website and you need to make sure you're getting the real output. You run it like this:

```
1   curl http://127.0.0.1:5000
```

We'll get into what all of that means later, but just remember Curl is your tool for looking at the full text of a website.

The ps command lists the processes that are currently running. A process is simply one of the programs you've ran, and this situation comes up usually when you have multiple Terminal windows or multiple tabs open. You might have a command that you can kill with CTRL-C so you can use ps to find it, and kill to kill it. First do this:

```
1  Zeds-iMac-Pro:~ zedshaw$ ps
2    PID TTY           TIME CMD
3    677 ttys000    0:00.03 /Applications/iTerm.app/Contents/MacOS/iTerm2
4    679 ttys000    0:00.05 -bash
5   1684 ttys001    0:00.03 /Applications/iTerm.app/Contents/MacOS/iTerm2
6   1686 ttys001    0:00.01 -bash
```

That will list all of the processes running at the moment, and you can see my output shows a couple of Terminals open. The PID is the "process ID," and that number lets you kill the process from another window. Just grab the PID, go to a new window, and type:

```
1  kill -KILL 679
```

You can also use kill -TERM PID to be a little nicer about it. Usually I try TERM, and if that doesn't work, I do KILL.

Crash Landing

This is definitely not enough to be a master of the bash, but it should be enough to understand what I'm doing in the rest of the course and to have enough to follow along.

Advanced Developer Tools

This exercise is all about avoiding "footguns." A "footgun" is a gun specifically designed to shoot yourself right in the foot. It points straight down all the time and has no safety latch, so every time you try to aim a footgun, you just blast your toe off. Software is full of these footguns because of limitations in the software, bad configuration designs, or other oversights of usability.

INFO If you have problems with these instructions and you're reading them in a printed version of the course, then please visit https://learncodethehardway.com/setup/python/ for the latest fixes and install instructions.

Managing conda Environments

Python has a useful feature called "environments," where you can install software specific to a project in a safe place. You "activate" your environment for a project, do your work, and deactivate when you're done. This feature is necessary because you can have conflicting requirements between different projects making it difficult to work on different projects on the same machine.

You create and activate a new environment named "lpythw" with conda:

```
1   conda create --name lpythw
2   conda activate lpythw
```

Once you do this, you should see your Shell prompt change to mention lpythw, so you know you're in that environment. After this you can install all the software you need, and when you're done, you deactivate it:

```
1   conda deactivate
```

You should use a new environment for all of your projects and don't install software in the base environment. This makes it easier to recover from bad installs.

Finally, you can list environments with conda info --envs:

```
1   $ conda info --envs
2   # conda environments:
3   #
4   base                     /Users/Zed/anaconda3
5   lpythw              *    /Users/Zed/anaconda3/envs/lpythw
```

You can list the packages in an environment with conda list.

Adding conda-forge

The official Anaconda repository has a lot of software, but sometimes you need more. To get more software use the very nice conda-forge project. This is a community-led stream of additional packages to augment the base conda packages. To set up conda-forge do this:

```
1  # confirm version >= 4.9
2  conda --version
3
4  # get to base env
5  conda deactivate
```

This sets up your environment to be the latest and work reliably. Next, you'll want to install a faster "solver," which is the part of conda that determines what to install:

```
1  # speed up anaconda significantly
2  conda install -n base conda-libmamba-solver
3  conda config --set solver libmamba
```

The libmamba solver should install, but if you get errors with libarchive.19, then you can't use mamba without deleting your Anaconda install and starting over fresh. Either way, you can now do your update:

```
1  # this can take a while
2  conda update -n base conda
```

You can then add the conda-forge channel to gain access to extra software; however, I'll have you install it using the "safe" way, which gives it *less* priority than the official software from Anaconda:

```
1  # add the conda-forge channel
2  conda config --append channels conda-forge
3  # make conda-forge versions priority
4  conda config --set channel_priority strict
```

I've tried to use it a different way, and placing conda-forge ahead of the default channel causes significant install problems with version numbers.

Finally, let's make an environment you can use from now on to do your work:

```
1  # create your environment
2  conda create -n lpythw
3  conda activate lpythw
```

Once you do this, you'll have access to almost everything you need, but you *might* need to use another command called pip. I recommend reading the Tips and Tricks for additional information, especially if you use an Apple CPU Mac and need to install software.

Using pip

The pip command is the most common method for installing software in a generic Python project. The pip command installs software from a different source than the conda command, so if you run pip inside an Anaconda environment, you can get version conflicts. If conda has software that needs a project version 1.2 but pip installs version 2.6, then you'll have weird software bugs and crashes. This is especially true if the module you install uses a compiled binary component.

With conda-forge enabled you will most likely have everything you'd need from pip, but if there *is* a module you need that is not available in conda-forge, then there are two ways you can use pip if you're desperate. First, you can make a new environment that *has only pip installs*:

```
1   conda create --name newenv-pip
2   conda activate newenv-pip
3   pip install package
4   # use only pip after this
```

I tag these environments with -pip at the end of their names so I know they use only pip. If you absolutely have to use a mix of conda and pip projects, then you'll need to create a new environment, but use conda before you use pip:

```
1   conda create --name new-condapip
2   conda activate new-condapip
3   conda install x-package
4   conda install y-package
5   pip install z-package
```

This works because conda knows about pip, so you can do first installs using conda, and then pip will work. If you do it the other way, pip doesn't know about conda, so it'll mess up the conda installs. You should also notice I tack on -condapip so I know what kind of environment this is.

Using a .condarc

There should be a file named .condarc in your home directory that currently has these contents:

```
1   channels:
2     - conda-forge
3     - defaults
4   channel_priority: strict
```

This file holds configuration values for conda, which you probably don't need to change, but if you ever do, you can find the documentation for it at the official documentation.

General Editing Tips

This advice applies to most editors, not just Geany:

1. Don't use `tab` characters unless the actual language demands it. Some programmers think that tabs are more usable, but they easily get mangled by various editors because of differences in configurations. Emacs is notorious for "compressing" `tab` characters to be three or five spaces and then having to add extra spaces when it saves a file. This changes the indentation in bad ways and gets sent to other programmers who have different configurations causing all hell to break loose, especially in Python. Other editors do this, and since nobody can absolutely guarantee that a `tab` will always be an even number of spaces and never "compressed," it's best to avoid them.

2. You might want to turn on "visible spaces" in your editor when working with Python. In Geany this is set with *View->Show White Space* and will show each `tab` and space character with small gray symbols. Most editors have a similar setting, so research it. In other languages this isn't as useful but doesn't hurt.

3. Save constantly in most editors. You can usually hit CTRL-S repeatedly while you work to make sure it's saved. I use an editor named Vim, which mostly does this for me, but I do save quite often still.

4. Geany is pretty great, but you should try as many editors as you can. You never know when you'll stumble on an editor that just sings to you in your dreams. Eventually you'll land on one that works for you, and you can fine-tune it to your exact work style.

5. Start changing your configuration in the editor you use to solve problems you might have. Every editor lets you change fonts, colors, background, and orientation of windows, and many have plugins. Geany has a nice list of plugins for many things you may want, so try them. You can even write plugins in Python using Geanypy, so if there's something very specific, this might be a fun project for you. Visual Studio Code also has a massive number of plugins that are easy to install.

6. If you're working on a platform that has a specific IDE, then don't fight it, and just use that company's IDE. If I'm writing software for an Android phone, then I'm using Android Studio. If I'm writing software for an iPhone, then–you guessed it–I'm using Xcode. I do prefer the power and freedom of using Vim, but fanaticism just gets in the way of reaching my goals.

Going Further

The overall advice I can give you about working as a programmer is to assume you own your experience with your computer. If you're using an editor and hate the font, change it. Need "dark mode" but it's not supported? Find a way to change it or use a different editor. Don't just accept things the way they are, and learn to change your computer to help you be more productive, comfortable, or happy while you work.

A Project Skeleton

This exercise is completely optional but useful if you want to create your own package to use in other projects. I will show you how to create a project for your code, install it locally in your conda environment, and use it. I won't cover how to publish it to PyPI or Anaconda's channels, but there's plenty of documentation online if you get to that point.

As you go through this documentation, you'll run into dead ends where the install doesn't work. Any time you run into errors, I recommend you delete your test_project and try it again. Usually it's because you missed a step, and attempting the install again will probably get it right. This works for almost any software you need to install.

Activate an Environment

Whatever you do, do not test this while in the base environment. Switch to the lpythw environment or any one that you have already:

```
1  conda activate lpythw
```

This will ensure that if you break the environment with your install, you can remove it and recover.

Just Use cookiecutter

Audrey and Danny Roy Greenfeld are two friends of mine who created the cookiecutter project. This project generates other files and projects in consistent ways so you don't have to remember every little thing about specific file formats or directory structures. We'll use it here to create a basic conda project using the cookiecutter-conda-python module:

```
1  conda install cookiecutter
```

Once cookiecutter is installed, you can create a quick test_project to play with:

```
1  cookiecutter https://github.com/conda/cookiecutter-conda-python.git
2  full_name [Full Name]: Zed Shaw
3  email [Email Address]: help@learncodethehardway.com
4  github_username [Destination github org or username]: lcthw
5  repo_name [repository-name]: test_project
6  package_name [test_project]: test_project
7  project_short_description [Short description]: A test project.
8  noarch_python [y]: y
9  include_cli [y]: y
```

```
10  Select open_source_license:
11  1 - MIT
12  2 - BSD
13  3 - ISC
14  4 - Apache
15  5 - GNUv3
16  6 - Proprietary
17  Choose from 1, 2, 3, 4, 5, 6 [1]: 1
```

I chose the MIT license just for a test, but if you chose 6 - Proprietary, then it doesn't make a LICENSE file for you, and that causes later steps to fail. If you did this, then just make an empty LICENSE file in the test_project directory.

Now that you've created the directory, you can start to work on it:

```
1  cd test_project
2  # make the LICENSE if you picked 6 above
3  ls
```

You should spend some time now to explore the contents of this directory and then create a file to play with later in test_project/testing.py:

```
1  def hello():
2      print("Hello!")
```

Building Your Project

You now need to tell conda to build the project with conda build conda.recipe. The conda.recipe directory contains all the build information, mostly in the conda.recipe/meta.yaml file. If you run into problems, check in that file, especially if you didn't make a LICENSE file.

```
1  conda build conda.recipe
2  # tons of output
3  # look for this line
4  TEST END: /Users/USER/anaconda3/conda-bld/noarch/test-project-0+unknown-py_0
       ↳ .tar.bz2
```

If you have errors, see the *Common Errors* section to see if it's a common error.

Installing Your Project

When you run the build, it puts the resulting test-project-0+unknown-py_0.tar.bz2 in an ... interesting location on your computer. In the install instructions I had you look for the TEST END line:

```
1  TEST END: /Users/USER/anaconda3/conda-bld/noarch/test-project-0+unknown-py_0
       ↳ .tar.bz2
2
```

```
3  # on windows it's
4  TEST END: C:\Users\lcthw\anaconda3\conda-bld\noarch\test-project-0+unknown-
      ↳ py_0.tar.bz2
```

That's where your package is, so now you can install it with `conda install`:

```
1  conda install /Users/USER/anaconda3/conda-bld/noarch/test-project-0+unknown-
      ↳ py_0.tar.bz2
2  Downloading and Extracting Packages
3  Downloading and Extracting Packages
4  Preparing transaction: done
5  Verifying transaction: done
6  Executing transaction: done
```

Once it's installed, you should see it in the list of packages:

```
1  $ conda list test-project
2  # packages in environment at /Users/USER/anaconda3/envs/lpythw:
3  #
4  # Name                    Version                   Build   Channel
5  test-project              0+unknown                 py_0    local
```

Notice that it renamed the project `test-project`, but if you name your project with a - like this, it will have an error. See the *Common Errors* section for more information on that.

Testing the Install

The final step in learning how to install this is to test that it's actually installed by importing it in an `ex41.py` file. Be sure to make this file in a directory *outside* of the `test_project` directory.

Listing 41.1: ex41.py

```
1  from test_project import testing
2
3  testing.hello()
```

If your install works, then this code should run successfully. If not, then time to debug why the `hello()` function is missing.

Remove `test-project`

If you're done testing the installation, then you should remove `test-project` just in case:

```
1  conda remove test-project
```

With that you're ready to make your own projects to install or share.

Common Errors

The errors that `conda build` produces are horrendous. I suggest if you get errors, just delete the project and try again. To find these errors, you have to scroll back very far and look for the red `error` text. It's tough, but here are my best clues:

- *error: metadata-generation-failed*—If you see the error `error in test-project setup`
  `↳ command: Problems to parse EntryPoint(name='test-project', value='test`
  `↳ -project.cli:cli', group='console_scripts')`, then it's because you named your project with a - as in `test-project` instead of `test_project`

- `ValueError: License file given in about/license_file`—Once again, scroll up and you'll see this line mentioning the `about/license_file`, and it means you're missing the `LICENSE` file

Study Drills

1. Repeat this process, but use some Python code you've been working on lately. You should package it, install it, and use it in another project where you need it.

2. Try using your project in `jupyter-lab` to see if it works. You might have to activate your `lpythw` environment to make this work.

3. Read the documentation for `conda build` and the similar documentation for packaging projects for PyPI.

4. Research what it takes to publish your projects to Anaconda and PyPI. I think #3 and #4 can be tackled later when you actually want to do this.

5. Read more about the `cookiecutter` project and what you can do with it. It will be useful to you later.

Doing Things to Lists

Y ou have learned about lists. When you learned about while-loops, you "appended" numbers to the end of a list and printed them out. There were also Study Drills where you were supposed to find all the other things you can do to lists in the Python documentation. That was a while back, so review those topics if you do not know what I'm talking about.

Found it? Remember it? Good. When you did this, you had a list, and you "called" the function append() on it. However, you may not really understand what's going on, so let's see what we can do to lists.

When you write mystuff.append('hello'), you are actually setting off a chain of events inside Python to cause something to happen to the mystuff list. Here's how it works:

1. Python sees you mentioned mystuff and looks up that variable. It might have to look backward to see if you created it with =, if it is a function argument, or if it's a global variable. Either way it has to find mystuff first.

2. Once it finds mystuff, it reads the . (period) operator and starts to look at *variables* that are part of mystuff. Since mystuff is a list, it knows that mystuff has a bunch of functions associated that apply to lists.

3. It then hits append and compares the name to all the names that mystuff says it owns. If append is in there (it is), then Python grabs *that* to use.

4. Next, Python sees the ((parenthesis) and realizes, "Oh hey, this should be a function." At this point it *calls* (runs, executes) the function just like normally, but instead it calls the function with an *extra* argument.

5. That *extra* argument is ... mystuff! I know, weird, right? But that's how Python works, so it's best to just remember it and assume that's the result. What happens, at the end of all this, is a function call that looks like append(mystuff, 'hello') instead of what you read, which is mystuff.append('hello')

For the most part you do not have to know that this is going on, but it helps when you get error messages from Python like this:

```
1    $ python3
2    >>> class Thing(object):
3    ...      def test(message):
4    ...              print(message)
5    ...
6    >>> a = Thing()
7    >>> a.test("hello")
8    Traceback (most recent call last):
```

```
9    File "<stdin>", line 1, in <module>
10   TypeError: test() takes exactly 1 argument (2 given)
11   >>>
```

What was all that? Well, this is me typing into the Python shell and showing you some magic. You haven't seen class yet, but we'll get into that later. For now, you see how Python said test() takes exactly 1 argument (2 given). If you see this, it means that Python changed a.test("hello") to test (a, "hello") and that somewhere someone messed up and didn't add the argument for a.

This might be a lot to take in, but we're going to spend a few exercises getting this concept firm in your brain. To kick things off, here's an exercise that mixes strings and lists for all kinds of fun:

Listing 42.1: ex42.py

```
1    ten_things = "Apples Oranges Crows Telephone Light Sugar"
2
3    print("Wait there are not 10 things in that list. Let's fix that.")
4
5    stuff = ten_things.split(' ')
6    more_stuff = ["Day", "Night", "Song", "Frisbee",
7                  "Corn", "Banana", "Girl", "Boy"]
8
9    while len(stuff) != 10:
10       next_one = more_stuff.pop()
11       print("Adding: ", next_one)
12       stuff.append(next_one)
13       print(f"There are {len(stuff)} items now.")
14
15   print("There we go: ", stuff)
16
17   print("Let's do some things with stuff.")
18
19   print(stuff[1])
20   print(stuff[-1]) # whoa! fancy
21   print(stuff.pop())
22   print(' '.join(stuff)) # what? cool!
23   print('#'.join(stuff[3:5])) # super stellar!
```

What You Should See

```
1    Wait there are not 10 things in that list. Let's fix that.
2    Adding:  Boy
3    There are 7 items now.
4    Adding:  Girl
5    There are 8 items now.
6    Adding:  Banana
7    There are 9 items now.
8    Adding:  Corn
```

```
 9  There are 10 items now.
10  There we go:  ['Apples', 'Oranges', 'Crows', 'Telephone', 'Light', 'Sugar',
        ↳ 'Boy', 'Girl', 'Banana', 'Corn']
11  Let's do some things with stuff.
12  Oranges
13  Corn
14  Corn
15  Apples Oranges Crows Telephone Light Sugar Boy Girl Banana
16  Telephone#Light
```

What Lists Can Do

Let's say you want to create a computer game based on Go Fish. If you don't know what Go Fish is, take the time now to go read up on it on the internet. To do this you would need to have some way of taking the concept of a "deck of cards" and put it into your Python program. You then have to write Python code that knows how to work this imaginary version of a deck of cards so that a person playing your game thinks that it's real, even if it isn't. What you need is a "deck of cards" structure, and programmers call this kind of thing a "data structure."

What's a data structure? If you think about it, a "data structure" is just a formal way to *structure* (organize) some *data* (facts). It really is that simple. Even though some data structures can get insanely complex, all they are is just a way to store facts inside a program so you can access them in different ways. They structure data.

I'll be getting into this more in the next exercise, but lists are one of the most common data structures programmers use. They are simply ordered lists of facts you want to store and access randomly or linearly by an index. What?! Remember what I said, though: just because a programmer said "a list is a list" doesn't mean that it's any more complex than what a list already is in the real world. Let's look at the deck of cards as an example of a list:

1. You have a bunch of cards with values

2. Those cards are in a stack, list, or list from the top card to the bottom card

3. You can take cards off the top, the bottom, and the middle at random

4. If you want to find a specific card, you have to grab the deck and go through it one at a time

Let's look at what I said:

• "An ordered list"—Yes, a deck of cards is in order with a first and a last

• "of things you want to store"—Yes, cards are things I want to store

• "and access randomly"—Yes, I can grab a card from anywhere in the deck

• "or linearly"—Yes, if I want to find a specific card, I can start at the beginning and go in order

• "by an index"—Almost, since with a deck of cards if I told you to get the card at index 19, you'd have to count until you found that one. In our Python lists, the computer can just jump right to any index you give it

That is all a list does, and this should give you a way to figure out concepts in programming. Every concept in programming usually has some relationship to the real world. At least the useful ones do. If you can figure out what the analog in the real world is, then you can use that to figure out what the data structure should be able to do.

When to Use Lists

You use a list whenever you have something that matches the list data structure's useful features:

1.   If you need to maintain order. Remember, this is listed order, not *sorted* order. Lists do not sort for you.

2.   If you need to access the contents randomly by a number. Remember, this is using *cardinal* numbers starting at 0.

3.   If you need to go through the contents linearly (first to last). Remember, that's what for-loops are for.

Then that's when you use a list.

Study Drills

1.   Take each function that is called, and go through the steps for function calls to translate them to what Python does. For example, more_stuff.pop() is pop(more_stuff).

2.   Translate these two ways to view the function calls in English. For example, more_stuff. ↳ pop() reads as "Call pop on more_stuff." Meanwhile, pop(more_stuff) means "Call pop with argument more_stuff." Understand how they are really the same thing.

3.   Go read about "object-oriented programming" online. Confused? I was too. Do not worry. You will learn enough to be dangerous, and you can slowly learn more later.

4.   Read up on what a "class" is in Python. *Do not read about how other languages use the word "class."* That will only mess you up.

5.   Do not worry if you do not have any idea what I'm talking about. Programmers like to feel smart, so they invented object-oriented programming, named it OOP, and then used it way too much. If you think that's hard, you should try to use "functional programming."

6.   Find 10 examples of things in the real world that would fit in a list. Try writing some scripts to work with them.

Common Student Questions

Didn't you say to not use `while-loops`?   Yes, so just remember sometimes you can break the rules if you have a good reason. Only idiots are slaves to rules all the time.

Why does `join(' ', stuff)` **not work?**   The way the documentation for `join` is written doesn't make sense. It does not work like that and is instead a method you call on the *inserted* string to put between the list to be joined. Rewrite it like `' '.join(stuff)`.

Why did you use a `while-loop`?   Try rewriting it with a `for-loop` and see if that's easier.

What does `stuff[3:5]` **do?**   That extracts a "slice" from the `stuff` list that is from element 3 to element 4, meaning it does *not* include this element 5. It's similar to how `range(3,5)` would work.

Doing Things to Dictionaries

You are now going to learn about the dictionary data structure in Python. A dictionary (or "dict") is a way to store data just like a list, but instead of using only numbers to get the data, you can use almost anything. This lets you treat a dict like it's a database for storing and organizing data.

Let's compare what dicts can do to what lists can do. You see, a list lets you do this:

Listing 43.1: ex43_pycon_out.py

```
1   >>> things = ['a', 'b', 'c', 'd']
2   >>> print(things[1])
3   b
4   >>> things[1] = 'z'
5   >>> print(things[1])
6   z
7   >>> things
8   ['a', 'z', 'c', 'd']
```

You can use numbers to "index" into a list, meaning you can use numbers to find out what's in lists. You should know this about lists by now, but make sure you understand that you can *only* use numbers to get items out of a list.

What a dict does is let you use *anything*, not just numbers. Yes, a dict associates one thing to another, no matter what it is. Take a look:

Listing 43.2: ex43_pycon_out.py

```
1    >>> stuff = {'name': 'Zed', 'age': 39, 'height': 6 * 12 + 2}
2    >>> print(stuff['name'])
3    Zed
4    >>> print(stuff['age'])
5    39
6    >>> print(stuff['height'])
7    74
8    >>> stuff['city'] = "SF"
9    >>> print(stuff['city'])
10   SF
```

You will see that instead of just numbers we're using strings to say what we want from the stuff dictionary. We can also put new things into the dictionary with strings. It doesn't have to be strings, though. We can also do this:

Listing 43.3: ex43_pycon_out.py

```
1   >>> stuff[1] = "Wow"
2   >>> stuff[2] = "Neato"
3   >>> print(stuff[1])
4   Wow
5   >>> print(stuff[2])
6   Neato
```

In this code I used numbers, and then you can see there are numbers and strings as keys in the dict when I print it. I could use anything. Well, almost anything, but just pretend you can use anything for now.

Of course, a dictionary that you can only put things in is pretty stupid, so here's how you delete things, with the pop( ) function:

Listing 43.4: ex43_pycon_out.py

```
1   >>> stuff.pop('city')
2   'SF'
3   >>> stuff.pop(1)
4   'Wow'
5   >>> stuff.pop(2)
6   'Neato'
7   >>> stuff
8   {'name': 'Zed', 'age': 39, 'height': 74}
9   >>>
```

A Dictionary Example

We'll now do an exercise that you *must* study very carefully. I want you to type this code in and try to understand what's going on. Take note of when you put things in a dict, get them from a hash, and all the operations you use. Notice how this example is mapping states to their abbreviations and then the abbreviations to cities in the states. Remember, "mapping" or "associating" is the key concept in a dictionary.

Listing 43.5: ex43.py

```
1   # create a mapping of state to abbreviation
2   states = {
3       'Oregon': 'OR',
4       'Florida': 'FL',
5       'California': 'CA',
6       'New York': 'NY',
7       'Michigan': 'MI'
8   }
9
```

```python
10   # create a basic set of states and some cities in them
11   cities = {
12       'CA': 'San Francisco',
13       'MI': 'Detroit',
14       'FL': 'Jacksonville'
15   }
16
17   # add some more cities
18   cities['NY'] = 'New York'
19   cities['OR'] = 'Portland'
20
21   # print out some cities
22   print('-' * 10)
23   print("NY State has: ", cities['NY'])
24   print("OR State has: ", cities['OR'])
25
26   # print some states
27   print('-' * 10)
28   print("Michigan's abbreviation is: ", states['Michigan'])
29   print("Florida's abbreviation is: ", states['Florida'])
30
31   # do it by using the state then cities dict
32   print('-' * 10)
33   print("Michigan has: ", cities[states['Michigan']])
34   print("Florida has: ", cities[states['Florida']])
35
36   # print every state abbreviation
37   print('-' * 10)
38   for state, abbrev in list(states.items()):
39       print(f"{state} is abbreviated {abbrev}")
40
41   # print every city in state
42   print('-' * 10)
43   for abbrev, city in list(cities.items()):
44       print(f"{abbrev} has the city {city}")
45
46   # now do both at the same time
47   print('-' * 10)
48   for state, abbrev in list(states.items()):
49       print(f"{state} state is abbreviated {abbrev}")
50       print(f"and has city {cities[abbrev]}")
51
52   print('-' * 10)
53   # safely get a abbreviation by state that might not be there
54   state = states.get('Texas')
55
56   if not state:
57       print("Sorry, no Texas.")
58
59
60
```

```
61   # get a city with a default value
62   city = cities.get('TX', 'Does Not Exist')
63   print(f"The city for the state 'TX' is: {city}")
```

What You Should See

```
1    ----------
2    NY State has:  New York
3    OR State has:  Portland
4    ----------
5    Michigan's abbreviation is:  MI
6    Florida's abbreviation is:  FL
7    ----------
8    Michigan has:  Detroit
9    Florida has:  Jacksonville
10   ----------
11   Oregon is abbreviated OR
12   Florida is abbreviated FL
13   California is abbreviated CA
14   New York is abbreviated NY
15   Michigan is abbreviated MI
16   ----------
17   CA has the city San Francisco
18   MI has the city Detroit
19   FL has the city Jacksonville
20   NY has the city New York
21   OR has the city Portland
22   ----------
23   Oregon state is abbreviated OR
24   and has city Portland
25   Florida state is abbreviated FL
26   and has city Jacksonville
27   California state is abbreviated CA
28   and has city San Francisco
29   New York state is abbreviated NY
30   and has city New York
31   Michigan state is abbreviated MI
32   and has city Detroit
33   ----------
34   Sorry, no Texas.
35   The city for the state 'TX' is: Does Not Exist
```

What Dictionaries Can Do

Dictionaries are another example of a data structure, and, like lists, they are one of the most commonly used data structures in programming. A dictionary is used to "map" or "associate" things you want to store to keys you use to get them. Again, programmers don't use a term like "dictionary" for something that doesn't work like an actual dictionary full of words, so let's use that as our real-world example.

Let's say you want to find out what the word "Honorificabilitudinitatibus" means. Today you would simply copy-paste that word into a search engine and then find out the answer, and we could say a search engine is like a really huge super-complex version of the *Oxford English Dictionary* (OED). Before search engines, what you would do is this:

1. Go to your library and get "the dictionary." Let's say it's the OED.

2. You know "honorificabilitudinitatibus" starts with the letter "H," so you look on the side of the book for the little tab that has "H" on it.

3. Then you skim the pages until you are close to where "hon" started.

4. Then you skim a few more pages until you find "honorificabilitudinitatibus" or hit the beginning of the "hp" words and realize this word isn't in the OED.

5. Once you find the entry, you read the definition to figure out what it means.

This process is nearly exactly the way a dict works, and you are basically "mapping" the word "honorificabilitudinitatibus" to its definition. A dict in Python is just like a dictionary in the real world such as the OED.

Study Drills

1. Do this same kind of mapping with cities and states/regions in your country or some other country.

2. Find the Python documentation for dictionaries and try to do even more things to them.

3. Find out what you *can't* do with dictionaries. A big one is that they do not have order, so try playing with that.

Common Student Questions

What is the difference between a list and a dictionary? A list is for an ordered list of items. A dictionary (or dict) is for matching some items (called "keys") to other items (called "values").

What would I use a dictionary for? Use one when you have to take one value and "look up" another value. In fact, you could call dictionaries "lookup tables."

What would I use a list for? Use a list for any sequence of things that need to be in order and you only need to look them up by a numeric index.

What if I need a dictionary, but I need it to be in order? Take a look at the `collections.`
`↳ OrderedDict` data structure in Python. Python 3.7 and beyond now guarantees dictionaries are ordered.

From Dictionaries to Objects

Y ou should review the following exercises before doing this one:

- Exercise 24, *Introductory Dictionaries*, to refresh your understanding of Dictionaries

- Exercise 25, *Dictionaries and Functions*, for how you can put functions in dictionaries and call them

- Exercise 26, *Dictionaries and Modules*, for how modules are just dictionaries behind the scenes and how changing the underlying __dict__ changes the module

In this exercise you'll learn about Object-Oriented Programming by creating your own little object system using the previous information.

Step 1: Passing a Dict to a Function

Imagine you want to record information about people and then have them say things. Maybe this is a little video game with little people growing food in a small town. You want to know their name, age, and hair color. You also need a way to make them talk. Using what you know, you may invent this code:

Listing 44.1: ex44_1.py

```
1    becky = {
2        "name": "Becky",
3        "age": 34,
4        "eyes": "green"
5    }
6
7    def talk(who, words):
8        print(f"I am {who['name']} and {words}")
9
10   talk(becky, "I am talking here!")
```

Let's break this down to confirm you understand the code:

1. I create a becky variable that has all the information about Becky

2. I then have a function named talk that accepts this becky variable and prints out a little dialogue from that character

3. Then I call this function, passing in the becky variable and something for Becky to say

What's interesting is you can use this function on anything that has the same "signature" as the becky variable. If you created 1,000 characters with this same dict, the talk() function would still work.

What You Should See

When you run the code for *Step 1*, you should see this output:

```
1  I am Becky and I am talking here!
```

This doesn't change in the later versions of this code.

Step 2: talk inside the Dict

The first problem with this design is any part of your code that wants to make these characters talk has to know about the talk() function. That's not too large a problem, but maybe you want each character to have special talk() functions that do something different.

One way to fix this is to "attach" the talk() function to the dict itself like this:

Listing 44.2: ex44_2.py

```
1    def talk(who, words):
2        print(f"I am {who['name']} and {words}")
3
4    becky = {
5        "name": "Becky",
6        "age": 34,
7        "eyes": "green",
8        "talk": talk # see this?
9    }
10
11   becky['talk'](becky, "I am talking here!")
```

The differences between this version and the first one are:

1. I move the talk() function to the top so we can reference it later.

2. I then put the function in the becky dictionary with "talk": talk. *Remember*, a function is just like any other variable, which means you can pass it to other functions and place it in a list or dict

3. Then the last line calls the talk() function in one move.

That last line *might* cause you problems, so let's break just that line down:

1. becky['talk']: Python gets the contents of the becky dictionary assigned the 'talk' key. It's exactly like if you did print(becky['age']) to get the age key of becky. Don't get confused by the characters after this.

2. `(becky, "I am talking here!")`: You know that Python sees `()` after a variable as a function call, and you just got the contents of `becky['talk']`, so this calls those contents as a function. It then passes the variable becky to it and the string `"I am talking here!"`

You can take the next step to study this code by breaking it apart into two lines of code like this:

```
1   becky_talk = becky['talk']
2   becky_talk(becky, "I am talking here!")
```

What confuses people is they see all those characters in the original "one-liner" and their brain treats it like one big word. The way you analyze these is to break them apart into separate lines using variables.

Step 3: Closures

The next thing to learn is the concept of a "closure." A closure is any function that's created inside another function but accesses data in its parent. Let's look at this code to see a closure in action:

Listing 44.3: ex44_3.py

```
1    # this function makes functions
2    def constructor(color, size):
3        print(">>> constructor color:", color, "size:", size)
4
5        # watch the indent!
6        def repeater():
7            # notice this function is using color, size
8            print("### repeater color:", color, "size:", size)
9
10       print("<<< exit constructor");
11       return repeater
12
13   # what's returned are repeater functions
14   blue_xl = constructor("blue", "xl")
15   green_sm = constructor("green", "sm")
16
17   # see how these repeaters "know" the parameters?
18   for i in range(0,4):
19       blue_xl()
20       green_sm()
```

Breaking down this code, we have the following:

1. I start a function named def `constructor(color, size)`, which will create functions for me.

2. I start off with a simple `print()` to trace this function.

3. Then I define the `repeater()` function, but notice it gets indented under `constructor`. This places that function inside `constructor` so that it's only usable in that block.

4. Under def repeater(), I do a print(), but *carefully* look at what this print() line is using. It's using the variables color and size from the def constructor(color, size), but those are function parameters. That means they're temporary, and when constructor exits, they "die," right? Nope.

5. Then I print another tracing line saying the constructor is exiting.

6. I return repeater() so the caller can have it, but remember color and size should be dead, right? Isn't this an error?

7. After I've defined constructor, I use it to craft two repeater() functions named blue_xl and green_sm

8. I then have a for-loop that uses those two functions to repeatedly print the *correct* size and color I gave to constructor

9. This means that functions created inside other functions *keep access to the variables they use*.

The key here is how def repeater() is indented *under* the def constructor but tries to use color and size. Python detects this and creates a *closure*, which is a function that keeps references to any variables it used. These references are retained even when the parent function has long exited.

What You Should See

When you run this closure code, you should see the following output:

```
1   >>> constructor color: blue size: xl
2   <<< exit constructor
3   >>> constructor color: green size: sm
4   <<< exit constructor
5   ### repeater color: blue size: xl
6   ### repeater color: green size: sm
7   ### repeater color: blue size: xl
8   ### repeater color: green size: sm
9   ### repeater color: blue size: xl
10  ### repeater color: green size: sm
11  ### repeater color: blue size: xl
12  ### repeater color: green size: sm
```

If you get something different, review your constructor() to make sure you've indented things correctly.

Step 4: A Person Constructor

What happens when you want to create 100 people? In the *Step 2* code you'd have to manually create every dict and put the talk() function in it, which is ridiculous. We have computers for repetitive boring work, so let's use what we know so far to create a new constructor() for our people.

We'll use everything you know so far to create a function that "constructs" people:

Listing 44.4: ex44_4.py

```
1    def Person_new(name, age, eyes):
2        person = {
3            "name": name,
4            "age": age,
5            "eyes": eyes,
6        }
7
8        def talk(words):
9            print(f"I am {person['name']} and {words}")
10
11        person['talk'] = talk
12
13        return person
14
15   becky = Person_new("Becky", 39, "green")
16
17   becky['talk']("I am talking here!")
```

This code is using the following concepts:

1. Person_new() is a constructor, which means it creates a new person dict and attaches the talk() function to it.

2. The talk() function is a closure, which means it has access to the person that is created at the top of the Person_new() function.

3. It adds this talk() function to the person just like you did in *Step 2*, but since this is a closure from *Step 3*, we don't have to manually give it the person

4. It returns this new person with its closure-based talk(), and then we can use it just like before, but it's a bit cleaner.

If we compare the *Step 2* final line with this line, we have the following:

```
1    # from step 2, see the two becky uses?
2    becky['talk'](becky, "I am talking here!")
3
4    # from step 4, now only one becky
5    becky['talk']("I am talking here!")
```

With the Person_new() constructor, we can remove this extra becky variable, which makes it *far* more reliable to use. This also means we could potentially give different kinds of people different talk() functions if we wanted.

Study Drills

1. Use Person_new( ) to create a few more people.

2. Add a new function hit( ), which makes one person hit another person.

3. Give people hit points in their dict and have hit( ) randomly reduce each person's hit points. You'll need random( ) for this.

4. Add a job attribute to person and give different jobs different hit points, damage, and dialogue. For example, a "boxer" would have more HP and damage than a person with the job "baby." Python has way better tools for this same problem, but for this code it is a fun challenge.

5. Finally, have your code run a little fight club using loops to make different people battle.

Basic Object-Oriented Programming

I n Exercise 44 you learned how to use a function to create special dict containers with functions attached to them. In this exercise you'll learn the "right" way to do the same thing using Python's class keyword and the object-oriented programming (OOP) features.

OOP is *very* complicated to understand and explain, so we'll focus on code to start and slowly build up your understanding of the concept. The most important thing for you to remember when studying this is that *OOP is weird*. Humans don't think about the world like this, and most of the theory behind OOP has been debunked by modern psychology and neurology. This means you need to keep grinding OOP code until you get it. It just takes time and exposure, so don't give up.

Python's People

We'll start by reviewing this code that implements the same output, but using Python's official OOP system. Get this code to work and then place it side by side with the ex44.py file to compare.

Listing 45.1: ex45.py

```
1   class Person(object):
2
3       # this is double underscores around init
4       def __init__(self, name, age, eyes):
5           self.name = name
6           self.age = age
7           self.eyes = eyes
8
9       def talk(self, words):
10          print(f"I am {self.name} and {words}")
11
12  becky = Person("Becky", 39, "green")
13  becky.talk("I am talking here!")
```

This will produce the same output, but it's implemented very differently. Let's break down this code and compare it to the code you already wrote in ex44.py.

1. I use the class keyword to define a Person class. A class defines what data and functions your Person will have when you create it.

2. I then have a def __init__() function, which is similar to the Person_new() function from the DIY version. Its job is to configure any Person you create with the data it needs.

NOTE: The __init__() has two underscores and is typically called a "double underscore" or "dunder" function.

3. The __init__() takes the same parameters of name, age, and eyes, but also an additional parameter named self, which is the person from the ex44.py code.

4. Inside the __init__() I assign each of name, age, and eyes to the self with self.name = name. This is like doing self['name'] = name, and behind the scenes Python actually does this.

5. Then I have a def talk() function, which takes parameters self and words. Remember, self is like the person from ex44.py, but Python handles binding this for you where in ex44.py you had to manually bind it to your talk() function.

6. After this definition we create an *object* using the Person constructor. We name this object becky so the class Person is turned into a "constructor function" like the Person_new in ex44.py. Python is doing a *lot* more than the DIY Person_new(), but they're similar in purpose and usage.

7. I finally call becky.talk("I am talking here!") to make Becky talk, and that code is nearly the same as becky['talk']("I am talking here!") in the ex44.py code.

If you're comparing ex44.py and ex45.py, you should be able to see how they're similar. The DIY version in ex44.py is definitely inferior to the official Python OOP version in ex45.py, but it's intended to be a "bridge" from what you know about functions and dictionaries to how classes and objects work in Python.

The class version in ex45.py also has a far more solid foundation and supports many additional features, so after this, never do OOP the way I did in ex44.py. It was only for training.

Using dir() and __dict__

Many Python developers think that Python's objects are completely different from the dict, but we can actually find the dict that's inside objects *and* classes. Add these lines right after you create the becky object:

```
1  # this is the becky line
2  becky = Person("Becky", 39, "green")
3  # add this line
4  print(becky.__dict__)
```

Run the ex45.py file again, and you should see this:

```
1  {'name': 'Becky', 'age': 39, 'eyes': 'green'}
2  I am Becky and I am talking here!
```

Do you remember when you accessed the __dict__ in a module? Python's objects also have a __dict__ that contains all of the attributes you set in the __init__. Here's some other things to try:

```
1    # the class that becky comes from
2    print(becky.__class__)
3
4    # the contents of that class
5    print(becky.__class__.__dict__)
6
7    # a list of strings for everything
8    print(dir(becky))
9
10   # these two do the same thing
11   print(becky.talk)
12   print(getattr(becky, 'talk'))
13
14   # this is the class's version of talk
15   print(becky.__class__.__dict__['talk'])
```

The last two lines are interesting because they output different things:

```
1    <bound method Person.talk of
2        <__main__.Person object at 0x7fc338253cd0>>
3    <function Person.talk at 0x7fc3280b9750>
```

The difference is the bound method means it's like the closure you made in ex44.py, so it's been bound to the object and has access to a self parameter by default. The second one is the base function in the class that hasn't been bound. See the *Study Drills* section for an experiment with this.

About the Dot (.)

In ex44.py you had to manually access functions using the dict syntax like this:

```
1    becky = Person_new("Becky", 39, "green")
2    becky['talk']("I am talking here!")
```

In ex45.py you used the . (dot) operator instead:

```
1    becky = Person("Becky", 39, "green")
2    becky.talk("I am talking here!")
```

You've used this . (dot) syntax in the past many times without really understanding it. Let's fix that understanding now that you can define classes and use them to create objects.

A primary cause of confusion in people new to OOP is lines of code like becky.talk("I am talking ↳ here!") because they see this as a *single* operation, when it is actually multiple operations done for you. If we break down *only* this line, we get the following:

1. The becky is your class Person object you want to access.

2. . tells Python you want to access–or get–something in this object. It's similar to the ['key'] syntax with dict variables.

3. talk becomes the key you want to get out of the becky object.

4. Python then looks inside your becky object to see if you have an attribute you've set named talk. Remember from the dir(becky) test previously it is in there, so the function is returned.

5. Python then finds the talk() function inside dir(becky) and returns that for you to call.

With that we now know that the . (dot) operator stops at this point, and the remaining part of becky. ↳ talk("I am talking here!") is *only* a call of that function. That means it's actually *two* lines of code like this:

```
1    talk = becky.talk
2    talk("I am talking here!")
```

Any time you're confused about a single line of code, convert it to two (or more) lines like this.

Terminology

There are a few terms used by OOP people that you should know:

- class—This is the definition used to construct objects. Think of it like a blueprint. This is class Person in our code.

- object—Each time you use a class, it creates an object. This is the becky variable.

- instance—This is another name for an object, as in "this is an instance of a Person."

- instantiate—This is a way to say "create an object" or "create an instance."

- attribute—This is any data that is part of the objects as defined by the class you used to create it. This is self.name or self.age in our code.

- method—It's just a function that's been attached to a class. Don't get confused when people claim a method is radically different from a function. If someone claims this, ask them if they think a salmon is totally different from a fish.

- inheritance—This is a complicated topic we'll cover later, but you can have a class that gets additional features from another class. It's similar to how you inherited certain features from your parents.

- members—The members of a class are just the attributes and methods defined in the class.

- polymorphism—This is a protocol for what happens when classes of different inheritance are used. This is a complex topic, and honestly it's a lot more trouble than it's worth.

A Word on `self`

You may have wondered where this `self` variable comes from or why you need it. Imagine you have this code:

```
1    # make some objects
2    frank = Person("Frank", 100, "green")
3    mary = Person("Mary", 20, "brown")
```

If you look inside the __init__ of `Person`, you'll see the lines that use `self` to set each person's name, age, and eyes:

```
1    def __init__(self, name, age, eyes):
2        self.name = name
3        self.age = age
4        self.eyes = eyes
```

When Python calls this __init__() function, it needs some temporary variable for you to work on. In the make some objects code, the `frank =` happens *after* the call to `Person()`. Remember, Python executes the right-hand side and *then* assigns the result to the left-hand side.

That means, at the time __init__() is called, there is no `frank`. To solve this problem, Python makes a temporary variable, passes it as `self` to your __init__() so you can set it up, and *then* returns that so it can be assigned to `frank` or `mary` above.

It makes sense that you need a temporary variable for __init__(), but what about `talk(self, word)` and its `self`? Even though `frank` or `mary` exists, how would your `talk()` function know about them? They're outside of this function, and you define `talk()` separately from these other variables. To solve this problem, when you use a . operator, Python "remembers" that `talk()` is attached to `frank` or `mary` and passes that in as the `self` parameter. That way, you don't have to know about anything but `self` for your `Person` to work.

The only problem with this design is you'll run into errors like this:

```
1    Traceback (most recent call last):
2      File "ex45.py", line 13, in <module>
3        becky.talk("I am talking here!")
4    TypeError: Person.talk() takes 1 positional argument but 2 were given
```

This error is really confusing, but it's basically saying you forgot `self` when you defined def `talk()` in the `Person` class.

Study Drills

1. Python 3 allows you to write classes as `class Person` or using `class Person(object)`. Research why they have this second form and whether you really need to use it in Python 3.

2. Use your `Person` class to make 1,000 people in a loop and store them in a `list`.

3. Repeat the same Study Drills from Exercise 44 where you made people who can fight each other. That means adding hit points, a way to have one person attack another, and a `job` that gives people different combat abilities.

4. Compare this solution to the one you made in Exercise 44. Which one do you prefer? Even if you prefer the previous, please don't write more code like that. It's only a training exercise.

5. Remember how you could get the `talk()` function from `becky.__class__.__dict__` but it was different from `becky.talk`? Try calling it and see what error you get. Can you fix the error?

Common Student Questions

Why should I use Object-Oriented Programming?   Because the language you're using features OOP as the primary way to structure code. If it's a language like Python, Java, C++, Ruby, or C#, then OOP is going to be easier. Other languages rely more on functions and modules as the primary way you structure your code, so OOP will be painful to use.

Inheritance and Advanced OOP

An important concept that you have to understand is the difference between a class and an object. The problem is, there is no real "difference" between a class and an object. They are actually the same thing at different points in time. I will demonstrate by a Zen koan:

```
1   What is the difference between a fish and a salmon?
```

Did that question sort of confuse you? Really sit down and think about it for a minute. I mean, a fish and a salmon are different, but, wait, they are the same thing, right? A salmon is a *kind* of fish, so I mean it's not different. But at the same time, a salmon is a particular *type* of fish, so it's actually different from all other fish. That's what makes it a salmon and not a halibut. So a salmon and a fish are the same but different. Weird.

This question is confusing because most people do not think about real things this way, but they intuitively understand them. You do not need to think about the difference between a fish and a salmon because you *know* how they are related. You know a salmon is a *kind* of fish and that there are other kinds of fish without having to understand that.

Let's take it one step further. Let's say you have a bucket full of three salmon and because you are a nice person, you have decided to name them Frank, Joe, and Mary. Now, think about this question:

```
1   What is the difference between Mary and a salmon?
```

Again, this is a weird question, but it's a bit easier than the fish versus salmon question. You know that Mary is a salmon, so she's not really different. She's just a specific "instance" of a salmon. Joe and Frank are also instances of salmon. What do I mean when I say "instance"? I mean they were created from some other salmon and now represent a real thing that has salmon-like attributes.

Now for the mind-bending idea: Fish is a class, Salmon is a class, and Mary is an object. Think about that for a second. Let's break it down slowly and see if you get it.

A fish is a class, meaning it's not a *real* thing, but rather a word we attach to instances of things with similar attributes. Got fins? Got gills? Lives in water? Alright it's probably a fish.

Someone with a Ph.D. then comes along and says, "No, my young friend, *this* fish is actually *Salmo salar*, affectionately known as a salmon." This professor has just clarified the fish further and made a new class called Salmon that has more specific attributes. Longer nose, reddish flesh, big, lives in the ocean or fresh water, tasty? Probably a salmon.

Finally, a cook comes along and tells the Ph.D., "No, you see this salmon right here, I'll call her Mary, and I'm going to make a tasty fillet out of her with a nice sauce." Now you have this *instance* of a salmon (which also is an instance of a fish) named Mary turned into something real that is filling your belly. It has become an object.

There you have it: Mary (the object) is a kind of salmon (a class) that is a kind of fish (the parent class)— object is an instance of a subclass of a class.

How This Looks in Code

This is a weird concept, but to be very honest you have to worry about it only when you make new classes and when you use a class. I will show you two tricks to help you figure out whether something is a class or an object.

First, you need to learn two catch phrases: "is-a" and "has-a." You use the phrase is-a when you talk about objects and classes being related to each other by a class relationship. You use has-a when you talk about objects and classes that are related only because they *reference* each other.

Now, go through this piece of code and replace each ##?? comment with a comment that says whether the next line represents an is-a or a has-a relationship and what that relationship is. In the beginning of the code, I've laid out a few examples, so you just have to write the remaining ones.

Remember, is-a is the relationship between fish and salmon, while has-a is the relationship between salmon and gills.

Listing 46.1: ex46.py

```
1    ## Animal is-a object (yes, sort of confusing) look at the extra credit
2    class Animal(object):
3        pass
4
5    ## ??
6    class Dog(Animal):
7
8        def __init__(self, name):
9            ## ??
10           self.name = name
11
12   ## ??
13   class Cat(Animal):
14
15       def __init__(self, name):
16           ## ??
17           self.name = name
18
19   ## ??
```

```
20   class Person(object):
21
22       def _init_(self, name):
23           ## ??
24           self.name = name
25
26           ## Person has-a pet of some kind
27           self.pet = None
28
29   ## ??
30   class Employee(Person):
31
32       def _init_(self, name, salary):
33           ## ?? hmm what is this strange magic?
34           super(Employee, self)._init_(name)
35           ## ??
36           self.salary = salary
37
38   ## ??
39   class Fish(object):
40       pass
41
42   ## ??
43   class Salmon(Fish):
44       pass
45
46   ## ??
47   class Halibut(Fish):
48       pass
49
50
51   ## rover is-a Dog
52   rover = Dog("Rover")
53
54   ## ??
55   satan = Cat("Satan")
56
57   ## ??
58   mary = Person("Mary")
59
60   ## ??
61   mary.pet = satan
62
63   ## ??
64   frank = Employee("Frank", 120000)
65
66   ## ??
67   frank.pet = rover
68
69   ## ??
70   flipper = Fish()
```

```
71    ## ??
72    crouse = Salmon()
73
74    ## ??
75    harry = Halibut()
```

About class Name(object)

In Python 3 you do not need to add the (object) after the name of the class, but the Python community believes in "explicit is better than implicit," so I and other Python experts have decided to include it. You may run into code that does not have (object) after simple classes, and those classes are perfectly fine and will work with classes you create that do have (object). At this point it is simply extra documentation and has no impact on how your classes work.

In Python 2 there was a difference between the two types of classes, but now you don't have to worry about it. The only tricky part to use (object) involves the mental gymnastics of saying "class Name is a class of type object." That may sound confusing to you now, since it's a class that's a name object that's a class, but don't feel bad about that. Just think of class Name(object) as saying "this is a basic simple class" and you'll be fine.

Finally, in the future, the styles and tastes of Python programmers may change, and this explicit use of (object) might be seen as a sign that you are a bad programmer. If that happens, simply stop using it, or tell them, "Python Zen says explicit is better than implicit."

Study Drills

1. Research why Python added this strange object class and what that means.

2. Is it possible to use a class like it's an object?

3. Fill out the animals, fish, and people in this exercise with functions that make them do things. See what happens when functions are in a "base class" like Animal versus in, say, Dog.

4. Find other people's code and work out all the is-a and has-a relationships.

5. Make some new relationships that are lists and dictionaries so you can also have "has-many" relationships.

6. Do you think there's such thing as an "is-many" relationship? Read about "multiple inheritance," and then avoid it if you can.

Common Student Questions

What are these ## ?? **comments for?**   Those are "fill-in-the-blank" comments that you are supposed to fill in with the right "is-a," "has-a" concepts. Read this exercise again and look at the other comments to see what I mean.

What is the point of self.pet = None?   That makes sure that the self.pet attribute of that class is set to a default of None.

What does super(Employee, self).__init__(name) **do?**   That's how you can run the __init__ method of a parent class reliably. Search for "python3 super" and read the various advice on it being evil and good for you.

Basic Object-Oriented Analysis and Design

I'm going to describe a process to use when you want to build something using Python, specifically with object-oriented programming (OOP). What I mean by a "process" is that I'll give you a set of steps that you do in order but that you aren't meant to be a slave to or that will totally always work for every problem. They are just a good starting point for many programming problems and shouldn't be considered the *only* way to solve these types of problems. This process is just one way to do it that you can follow.

The process is as follows:

1. Write or draw about the problem

2. Extract key concepts from Step #1 and research them

3. Create a class hierarchy and object map for the concepts

4. Code the classes and a test to run them

5. Repeat and refine

The way to look at this process is that it is "top down," meaning it starts from the very abstract loose idea and then slowly refines it until the idea is solid and something you can code.

I start by just writing about the problem and trying to think up anything I can about it. Maybe I'll even draw a diagram or two, maybe a map of some kind, or even write myself a series of emails describing the problem. This gives me a way to express the key concepts in the problem and also explore what I might already know about it.

Then I go through these notes, drawings, and descriptions, and I pull out the key concepts. There's a simple trick to doing this: Simply make a list of all the *nouns* and *verbs* in your writing and drawings, then write out how they're related. This gives me a good list of names for classes, objects, and functions in the next step. I take this list of concepts and then research any that I don't understand so I can refine them further if needed.

Once I have my list of concepts, I create a simple outline/tree of the concepts and how they are related as classes. You can usually take your list of nouns and start asking "Is this one like other concept nouns? That means they have a common parent class, so what is it called?" Keep doing this until you have a class hierarchy that's just a simple tree list or a diagram. Then take the *verbs* you have and see if those are function names for each class and put them in your tree.

With this class hierarchy figured out, I sit down and write some basic skeleton code that has just the classes, their functions, and nothing more. I then write a test that runs this code and makes sure the classes I've made make sense and work right. Sometimes I may write the test first, though, and other times I might write a little test, a little code, a little test, etc., until I have the whole thing built.

Finally, I keep cycling over this process, repeating it and refining as I go and making it as clear as I can before doing more implementation. If I get stuck at any particular part because of a concept or problem I haven't anticipated, then I sit down and start the process over on just that part to figure it out more before continuing.

I will now go through this process while coming up with a game engine and a game for this exercise.

The Analysis of a Simple Game Engine

The game I want to make is called "Gothons from Planet Percal #25," and it will be a small space adventure game. With nothing more than that concept in my mind, I can explore the idea and figure out how to make the game come to life.

Write or Draw About the Problem

I'm going to write a little paragraph for the game:

"Aliens have invaded a space ship, and our hero has to go through a maze of rooms defeating them so he can escape into an escape pod to the planet below. The game will be more like a Zork or Adventure type of game with text outputs and funny ways to die. The game will involve an engine that runs a map full of rooms or scenes. Each room will print its own description when the player enters it and then tell the engine what room to run next out of the map."

At this point I have a good idea for the game and how it would run, so now I want to describe each scene:

- *Death*—This is when the player dies and should be something funny.
- *Central Corridor*—This is the starting point and has a Gothon already standing there that the players have to defeat with a joke before continuing.
- *Laser Weapon Armory*—This is where the hero gets a neutron bomb to blow up the ship before getting to the escape pod. It has a keypad the hero has to guess the number for.
- *The Bridge*—This is another battle scene with a Gothon where the hero places the bomb.
- *Escape Pod*—This is where the hero escapes but only after guessing the right escape pod.

At this point I might draw a map of these and maybe write more descriptions of each room—whatever comes to mind as I explore the problem.

Extract Key Concepts and Research Them

I now have enough information to extract some of the nouns and analyze their class hierarchy. First I make a list of all the nouns:

- Alien
- Player
- Ship
- Maze
- Room
- Scene
- Gothon
- Escape Pod
- Planet
- Map
- Engine
- Death
- Central Corridor
- Laser Weapon Armory
- The Bridge

I would also possibly go through all the verbs and see if they are anything that might be good function names, but I'll skip that for now.

At this point you might also research each of these concepts and anything you don't know right now. For example, I might play a few of these types of games and make sure I know how they work. I might research how ships are designed or how bombs work. Maybe I'll research some technical issue like how to store the game's state in a database. After I've done this research, I might start over at step #1 based on new information I have and rewrite my description and extract new concepts.

Create a Class Hierarchy and Object Map for the Concepts

Once I have that, I turn it into a class hierarchy by asking "What is similar to other things?" I also ask, "What is basically just another word for another thing?"

Right away I see that "Room" and "Scene" are basically the same thing depending on how I want to do things. I'm going to pick "Scene" for this game. Then I see that all the specific rooms like "Central Corridor" are basically just "Scenes." I see also that "Death" is basically a "Scene," which confirms my choice of "Scene" over "Room" since you can have a death scene, but a death room is kind of odd.

"Maze" and "Map" are basically the same, so I'm going to go with "Map" since I used it more often. I don't want to do a battle system, so I'm going to ignore "Alien" and "Player" and save that for later. The "Planet" could also just be another scene instead of something specific.

After all of that thought process, I start to make a class hierarchy that looks like this in my text editor:

```
1  * Map
2  * Engine
3  * Scene
4    * Death
5    * Central Corridor
6    * Laser Weapon Armory
7    * The Bridge
8    * Escape Pod
```

I would then go through and figure out what actions are needed on each thing based on verbs in the description. For example, I know from the description I'm going to need a way to "run" the engine, "get the next scene" from the map, get the "opening scene," and "enter" a scene. I'll add those like this:

```
1  * Map
2    - next_scene
3    - opening_scene
4  * Engine
5    - play
6  * Scene
7    - enter
8    * Death
9    * Central Corridor
10    * Laser Weapon Armory
11    * The Bridge
12    * Escape Pod
```

Notice how I just put -enter under Scene since I know that all the scenes under it will inherit it and have to override it later.

Code the Classes and a Test to Run Them

Once I have this tree of classes and some of the functions, I open up a source file in my editor and try to write the code for it. Usually I'll just copy-paste the tree into the source file and then edit it into classes. Here's a small example of how this might look at first, with a simple little test at the end of the file:

Listing 47.1: ex47_classes.py

```
1  class Scene(object):
2
3      def enter(self):
4          pass
5
6
```

```
 7    class Engine(object):
 8
 9        def _init_(self, scene_map):
10            pass
11
12        def play(self):
13            pass
14
15    class Death(Scene):
16
17        def enter(self):
18            pass
19
20    class CentralCorridor(Scene):
21
22        def enter(self):
23            pass
24
25    class LaserWeaponArmory(Scene):
26
27        def enter(self):
28            pass
29
30    class TheBridge(Scene):
31
32        def enter(self):
33            pass
34
35    class EscapePod(Scene):
36
37        def enter(self):
38            pass
39
40
41    class Map(object):
42
43        def _init_(self, start_scene):
44            pass
45
46        def next_scene(self, scene_name):
47            pass
48
49        def opening_scene(self):
50            pass
51
52
53    a_map = Map('central_corridor')
54    a_game = Engine(a_map)
55    a_game.play()
```

In this file you can see that I simply replicated the hierarchy I wanted and then added a little bit of code at the end to run it and see if it all works in this basic structure. In the later sections of this exercise, you'll fill in the rest of this code and make it work to match the description of the game.

Repeat and Refine

The last step in my little process isn't so much a step as it is a `while-loop`. You don't ever do this as a one-pass operation. Instead, you go back over the whole process again and refine it based on information you've learned from later steps. Sometimes I'll get to step #3 and realize that I need to work on 1 and 2 more, so I'll stop and go back and work on those. Sometimes I'll get a flash of inspiration and jump to the end to code up the solution in my head while I have it there, but then I'll go back and do the previous steps to make sure I cover all the possibilities I have.

The other idea in this process is that it's not just something you do at one single level but something that you can do at every level when you run into a particular problem. Let's say I don't know how to write the `Engine.play` method yet. I can stop and do this whole process on *just* that one function to figure out how to write it.

Top Down versus Bottom Up

The process is typically labeled "top down" since it starts at the most abstract concepts (the top) and works its way down to actual implementation. I want you to use this process I just described when analyzing problems in the book from now on, but you should know that there's another way to solve problems in programming that starts with code and goes "up" to the abstract concepts. This other way is labeled "bottom up." Here are the general steps you follow to do this:

1. Take a small piece of the problem; hack on some code and get it to run barely

2. Refine the code into something more formal with classes and automated tests

3. Extract the key concepts you're using and try to find research for them

4. Write a description of what's really going on

5. Go back and refine the code, possibly throwing it out and starting over

6. Repeat, moving on to some other piece of the problem

I find this process is better once you're more solid at programming and are naturally thinking in code about problems. This process is very good when you know small pieces of the overall puzzle but maybe don't have enough information yet about the overall concept. Breaking it down in little pieces and exploring with code then helps you slowly grind away at the problem until you've solved it. However, remember that your solution will probably be meandering and weird, so that's why my version of this process involves going back and finding research and then cleaning things up based on what you've learned.

The Code for "Gothons from Planet Percal #25"

Stop! I'm going to show you my final solution to the preceding problem, but I don't want you to just jump in and type this up. I want *you* to take the rough skeleton code I did and try to make it work based on the description. Once you have your solution, then you can come back and see how I did it.

I'm going to break this final file ex47.py down into sections and explain each one rather than dump all the code at once.

Listing 47.2: ex47.py

```
1    from sys import exit
2    from random import randint
3    from ex47_dialogue import DIALOGUE
```

This is just our basic imports for the game. The only new thing is the import of the DIALOGUE data from the ex47_dialogue.py module. This module contains all of the dialogue text for the game so you don't have to type in all the text. You can download the file from the learncodethehardway.com Python resources and save it to your computer. If you can't access the internet, then here's the entire file:

Listing 47.3: ex47_dialogue.py

```
1    DIALOGUE = {
2        "CentralCorridor_enter": """
3    The Gothons of Planet Percal #25 have invaded your ship and
4    destroyed your entire crew.  You are the last surviving
5    member and your last mission is to get the neutron destruct
6    bomb from the Weapons Armory, put it in the bridge, and blow
7    the ship up after getting into an escape pod.
8
9    You're running down the central corridor to the Weapons
10   Armory when a Gothon jumps out, red scaly skin, dark grimy
11   teeth, and evil clown costume flowing around his hate filled
12   body.  He's blocking the door to the Armory and about to
13   pull a weapon to blast you.
14   """,
15   "CentralCorridor_shoot": """
16   Quick on the draw you yank out your blaster and fire it at
17   the Gothon.  His clown costume is flowing and moving around
18   his body, which throws off your aim.  Your laser hits his
19   costume but misses him entirely.  This completely ruins his
20   brand new costume his mother bought him, which makes him fly
21   into an insane rage and blast you repeatedly in the face
22   until you are dead.  Then he eats you.
23   """,
24   "CentralCorridor_dodge": """
25   Like a world class boxer you dodge, weave, slip and slide
26   right as the Gothon's blaster cranks a laser past your head.
```

```
27    In the middle of your artful dodge your foot slips and you
28    bang your head on the metal wall and pass out.  You wake up
29    shortly after only to die as the Gothon stomps on your head
30    and eats you.
31    """,
32    "CentralCorridor_joke": """
33    Lucky for you they made you learn Gothon insults in the
34    academy.  You tell the one Gothon joke you know: Lbhe zbgure
35    vf fb sng, jura fur fvgf nebhaq gur ubhfr, fur fvgf nebhaq
36    gur ubhfr.  The Gothon stops, tries not to laugh, then busts
37    out laughing and can't move.  While he's laughing you run up
38    and shoot him square in the head putting him down, then jump
39    through the Weapon Armory door.
40    """,
41    "LaserWeaponArmory_enter": """
42    You do a dive roll into the Weapon Armory, crouch and scan
43    the room for more Gothons that might be hiding.  It's dead
44    quiet, too quiet.  You stand up and run to the far side of
45    the room and find the neutron bomb in its container.
46    There's a keypad lock on the box and you need the code to
47    get the bomb out.  If you get the code wrong 10 times then
48    the lock closes forever and you can't get the bomb.  The
49    code is 3 digits.
50    """,
51    "LaserWeaponArmory_guess": """
52    The container clicks open and the seal breaks, letting gas
53    out.  You grab the neutron bomb and run as fast as you can
54    to the bridge where you must place it in the right spot.
55    """,
56    "LaserWeaponArmory_fail": """
57    The lock buzzes one last time and then you hear a sickening
58    melting sound as the mechanism is fused together.  You
59    decide to sit there, and finally the Gothons blow up the
60    ship from their ship and you die.
61    """,
62    "TheBridge_enter": """
63    You burst onto the Bridge with the netron destruct bomb
64    under your arm and surprise 5 Gothons who are trying to take
65    control of the ship.  Each of them has an even uglier clown
66    costume than the last.  They haven't pulled their weapons
67    out yet, as they see the active bomb under your arm and
68    don't want to set it off.
69    """,
70    "TheBridge_throw_bomb": """
71    In a panic you throw the bomb at the group of Gothons and
72    make a leap for the door.  Right as you drop it a Gothon
73    shoots you right in the back killing you.  As you die you
74    see another Gothon frantically try to disarm the bomb. You
75    die knowing they will probably blow up when it goes off.
76    """,
77
```

```
78    "TheBridge_place_bomb": """
79    You point your blaster at the bomb under your arm and the
80    Gothons put their hands up and start to sweat.  You inch
81    backward to the door, open it, and then carefully place the
82    bomb on the floor, pointing your blaster at it.  You then
83    jump back through the door, punch the close button and blast
84    the lock so the Gothons can't get out.  Now that the bomb is
85    placed you run to the escape pod to get off this tin can.
86    """,
87    "EscapePod_enter":"""
88    You rush through the ship desperately trying to make it to
89    the escape pod before the whole ship explodes.  It seems
90    like hardly any Gothons are on the ship, so your run is
91    clear of interference.  You get to the chamber with the
92    escape pods, and now need to pick one to take.  Some of them
93    could be damaged but you don't have time to look.  There's 5
94    pods, which one do you take?
95    """,
96    "EscapePod_death":"""
97    You jump into pod {guess} and hit the eject button.  The pod
98    escapes out into the void of space, then implodes as the
99    hull ruptures, crushing your body into jam jelly.
100   """,
101   "EscapePod_escape":"""
102   You jump into pod {guess} and hit the eject button.  The pod
103   easily slides out into space heading to the planet below.
104   As it flies to the planet, you look back and see your ship
105   implode then explode like a bright star, taking out the
106   Gothon ship at the same time.  You won!
107   """,
108   }
```

I suggest you only create this file's structure with small notes for the actual dialogue until you can download the file.

Listing 47.4: ex47.py

```
1    class Scene(object):
2
3        def enter(self):
4            print("This scene is not yet configured.")
5            print("Subclass it and implement enter().")
6            exit(1)
```

As you saw in the skeleton code, I have a base class for Scene that will have the common things that all scenes do. In this simple program they don't do much, so this is more a demonstration of what you would do to make a base class.

Listing 47.5: ex47.py

```
1    class Engine(object):
2
3        def _init_(self, scene_map):
4            self.scene_map = scene_map
5
6        def play(self):
7            current_scene = self.scene_map.opening_scene()
8            last_scene = self.scene_map.next_scene('finished')
9
10           while current_scene != last_scene:
11               next_scene_name = current_scene.enter()
12               current_scene = self.scene_map.next_scene(next_scene_name)
13
14           # be sure to print out the last scene
15           current_scene.enter()
```

I also have my Engine class, and you can see how I'm already using the methods for Map.opening_
↳ scene and Map.next_scene. Because I've done a bit of planning, I can just assume I'll write those
methods and then use them before I've written the Map class.

Listing 47.6: ex47.py

```
1    class Death(Scene):
2
3        quips = [
4            "You died.  You kinda suck at this.",
5            "Your Mom would be proud...if she were smarter.",
6            "Such a luser.",
7            "I have a small puppy that's better at this.",
8            "You're worse than your Dad's jokes."
9
10       ]
11
12       def enter(self):
13           print(Death.quips[randint(0, len(self.quips)-1)])
14           exit(1)
```

My first scene is the odd scene named Death, which shows you the simplest kind of scene you can
write.

Listing 47.7: ex47.py

```
1    class CentralCorridor(Scene):
2
3        def enter(self):
4            print(DIALOGUE["CentralCorridor_enter"])
5
```

```
6                action = input("> ")
7
8                if action == "shoot!":
9                    print(DIALOGUE["CentralCorridor_shoot"])
10                   return 'death'
11
12               elif action == "dodge!":
13                   print(DIALOGUE["CentralCorridor_dodge"])
14                   return 'death'
15
16               elif action == "tell a joke":
17                   print(DIALOGUE["CentralCorridor_joke"])
18                   return 'laser_weapon_armory'
19
20               else:
21                   print("DOES NOT COMPUTE!")
22                   return 'central_corridor'
```

After that I've created the `CentralCorridor`, which is the start of the game. I'm doing the scenes for the game before the Map because I need to reference them later.

Listing 47.8: ex47.py

```
1     class LaserWeaponArmory(Scene):
2
3         def enter(self):
4             print(DIALOGUE["LaserWeaponArmory_enter"])
5
6             code = f"{randint(1,9)}{randint(1,9)}{randint(1,9)}"
7             guess = input("[keypad]> ")
8             guesses = 0
9
10            while guess != code and guesses < 10:
11                print("BZZZZEDDD!")
12                guesses += 1
13                guess = input("[keypad]> ")
14
15            if guess == code:
16                print(DIALOGUE["LaserWeaponArmory_guess"])
17                return 'the_bridge'
18            else:
19                print(DIALOGUE["LaserWeaponArmory_fail"])
20                return 'death'
21
22
23
24    class TheBridge(Scene):
25
26        def enter(self):
```

```
27                  print(DIALOGUE["TheBridge_enter"])
28
29                  action = input("> ")
30
31                  if action == "throw the bomb":
32                      print(DIALOGUE["TheBridge_throw_bomb"])
33                      return 'death'
34
35                  elif action == "slowly place the bomb":
36                      print(DIALOGUE["TheBridge_place_bomb"])
37
38                      return 'escape_pod'
39                  else:
40                      print("DOES NOT COMPUTE!")
41                      return "the_bridge"
42
43
44      class EscapePod(Scene):
45
46          def enter(self):
47                  print(DIALOGUE["EscapePod_enter"])
48
49                  good_pod = randint(1,5)
50                  guess = input("[pod #]> ")
51
52
53                  if int(guess) != good_pod:
54                      print(DIALOGUE["EscapePod_death"]
55                          .format(guess=guess))
56                      return 'death'
57                  else:
58                      print(DIALOGUE["EscapePod_escape"]
59                          .format(guess=guess))
60
61                      return 'finished'
62
63      class Finished(Scene):
64
65          def enter(self):
66                  print("You won! Good job.")
67                  return 'finished'
```

This is the rest of the game's scenes, and since I know I need them and have thought about how they'll flow together, I'm able to code them up directly.

Incidentally, I wouldn't just type all this code in. Remember, I said to try to build this incrementally, one little bit at a time. I'm just showing you the final result.

Listing 47.9: ex47.py

```
1    class Map(object):
2
3        scenes = {
4            'central_corridor': CentralCorridor(),
5            'laser_weapon_armory': LaserWeaponArmory(),
6            'the_bridge': TheBridge(),
7            'escape_pod': EscapePod(),
8            'death': Death(),
9            'finished': Finished(),
10       }
11
12       def _init_(self, start_scene):
13           self.start_scene = start_scene
14
15       def next_scene(self, scene_name):
16           val = Map.scenes.get(scene_name)
17           return val
18
19       def opening_scene(self):
20           return self.next_scene(self.start_scene)
```

After that I have my Map class, and you can see it is storing each scene by name in a dictionary, and then I refer to that dict with Map.scenes. This is also why the map comes after the scenes because the dictionary has to refer to the scenes, so they have to exist.

Listing 47.10: ex47.py

```
1    a_map = Map('central_corridor')
2    a_game = Engine(a_map)
3    a_game.play()
```

Finally, I've got my code that runs the game by making a Map and then handing that map to an Engine before calling play to make the game work.

What You Should See

Make sure you understand the game and that you tried to solve it yourself first. One thing to do if you're stumped is cheat a little by reading my code and then continue trying to solve it yourself.

The length of this script is quite large, so rather than include it here, I'll assume you know how to run it.

Study Drills

1. Change it! Maybe you hate this game. It could be too violent, or maybe you aren't into sci-fi. Get the game working and then change it to what you like. This is your computer; you make it do what you want.

2. I have a bug in this code. Why is the door lock guessing 11 times?

3. Explain how returning the next room works.

4. Add cheat codes to the game so you can get past the more difficult rooms. I can do this with two words on one line.

5. Go back to my description and analysis and then try to build a small combat system for the hero and the various Gothons he encounters.

6. This is actually a small version of something called a "finite state machine." Read about them. They might not make sense, but try anyway.

Common Student Questions

Where can I find stories for my own games?   You can make them up, just like you would tell a story to a friend. Or you can take simple scenes from a book or movie you like.

Inheritance versus Composition

I n the fairy tales about heroes defeating evil villains there's always a dark forest of some kind. It could be a cave, a forest, another planet, or just some place that everyone knows the hero shouldn't go. Of course, shortly after the villain is introduced you find out, yes, the hero has to go to that stupid forest to kill the bad guy. It seems the hero just keeps getting into situations that require him to risk his life in this evil forest.

You rarely read fairy tales about the heroes who are smart enough to just avoid the whole situation entirely. You never hear a hero say, "Wait a minute, if I leave to make my fortunes on the high seas, leaving Buttercup behind, I could die, and then she'd have to marry some ugly prince named Humperdink. Humperdink! I think I'll stay here and start a Farm Boy for Rent business." If he did that, there'd be no fire swamp, dying, reanimation, sword fights, giants, or any kind of story really. Because of this, the forest in these stories seems to exist like a black hole that drags the hero in no matter what they do.

In object-oriented programming, inheritance is the evil forest. Experienced programmers know to avoid this evil because they know that deep inside the Dark Forest Inheritance is the Evil Queen Multiple Inheritance. She likes to eat software and programmers with her massive complexity teeth, chewing on the flesh of the fallen. But the forest is so powerful and so tempting that nearly every programmer has to go into it and try to make it out alive with the Evil Queen's head before they can call themselves real programmers. You just can't resist the Inheritance Forest's pull, so you go in. After the adventure, you learn to just stay out of that stupid forest and bring an army if you are ever forced to go in again.

This is basically a funny way to say that I'm going to teach you something you should use carefully called "inheritance." Programmers who are currently in the forest battling the Queen will probably tell you that you have to go in. They say this because they need your help since what they've created is probably too much for them to handle. But you should always remember this:

> Most of the uses of inheritance can be simplified or replaced with composition, and multiple inheritance should be avoided at all costs.

What Is Inheritance?

Inheritance is used to indicate that one class will get most or all of its features from a parent class. This happens implicitly whenever you write class Foo(Bar), which says "Make a class Foo that inherits from Bar." When you do this, the language makes any action that you do on instances of Foo also work as if they were done to an instance of Bar. Doing this lets you put common functionality in the Bar class and then specialize that functionality in the Foo class as needed.

When you are doing this kind of specialization, there are three ways that the parent and child classes can interact:

1. Actions on the child imply an action on the parent

2. Actions on the child override the action on the parent

3. Actions on the child alter the action on the parent

I will now demonstrate each of these in order and show you code for them.

Implicit Inheritance

First I will show you the implicit actions that happen when you define a function in the parent but *not* in the child:

Listing 48.1: ex48a.py

```
1   class Parent(object):
2
3       def implicit(self):
4           print("PARENT implicit()")
5
6   class Child(Parent):
7       pass
8
9   dad = Parent()
10  son = Child()
11
12  dad.implicit()
13  son.implicit()
```

The use of pass under the class Child: is how you tell Python that you want an empty block. This creates a class named Child but says that there's nothing new to define in it. Instead, it will inherit all of its behavior from Parent. When you run this code, you get the following:

```
1   PARENT implicit()
2   PARENT implicit()
```

Notice how even though I'm calling son.implicit() on line 13 and even though Child does *not* have an implicit() function defined, it still works, and it calls the one defined in Parent. This shows you that if you put functions in a base class (i.e., Parent), then all subclasses (i.e., Child) will automatically get those features. This is very handy for repetitive code you need in many classes.

Override Explicitly

The problem with having functions called implicitly is sometimes you want the child to behave differently. In this case you want to override the function in the child, effectively replacing the functionality. To do this just define a function with the same name in `Child`. Here's an example:

Listing 48.2: ex48b.py

```
1   class Parent(object):
2
3       def override(self):
4           print("PARENT override()")
5
6   class Child(Parent):
7
8       def override(self):
9           print("CHILD override()")
10
11  dad = Parent()
12  son = Child()
13
14  dad.override()
15  son.override()
```

In this example I have a function named `override` in both classes, so let's see what happens when you run it:

```
1   PARENT override()
2   CHILD override()
```

As you can see, when line 14 runs, it runs the `Parent.override()` function because that variable (dad) is a `Parent`. But when line 15 runs, it prints out the `Child.override` messages because son is an instance of `Child` and `Child` overrides that function by defining its own version.

Take a break right now and try playing with these two concepts before continuing.

Alter Before or After

The third way to use inheritance is a special case of overriding where you want to alter the behavior before or after the `Parent` class's version runs. You first override the function just like in the previous example, but then you use a Python built-in function named `super` to get the `Parent` version to call. Here's the example of doing that so you can make sense of this description:

Listing 48.3: ex48c.py

```
1    class Parent(object):
2
3        def altered(self):
4            print("PARENT altered()")
5
6    class Child(Parent):
7
8        def altered(self):
9            print("CHILD, BEFORE PARENT altered()")
10           super(Child, self).altered()
11           print("CHILD, AFTER PARENT altered()")
12
13   dad = Parent()
14   son = Child()
15
16   dad.altered()
17   son.altered()
```

The important lines here are 9–11, where in the Child I do the following when son.altered() is
called:

1. Because I've overridden Parent.altered, the Child.altered() version runs, and line 9
   executes like you'd expect.

2. In this case I want to do a before and after, so after line 9 I want to use super to get the
   Parent.altered() version.

3. On line 10 I call super(Child, self).altered(), which is aware of inheritance and will
   get the Parent class for you. You should be able to read this as "call super with arguments
   Child and self and then call the function altered on whatever it returns."

4. At this point, the Parent.altered() version of the function runs, and that prints out the
   Parent message.

5. Finally, this returns from Parent.altered(), and the Child.altered() function continues to print out the after message.

If you run this, you should see this:

```
1   PARENT altered()
2   CHILD, BEFORE PARENT altered()
3   PARENT altered()
4   CHILD, AFTER PARENT altered()
```

All Three Combined

To demonstrate all of these, I have a final version that shows each kind of interaction from inheritance in one file:

Listing 48.4: ex48d.py

```
1    class Parent(object):
2
3        def override(self):
4            print("PARENT override()")
5
6        def implicit(self):
7            print("PARENT implicit()")
8
9        def altered(self):
10           print("PARENT altered()")
11
12   class Child(Parent):
13
14       def override(self):
15           print("CHILD override()")
16
17       def altered(self):
18           print("CHILD, BEFORE PARENT altered()")
19           super(Child, self).altered()
20           print("CHILD, AFTER PARENT altered()")
21
22   dad = Parent()
23   son = Child()
24
25   dad.implicit()
26   son.implicit()
27
28   dad.override()
29   son.override()
30
31   dad.altered()
32   son.altered()
```

Go through each line of this code, and write a comment explaining what that line does and whether it's an override or not. Then run it and confirm you get what you expected:

```
1  PARENT implicit()
2  PARENT implicit()
3  PARENT override()
4  CHILD override()
5  PARENT altered()
6  CHILD, BEFORE PARENT altered()
```

```
7  PARENT altered()
8  CHILD, AFTER PARENT altered()
```

The Reason for super( )

This should seem like common sense, but then we get into trouble with a thing called "multiple inheritance." Multiple inheritance is when you define a class that inherits from one or *more* classes, like this:

```
1  class SuperFun(Child, BadStuff):
2      pass
```

This is like saying "Make a class named SuperFun that inherits from the classes Child and BadStuff at the same time."

In this case, whenever you have implicit actions on any SuperFun instance, Python has to look up the possible function in the class hierarchy for both Child and BadStuff, but it needs to do this in a consistent order. To do this, Python uses "method resolution order" (MRO) and an algorithm called C3 to get it straight.

Because the MRO is complex and a well-defined algorithm is used, Python can't leave it to you to get the MRO right. Instead, Python gives you the super( ) function, which handles all of this for you in the places that you need the altering type of actions as I did in Child.altered( ). With super( ) you don't have to worry about getting this right, and Python will find the right function for you.

Using super( ) with __init__( )

The most common use of super( ) is actually in __init__( ) functions in base classes. This is usually the only place where you need to do some things in a child and then complete the initialization in the parent. Here's a quick example of doing that in the Child:

```
1  class Child(Parent):
2
3      def _init_(self, stuff):
4          self.stuff = stuff
5          super(Child, self)._init_()
```

This is pretty much the same as the Child.altered( ) example, except I'm setting some variables in the __init__( ) before having the Parent initialize with its Parent.__init__( ).

Composition

Inheritance is useful, but another way to do the same thing is just to *use* other classes and modules, rather than rely on implicit inheritance. If you look at the three ways to exploit inheritance, two of the three involve writing new code to replace or alter functionality. This can easily be replicated by just calling functions in a module. Here's an example of doing this:

Listing 48.5: ex48e.py

```
 1    class Other(object):
 2
 3        def override(self):
 4            print("OTHER override()")
 5
 6        def implicit(self):
 7            print("OTHER implicit()")
 8
 9        def altered(self):
10            print("OTHER altered()")
11
12    class Child(object):
13
14        def _init_(self):
15            self.other = Other()
16
17        def implicit(self):
18            self.other.implicit()
19
20        def override(self):
21            print("CHILD override()")
22
23        def altered(self):
24            print("CHILD, BEFORE OTHER altered()")
25            self.other.altered()
26            print("CHILD, AFTER OTHER altered()")
27
28    son = Child()
29
30    son.implicit()
31    son.override()
32    son.altered()
```

In this code I'm not using the name Parent, since there is *not* a parent-child is-a relationship. This is a has-a relationship, where Child has-a Other that it uses to get its work done. When I run this, I get the following output:

```
1   OTHER implicit()
2   CHILD override()
3   CHILD, BEFORE OTHER altered()
4   OTHER altered()
5   CHILD, AFTER OTHER altered()
```

You can see that most of the code in Child and Other is the same to accomplish the same thing. The only difference is that I had to define a Child.implicit() function to do that one action. I could then ask myself if I need this Other to be a class, and could I just make it into a module named other.py?

When to Use Inheritance or Composition

The question of "inheritance versus composition" comes down to an attempt to solve the problem of reusable code. You don't want to have duplicated code all over your software, since that's not clean and efficient. Inheritance solves this problem by creating a mechanism for you to have implied features in base classes. Composition solves this by giving you modules and the capability to call functions in other classes.

If both solutions solve the problem of reuse, then which one is appropriate in which situations? The answer is incredibly subjective, but I'll give you my three guidelines for when to do which:

1. Avoid multiple inheritance at all costs, as it's too complex to be reliable. If you're stuck with it, then be prepared to know the class hierarchy and spend time finding where everything is coming from.

2. Use composition to package code into modules that are used in many different unrelated places and situations.

3. Use inheritance only when there are clearly related reusable pieces of code that fit under a single common concept or if you have to because of something you're using.

Do not be a slave to these rules. The thing to remember about object-oriented programming is that it is entirely a social convention programmers have created to package and share code. Because it's a social convention but one that's codified in Python, you may be forced to avoid these rules because of the people you work with. In that case, find out how they use things and then just adapt to the situation.

Study Drill

There is only one Study Drill for this exercise because it is a big exercise. Read http://www.python.org /dev/peps/pep-0008/ and start trying to use it in your code. You'll notice that some of it is different from what you've been learning in this book, but now you should be able to understand their recommendations and use them in your own code. The rest of the code in this book may or may not follow these guidelines depending on whether it makes the code more confusing. I suggest you also do this, as comprehension is more important than impressing everyone with your knowledge of esoteric style rules.

Common Student Questions

How do I get better at solving problems that I haven't seen before? The only way to get better at solving problems is to solve as many problems as you can *by yourself*. Typically people hit a difficult problem and then rush out to find an answer. This is fine when you have to get things done, but if you have the time to solve it yourself, then take that time. Stop and bang your head against the problem for as long as possible, trying every possible thing until you solve it or give up. After that the answers you find will be more satisfying, and you'll eventually get better at solving problems.

Aren't objects just copies of classes? In some languages (like JavaScript) that is true. These are called "prototype languages," and there are not many differences between objects and classes other than usage. In Python, however, classes act as templates that "mint" new objects, similar to how coins were minted using a die (template).

You Make a Game

You need to start learning to feed yourself. I hope as you have worked through this book, you have learned that all the information you need is on the internet. You just have to go search for it. The only things you have been missing are the right words and what to look for when you search. Now you should have a sense of it, so it's about time you struggled through a big project and tried to get it working.

Here are your requirements:

1. Make a different game from the one I made.

2. Use more than one file, and use `import` to use them. Make sure you know what that is.

3. Use *one class per room* and give the classes names that fit their purpose (like `GoldRoom`, `KoiPondRoom`).

4. Your runner will need to know about these rooms, so make a class that runs them and knows about them. There are plenty of ways to do this, but consider having each room return what room is next or setting a variable of what room is next.

Other than that, I leave it to you. Spend a whole week on this and make it the best game you can. Use classes, functions, dicts, lists, and anything you can to make it nice. The purpose of this lesson is to teach you how to structure classes that need other classes inside other files.

Remember, I'm not telling you *exactly* how to do this because you have to do this yourself. Go figure it out. Programming is problem solving, and that means trying things, experimenting, failing, scrapping your work, and trying again. When you get stuck, ask for help and show people your code. If they are mean to you, ignore them, and focus on the people who are not mean and offer to help. Keep working it and cleaning it until it's good, and then show it some more.

Good luck, and see you in a week with your game.

Evaluating Your Game

In this exercise you will evaluate the game you just made. Maybe you got partway through it and you got stuck. Maybe you got it working but just barely. Either way, we're going to go through a bunch of things you should know now and make sure you covered them in your game. We're going to study properly formatting a class, common conventions in using classes, and a lot of "textbook" knowledge.

Why would I have you try to do it yourself and then show you how to do it right? From now on in the book, I'm going to try to make you self-sufficient. I've been holding your hand mostly this whole time, and I can't do that for much longer. I'm now instead going to give you things to do, have you do them on your own, and then give you ways to improve what you did.

You will struggle at first and probably be very frustrated, but stick with it, and eventually you will build a mind for solving problems. You will start to find creative solutions to problems rather than just copy solutions out of textbooks.

Function Style

All the other rules I've taught you about how to make a nice function apply here, but add these things:

- For various reasons, programmers call functions that are part of classes "methods." It's mostly marketing, but just be warned that every time you say "function" they'll annoyingly correct you and say "method." If they get too annoying, just ask them to demonstrate the mathematical basis that determines how a "method" is different from a "function" and they'll shut up.

- When you work with classes, much of your time is spent talking about making the class "do things." Instead of naming your functions after what the functions do, name them as if they're commands you're giving to the class. Same as pop is saying "Hey list, pop this off." It isn't called `remove_from_end_of_list` because even though that's what it does, that's not a *command* to a list.

- Keep your functions small and simple. For some reason when people start learning about classes, they forget this.

Class Style

- Your class should use "camel case" like `SuperGoldFactory` rather than `super_gold_ ↳ factory`

- Try not to do too much in your `__init__()` functions. It makes them harder to use.

- Your other functions should use "underscore format," so write `my_awesome_hair` and not `myawesomehair` or `MyAwesomeHair`

- Be consistent in how you organize your function arguments. If your class has to deal with users, dogs, and cats, keep that order throughout unless it really doesn't make sense. If you have one function that takes (`dog`, `cat`, `user`) and the other takes (`user`, `cat`, `dog`), it'll be hard to use.

- Try not to use variables that come from the module or globals. They should be fairly self-contained.

- A foolish consistency is the hobgoblin of little minds. Consistency is good, but foolishly following some idiotic mantra because everyone else does is bad style. Think for yourself.

- Always, *always* have `class Name(object)` format or else you will be in big trouble.

Code Style

- Give your code vertical space so people can read it. You will find some very bad programmers who are able to write reasonable code but who do not add *any* spaces. This is bad style in any language because the human eye and brain use space and vertical alignment to scan and separate visual elements. Not having space is the same as giving your code an awesome camouflage paint job.

- If you can't read it out loud, it's probably hard to read. If you are having a problem making something easy to use, try reading it out loud. Not only does this force you to slow down and really read it, but it also helps you find difficult passages and things to change for readability.

- Try to do what other people are doing in Python until you find your own style.

- Once you find your own style, do not be a jerk about it. Working with other people's code is part of being a programmer, and other people have really bad taste. Trust me, you will probably have really bad taste too and not even realize it.

- If you find someone who writes code in a style you like, try writing something that mimics that style.

Good Comments

- Programmers will tell you that your code should be readable enough that you do not need comments. They'll then tell you in their most official sounding voice, "Ergo one should never write comments or documentation. QED." Those programmers are either consultants who get paid more if other people can't use their code or incompetents who tend to never work with other people. Ignore them and write comments.

- When you write comments, describe *why* you are doing what you are doing. The code already says how, but why you did things the way you did is more important.

- When you write doc comments for your functions, make the comments documentation for someone who will have to use your code. You do not have to go crazy, but a nice little sentence about what someone can do with that function helps a lot.

- While comments are good, too many are bad, and you have to maintain them. Keep your comments relatively short and to the point, and if you change a function, review the comment to make sure it's still correct.

Evaluate Your Game

I want you to now pretend you are me. Adopt a very stern look, print out your code, and take a red pen and mark every mistake you find, including anything from this exercise and from other guidelines you've read so far. Once you are done marking your code up, I want you to fix everything you came up with. Then repeat this a couple of times, looking for anything that could be better. Use all the tricks I've given you to break your code down into the smallest, tiniest little analysis you can.

The purpose of this exercise is to train your attention to detail on classes. Once you are done with this bit of code, find someone else's code and do the same thing. Go through a printed copy of some part of it and point out all the mistakes and style errors you find. Then fix it and see if your fixes can be done without breaking that program.

I want you to do nothing but evaluate and fix code for the week—your own code and other people's. It'll be pretty hard work, but when you are done, your brain will be wired tight like a boxer's hands.

Automated Testing

This final exercise of Module 3 will teach you how to create automated tests. An automated test is code that runs other code and confirms it's still working. As a programmer, your primary way to improve your work comes from automating things you do manually, and testing is one of the easiest things you can automate. Once you have a nice automated test suite, you can run it every time you make a change to test that everything is still working.

What Is the Purpose of Testing?

There's a lot of people who advocate for various reasons and styles of testing, but in my experience there's really only one big benefit of automated tests:

> A complete automated test suite confirms that new code doesn't break old code.

When you change code, there's a probability your new code might break something else you wrote. This becomes more true as the size of your software and the team writing it increases. Once you have more than two people, you'll run into situations where one person changes something that breaks another person's code. If you have a handful of modules connected to each other, a change in one can cause others to break.

This leads to an important consequence of having tests:

> You can completely rewrite old code because your tests help ensure everything keeps working.

You do get a few additional benefits from automating your testing:

1. It's automated, so you don't waste time typing the same thing over and over.
2. It'll be consistent so you won't forget one of your tests.
3. An automated test can help find bugs or bad designs in APIs you use, but this is less common if you're testing efficiently.
4. It can give you a new perspective on your code, which might help you simplify it. If your test is heinous, then maybe it's time to rewrite the code.

How to Test Efficiently

What's the most efficient way to write tests then? I've found this process to provide the most value for the least effort:

1. Write tests that pretend to be the user, whether that user is someone accessing your website or a programmer using your API. Your tests should pretend to be an actual person doing good and bad things.

2. Cause as many errors as possible and confirm they are actually reported. For example, on a registration form give bad email addresses, usernames, and passwords and then check for the errors. If your tests runs later and you have no errors, then you broke something for sure.

3. Use a coverage reporting tool to confirm that your tests are at a *minimum* hitting most of the code, including error handlers.

4. Any code you can't hit should be analyzed and either removed as useless or get separate tests if it's actually not useless. If you can't hit the code from the UI, then why is it in there? Just in case? "Just in case code" is a security time bomb, so just remove it. You can always bring it back later. If it's code that's run in a background job or simply not used by the user, then write a special test just for that code.

5. Finally, if your code uses any other services run by other people, then write tests that confirm those services keep working. You won't believe how often companies and people change their services without telling you. A test that checks their service can save you significant downtime in the future. The only problem with these tests is you typically can't run them in a usual developer workflow. It's better to run this separately in a monitoring tool or some other infrequent checking service. If your tests run service checks, you may take the service down–or worse–incur massive costs as you rack up thousands of requests a day on accident.

If you're working by yourself, you can get away with just steps #1–3, but as your code grows, you'll need to start doing the rest of these. These also aren't an exhaustive list of things you need to do when testing software. That's an entire book on its own.

Install PyTest

In Python the best testing system is PyTest, and it's easy to install using conda:

```
1  conda activate lpythw # don't forget this
2  conda install pytest
```

You'll also want to install a "coverage" tool, which will tell you if your tests are reaching the code you want:

```
1  # don't forget to activate
2  conda install pytest-cov
```

I'll show you how to use the coverage tool after you learn how to write a simple test.

Simple PyTest Demo

For this simple test you'll need two files, one with some code and an ex50_test.py file to test it. I'll implement a simple combat system using a Person class you've seen before:

Listing 50.1: ex50.py

```
1   class Person:
2       def __init__(self, name, hp, damage):
3           self.name = name
4           self.hp = hp
5           self.damage = damage
6
7       def hit(self, who):
8           self.hp -= who.damage
9
10      def alive(self):
11          return self.hp > 0
```

The test imports this Person from module ex50 and then confirms that a boxer can hit a zombie named Zed:

Listing 50.2: ex50_test.py

```
1   from ex50 import Person
2
3   def test_combat():
4       boxer = Person("Boxer", 100, 10)
5       zombie = Person("Zed", 1000, 1000)
6
7       # these asserts are bad, fix them
8       assert boxer.hp == 100, "Boxer has wrong hp."
9       assert zombie.hp == 1000, "Zombe has wrong hp."
10
11      boxer.hit(zombie)
12      assert zombie.alive(), "Zombie should be alive."
13
14      zombie.hit(boxer)
15      assert not boxer.alive(), "Boxer should be dead."
```

The assert keyword is standard Python and is used to check for a truth condition, aborting if this condition is false. PyTest uses assert to test that the Person works as you want, so you don't have to remember many testing functions. The format of an assert is:

```
1   assert TEST, "MESSAGE"
```

When the TEST is false, Python will print MESSAGE and raise an exception. The message can also be an f-string to give more information.

Running pytest

If you try to run this ex50_test.py file normally, it will produce no output. You need to run it with the pytest command like this:

```
1  pytest ex50_test.py
```

This works, but pytest is smart enough to find your tests for you, so you can also just run pytest on its own, and it will find and run any file that starts with test_ or ends with _test.py. Try this to see you get the same output.

Exceptions and try/except

An exception is a way for code to report an error to other code. An exception is "thrown" where there's an error and then "caught" by other code that handles the error. The following code examples "throw" and "catch" two different types of errors.

Listing 50.3: ex50_except.py

```
1  try:
2      count = int("hello")
3  except ValueError:
4      print("Bad number given.")
5
6  try:
7      assert 1 == 2, "One does not equal 2"
8  except Exception as what:
9      print("assert throws", type(what))
```

If you run this simple code, it'll attempt to convert "hello" with int() but fail. Normally this prints out an error message and Python exits, but you can "wrap" it with try and except to "catch" the error and do something different.

The second part shows you what assert throws, which will print out <class 'AssertionError'>. Here's the full run of this code:

```
1  Bad number given.
2  assert throws <class 'AssertionError'>
```

Exceptions are used all over Python, but you don't run into them often until you get further in your programming studies. Most likely right after this course you'll have to deal with them, and then they're not that difficult. Just read the official Python documentation, and you'll know everything you need when the time comes.

Getting Coverage Reports

You'll definitely want to verify your testing with coverage reports from pytest-cov. To get a basic report, you add the --cov=DIR where DIR is the directory of code to analyze. This is *not* the test directory but the directory where the code lives. Your setup is very simple, so use . for the directory:

```
1  pytest --cov=.
```

This will print out your test results, but also a table of all the files in the directory and how much code was "covered" with the test. Here's a small sample from my directory:

```
1  Name                    Stmts   Miss  Cover
2  -------------------------------------------
3  ex39.py                    29     29     0%
4  ex40.py                    10     10     0%
5  .. many files cut..
6  ex50.py                     9      0   100%
7  ex50_except.py              8      8     0%
8  ex50_test.py               10      0   100%
9  -------------------------------------------
10 TOTAL                     668    584    13%
```

I've cut many files out from my output, but you can see how it says some files have 0% coverage and other 100%. You can get an HTML report by passing --cov-report html:

```
1  pytest --cov-report html:coverage --cov=.
```

This will save an HTML coverage report in the directory coverage, which you can view with:

```
1  # PowerShell uses start
2  start coverage/index.html
3
4  # macOS uses open
5  open coverage/index.html
```

That should open the report in your browser, and if you click on a file, it will show you exactly what lines have been run. The lines that are not tested yet are highlighted in red.

Study Drills

This example test is only educational, but it could be vastly improved to make it easier to use later:

1. Make this test fail in various ways so you know what a failure looks like. Try breaking both the ex50_test.py and ex50.py files. Maybe do bad math in ex50.py so the self.hp is wrong; then in the ex50_test.py try giving bad data to an assert.

2.   The assert messages tell you nothing about why they're wrong. `"Boxer has wrong hp."` should tell you *what* the hp should be with and *why* it should be that. Use an `f""` string to give more information.

3.   The test is checking values inside the object with code `self.hp`, but that's usually a recipe for tests that are difficult to maintain. It'd be better if you didn't use that and instead used only external functions to confirm everything is working.

4.   Another *very* useful thing is to add an `__invariant__()` function to the `Person` class. This comes from a style of programming called Design by Contract created by Bertrand Meyer where you add instrumentation to your code that confirms things are working as expected. The `__invariant__()` function's job is to check the `Person` object's internal state and make sure that there are no "bad" conditions. For example, it would confirm that `self.damage` is never 0 and that the person is `alive()` when `self.hp > 0`. Write an `__invariant__()` function that your test can call that uses `assert` to validate the `Person` object's internal state for the test.

5.   The other side of the test is that the `Person` class doesn't provide any error checking. What happens if you give someone `-100` damage? Are they a healer now? Add some `assert` checks to your `__init__()` and other functions to protect against bad input and then use what you know of `try/except` to confirm these checks work.

Common Student Questions

Do I have to write my tests first?   Some test fanatics like to enforce a particular way to test your code they call "test first." Their claim is that the only one true way of testing your software is to write zero code before you've written test code. The problem is *nobody* who claims to do "test first" testing actually does this. What they *really* do is write a "spike" first, which is a quick hack to explore the problem. *Then* they write a test based on the spike and finally write the code based on both the test and spike. This means they don't follow their own edicts, and this is generally true about anyone who is absolute in their advice.

When should I write tests?   I'm a big advocate of starting with what you know first. Do you know how to write the code but not really what results you should get? Start with the code then. Do you know how you want to interact with the code, but not really how it works yet? Start with the test. Starting with what you know gets you started, and getting started is usually the hardest thing for most people.

How can I make my code 100% correct?   You can't. No software will ever be 100% correct, and anyone claiming their method, programming language, or system produces "correct" or "perfect" software is selling you a fantasy. The only thing you can do is reduce the probability of a defect, and tests help with that.

Do I have to reach 100% code coverage? No, that's not totally necessary, but if you can, then it'll help with reducing the probability of defects. Your main goal with coverage is to confirm that you're efficiently checking all the branches of your code. What you want to avoid is testing 1 line of code 200 times but ignoring 30 lines of error handling. Coverage will help you find these situations and make them more efficient, but it's not a measure of overall testing quality. It's only a measure of testing efficiency and a baseline quality goal.

Other people say start with the smallest unit first and never test the UI. Yes, some people say this, and usually those people are consultants who get paid by the hour. Try their advice, but use measurements to confirm their claims. Write some tests using both styles, use coverage to see how often you're testing code and what you're testing, and track how much time it takes you to reach your goal. When you're done, you'll have formed your *own* opinion on what's best for *you* using measurements.

MODULE 4

Python and Data Science

What Is Data Munging?

At this point in the course you know Python. You may not feel *confident* in Python, and you don't know *all* of Python, but neither do most of the people using Python. There are supposed professionals who actually don't know you can use dis( ) to study the Python bytecode. These "professionals" also have no idea that Python even *has* bytecode. Given that you know how to analyze the bytes Python uses to process your code I'd say you could be more knowledgeable than many Python programmers working today.

Does that mean you're good at Python? No, not at all. Memorizing arbitrary facts about programming languages does not make you capable with that language. To become a capable programmer, you have to combine your understanding of how Python works with actually using it to build software. Programming is a *creative practice* similar to music, writing, and painting. You can memorize every note on the fretboard, but if you can't actually play those notes, you don't know how to play guitar. You can memorize every rule of English grammar, but if you can't actually write a compelling story or essay, then you can't write. You can memorize every quality of every pigment, but if you can't use those pigments to paint a portrait, then you can't paint.

The goal of the final module is to take you from "I know *about* Python" to "I can *create software* with Python." I'm going to teach you how to convert the ideas in your head into working software, but I must warn you, this process is *very* frustrating. Many beginners find it difficult to even express their ideas well, let alone well enough to create software. The way you become better at expressing your ideas in code is through experience. You simply have to do it over and over again until it's easy to do. That's why it's so frustrating to learn because it feels like you're making no progress until finally you do.

To accomplish this goal, I'm going to present three things to you in the next six exercises:

1. An abstract or poorly defined challenge to solve. Don't take these challenges as attempts to trick you like a bad job interview. I'll tell you any secrets I think you need. Take the challenges as being "loose" so you have freedom to find your own solution. Since I don't give you an exact problem, I don't expect any specific solution.

2. A new advanced Python concept to incorporate into your solution. I suggest creating a first version of your solution any way you can and *then* doing a new version that uses the new Python concept.

3. More technologies to explore that might make the problem easier, or are related to the topic. Being able to explore new technologies is important as a programmer, but it's also half the fun sometimes.

In this first exercise, I'm going to also describe a process for taking your ideas and turning them into code. It's important you read this process carefully and use it until you feel confident in your own skills.

After you're comfortable with the process, you can modify it to suit how you work or experiment with new ways to turn your ideas into code.

Why Data Munging?

In this exercise I'll introduce you to one of my favorite topics called "data munging." Data munging is the practice of using code to clean up terrible data for use by other parts of your code. It comes up in *every* type of programming you'll ever do, not just data science. It's also a nearly perfect topic for beginning programmers for many reasons:

1. It's something nearly everyone can understand
2. You usually have a lot of time to work on it and can repeatedly interact with the problem until you solve it
3. It's easy to automate and test
4. The code is almost *always* terrible, mostly because the inputs are so gnarly
5. It's still an important part of many data science projects since without data you can't do the science

INFO When you're doing data munging, you're actually doing something called Extract, Transform, and Load, or ETL. This exercise is about the Extract stage where you find various media to extract data from. Usually you'll receive the data in a nice format, like JSON or CSV files. In the worst—and sometimes the most lucrative—cases the media is not in any format you can use, and you have to manually extract what you need.

The Problem

I'm your manager, and I had an idea last night while I drove my Tesla home. I walked into your team's office and mumbled, "US beer consumption as a service for mobile." I walked out, and your team immediately had a meeting to implement this brilliant idea. When they finished, the senior developer tasked you with finding out how much beer is manufactured in the United States every month, but you're only able to get the PDF data from the Alcohol, Tobacco, and Firearms Department (ATF). The ATF has the data in Excel (.xls) format, but the senior developer tells you to use PDF because "we paid for a license to Adobe Acrobat in 2010."

The beer statistics are from the TTB division of the ATF on ttb.gov, but use my copy of their 2022 data at https://learncodethehardway.com/setup/python/ttb/ instead.

Your job is to download that PDF and extract the following data:

- Reporting Period
- Report Date
- Production for Current Month, Prior Year, Cumulative to Date
- Stocks on Hand End of Month for Current Month, Prior Year Current Month
- The difference between Production and Stock on Hand End-of-Month to determine the actual sales that month

To get you started on the project, you'll use the `pdftotext` project, but you're free to use any project that can extract text from PDF files.

The Setup

To install `pdftotext`, use conda:

```
1  conda activate lpythw
2  conda install pdftotext
```

How to Code

It seems weird to explain how to code at the end of the course, but this is where I find students have the most problem getting the code to work. There's a specific process you can follow that will take you from start to working software. It won't be *great* software, which is why you should also rewrite your solution once you get it working. If you can do it again, you'll be confident that it was your actual skills and not "dumb luck."

The most viable beginner process is this:

1. Create a file or project right away. Believe it or not, lots of students will sit there staring at the screen with no files open. Simply making a file or an empty project can be enough to get you going.

2. Type a description of the problem into the file either directly from the original or in your own words. You may need to work on this step more in ways you're familiar with before you write it into your file. Are you good at drawing? Try doing a diagram of the problem. Can you write? Try writing yourself an email describing the problem. Then write what you've described into the file so you can convert it to code.

3. Convert this description into a series of comments that describe each step of the solution. To do this, break up the description from #2 into separate lines for each step, and then add any additional steps that you feel are not mentioned.

4. Pick one of the steps you can do and under the comment write out "pseudo-code" that might solve that step (also called "p-code"). Pseudo-code is fake code that looks like "rough" Python. It's a rough sketch of the Python you need to write that doesn't worry about syntax or correctness.

5. Once you have a line or two of p-code, convert it to Python code that does what you need. At this point you should be running the Python you write repeatedly. Don't go more than a few lines before you run it. If you write many lines and have many errors, then delete those lines and do it again.

6. Then go to the next step comment to solve, write more p-code, convert it to Python, run it repeatedly, and continue until you have some kind of solution.

7. Frequently when doing this you will have to go back to previous lines and fix them as you learn more information. Don't feel like this is a "mistake," because programming requires constant revision as you gather more information.

When you're done, take a look at your code and start cleaning it up. Most programmers don't take this extra step and their code suffers for it. If you spend some time cleaning out dead code, fixing comments, removing useless comments, and simplifying what you can, then you'll be ahead of many programmers.

Finally, when you get a solution, take a long break and then do it again from scratch. You don't have to delete your code, but at least move it out of the way and try to not look at it while you make the new one. If you keep repeating your solutions, you'll get to a point where you can code most solutions directly without many of these steps. I still use this process when I'm lost, but I have used it so many times that I don't need it all the time.

If doing it again is boring, then give yourself a small challenge. Maybe try a new piece of technology or a different but similar starting problem. Or, don't do it again and come back to it when you feel like it.

Process Example

I'll now give you a tiny example of the previous process. Create a file named ex51.py and put this in right away:

```
1  Your job is to download that PDF and extract the following data:
2
3  * Reporting Period
```

For the demo I'm doing only the first task. You do the rest.

Next I convert this to comments, but I'm going to change "download" to just "open" since I'll manually download the file:

```
1  # open the PDF
2  # extract the Reporting Period
```

Once I have those, I expand on them until it seems like I have a plan:

```
1  # import modules I need
2  # open the pdf
3  # convert it to text
4  # find Reporting Period
5  # print it
```

I now have a solid set of steps, so I can put some p-code under each one. I'll place p-code under all of them because this is a textual book. If I did each one, the book would be 900 pages long. You should do one at a time and get each one working before doing the next one.

```
1   # import modules I need
2   import pdftotext
3   import sys for argv
4
5   # open the pdf
6   infile = open sys argv[1]
7
8   # convert it to text
9   pdf = pdftotext infile
10
11  lines = split pdf
12
13  # find Reporting Period
14  for line in lines
15    if line starts with "Reporting Period"
16      # print it
17      print line
```

You'll notice the p-code is very similar to the Python, and eventually you'll just write the Python. Once I have the p-code, I convert it to Python and have this final result:

Listing 51.1: ex51.py

```
1   # import modules I need
2   import pdftotext
3   import sys
4
5   # open the pdf
6   infile = open(sys.argv[1], "rb")
7
8   # convert it to text
9   pdf = pdftotext.PDF(infile)
10
11  lines = "".join(pdf).split("\n")
12
13  # find Reporting Period
14  for line in lines:
```

```
15      if line.startswith("Reporting Period"):
16          # print it
17          print(line)
18      else:
19          print(line)
```

At this point though, the code is incomplete because it prints only that line, and you need the next line. This is on purpose, so you'll have to solve it yourself. I suggest taking the time to get this code working and then try to actually solve the given problem and get the *Reporting Period* from the input. It should be the next line.

Solution Strategies

The simplest thing to do is figure out when you receive numbers in the output and simply extract the right ones. This is a good first step to get something working, but counting lines is not very robust. It might work on one PDF and then next month it fails because one line moved.

The next thing you can try is using these two regular expressions:

```
1  numbers = re.compile(r"^[,\d\s]+$")
2  ignore = re.compile(r"^\s*$")
```

You can determine if a line has numbers or should be skipped with the .match() function like this:

```
1  numbers.match(line)
2  ignore.match(line)
```

A "regular expression" is a way to match patterns on the input, and regular expressions are *insanely* useful to learn at some point. For this exercise, you can just use the ones I gave you and read the official Python regex docs for more information.

With these regex matching lines, you have a way to filter out anything but numbers. If you can get a list of numbers, then simple indexing to the number you want will work better.

The next way to solve this is to detect every line by its pattern and fill in a large dict or class with all the data. As you find lines, you take out data that's in the line, ignore lines that have no data, and then confirm you're getting the right ones as expected. This version uses parsing to confirm that you're still getting the same format, so if you get a new PDF that has lines out of order, you detect it.

There are lots of other ways to solve this, but try these to see how you do it. I believe you could spend quite a while on this exercise, possibly a week or two. Data munging has quite a lot of depth to it for such a simple problem, and there's a lot of technology you can play with. Take your time and enjoy it.

Awesome ETL Tools

You've completed a small project to get a test of ETL. You should now spend some time researching and playing with more tools.

- https://github.com/spotify/luigi
- https://petl.readthedocs.io
- https://airflow.apache.org
- https://www.bonobo-project.org
- https://pypi.org/project/pdftotext/
- https://docs.python.org/3/library/re.html

All of these are projects for different aspects of the *Extract, Transform, and Load* process. Some like Luigi manage the entire process with various GUIs and tools to visualize what's happening.

I suggest you attempt to install and play with as many of these as you can if you're interested in this part of data science. There's always a need for people who like wrangling bad data, and it's not a difficult topic to learn. That's why I like it as a great beginner topic of study.

Study Drills

1. Run this on all of the PDFs for 2023 and produce a report on the reports.

2. If your parser isn't able to handle all the reports in 2023, then consider improving it so that it's more robust.

3. One thing all data munging tools needs is a "exception log." An exception log reports what parts of what inputs have badly formed data while possibly saving the actual data for later inspection. You need this because you don't want one bad PDF destroying the entire ETL process, but you do need to go back and fix the problem to rerun it. Make an exception logging system for your tool.

4. Look at the dbm module in Python to store the data to disk. For this application the dbm module isn't great, but it is useful for basic storage. The last three exercises will cover SQL and SQLite3, which is far better.

Scraping Data from the Web

The two most popular uses of Python are *data science* and *web scraping* because web scraping typically feeds data to your data science pipeline. If you have an application that needs beer sales, then scraping it off the ATF TTB website is probably your only solution. If you need to train a GPT model on text, then scraping it off various forum websites is a good option. The web has so much data available; it's just in unfriendly visual formats.

Web scraping is also a great beginner topic for many of the same reasons as data munging:

1. It's something everyone understands because they use browsers all day long. Most people have some concept of what a web page is.

2. Web scraping doesn't require a ton of theory or computer science knowledge. You just need a way to get a web page and parse raw HTML for what you want.

3. It's easy to manually download a page you want to study and then work on it for as long as you want.

4. Just like data munging, the code is almost never "elegant." You're free to create the worst hacks possible to get it working and then refine later.

5. It's also a very important part of many data science projects. *Data* science needs *data*. The web has a ton of *data*.

6. Web scraping *also* leads you to automated testing of web applications, so you can do double education by learning to test.

Introducing `with`

I want to include at least one advanced concept in each of these projects. In this project I want you to use the `with` keyword. The `with` keyword creates a block that ensures its resource is cleaned up when the block exits. It's used with files mostly but works with anything that needs to be open and closed reliably. Here's a simple example:

```
1  with open("test.txt") as f:
2      print(f.read())
```

This will `print()` the contents of the file `test.txt`, but when the `with` block exits, it will automatically call `f.close()` to clean it up. This means if `test.txt` isn't there, you won't have a dangling open file. In the starter code I show you how to use this to create a "cache" of the page you're working on to save time.

The Problem

The senior developer on the team rolls their chair to your desk, wipes Cheetos dust off their fingers, and slicks back their purple hair before asking, "So how's it going?" You explain that you manually download the PDFs, and the senior developer looks at you puzzled. "Man…ually? What's that? Like, you use your hands to download files off a website? Gross." They then slowly scoot their chair away from you mumbling "gross" every few pushes of their legs before reaching their desk, saying "eww," and turning to their own computer.

I guess you need to automatically download the PDF files? The senior developer is right. Downloading these PDF files manually is annoying and error prone. It's much better to write a Python script that downloads the files and extracts the data for you. Web pages may contain data, but they're designed for people to read, not computers. To solve this problem, you'll use a project to "scrape" the data off the web page and download the PDF files you need.

Your tasks are the following:

1. Write a python script that can download the PDFs for each month/year from the ttb.gov website.

2. Be nice to this website and limit your script to only five PDFs until it's working.

3. Use the disk to cache the pages and PDFs so you aren't hammering the website. This also helps you work quicker since you aren't waiting for the internet.

4. Once you're able to reliably get all the PDFs, you should integrate your statistics extraction from the previous exercise to produce full statistics.

5. It might be time to officially create a project and write automated tests for your code. The next exercise will require you to rewrite some of this, so having tests will make this quicker and easier.

Once again, this topic is very deep, and you could spend a good month exploring everything about web scraping. Take your time with this, and learn as much as possible.

The Setup

You should already have the BeautifulSoup project installed, but confirm that first:

```
1  $ conda list beautiful
2  # packages in environment at ~/anaconda3:
3  #
4  # Name  Version  Build  Channel
5  beautifulsoup4  4.12.2  py311hecd8cb5_0
```

You should also have the lxml project, but install the html5lib project as an alternative:

```
1  conda install html5lib
```

That will set you up for the rest of the exercise, but remember you can use anything that gets the job done. I give you suggestions so you can start quickly, but if you know of better tools, feel free to use them.

The Clue

To accomplish this problem, you'll need some basics:

1. How to download a URL

2. Saving it to disk so you don't have to rely on the network while you work

3. Loading it with `BeautifulSoup`

4. How to use `with`

Here's a small piece of starter code to get you going:

Listing 52.1: ex52.py

```
1    from bs4 import BeautifulSoup
2    from urllib import request
3    import os
4
5    if not os.path.exists("ttb_stats.json"):
6        with open("ttb_page.html", "wb") as f:
7            resp = request.urlopen("https://learncodethehardway.com/setup/
8                                ↳ python/ttb/")
9            body = resp.read()
10           f.write(body)
11   else:
12       with open("ttb_page.html") as f:
13           body = f.read()
14
15   # change this to lxml intead of html5lib if you can't use it
16   soup = BeautifulSoup(body, "html5lib")
17   print(soup.title)
```

I recommend that you read this code, take some notes, and then attempt to rebuild it from scratch so you can *own* this solution. My clues are mostly to get you going since that's usually the hardest part for beginners, but eventually you'll need to get started on your own. Might as well practice that now, even if you have a bit of help.

Awesome Scraping Tools

As with the data munging exercise, you can investigate many tools for web scraping:

*   `Requests` is an easier to use HTTP client than `urllib`

*   `Playwright` actually runs Chrome or Firefox to simulate an entire browser. If you need more complex web scraping, then this is where to go, but it is harder to use.

- Scrapy is a more extensive web scraping library that is maintained by Zyte, which also offers a scraping hosting system.

- commoncrawl.org is a free open repository of web crawl data. No point in crawling when they've done it for you.

Study Drills

1. Your caching system should look at the headers from `request.urlopen()` to determine when the website changed. You'll need to keep track of when these files changed, and if the website updates, you'll update your cache. Keep in mind you'll need to to do this for *each* file, not if one site changes. Also look into the `E-Tag` header as another indicator of change.

2. You can make an `OPTIONS` request to get the date of the files *before* downloading them. Figure out how to do that with `urllib`.

Getting Data from APIs

I n this exercise you'll access the application programmer interface (API) I use for my learncodethe-hardway.com website. In web development, an API is usually a combination of the following:

1.   A web server that you can access with the HTTP protocol. You used HTTP when you used `urllib` to get the beer production PDFs from the ttb.gov website. HTTP is also what your browser uses to display the web application to you.

2.   This web server responds in some data format that's easily parsed. This is what differentiates a PDF from an API. Sure, you're getting data on beer production from ttb.gov, but *you* have to parse that data out of a PDF. An API gives you the data ready to go in a format that loads directly into your application with no manual parsing.

3.   A higher level API will provide features to discover how the API works automatically. This is a more advanced feature of APIs, but many of them will have an initial URL that describes the API, and then each piece of data will describe what's allowed and link to related elements. There is no official standard on how this is done, but if it's available, it's nice to have.

I use an API in my web application that conforms to #1 and #2, but only partially to #3 since I don't actually care if other people can dynamically figure out how to use my API. List item #3 is a common practice since private APIs are made for a specific application written by the API owners, while public APIs are intended for anyone to use and discover. I chose my private API because *many* times those are the most useful because other people are too lazy to reverse engineer them.

INFO Please do not download the raw video or HTML files for the course since that will most definitely crush my little web server. This also violates the TOS.

Introducing JSON

The primary format you'll encounter in APIs is JavaScript Object Notation (JSON). JSON is a standard data format for transmitting data with a simple strict format that people can still read. The syntax comes from JavaScript, but it's generic and looks similar to Python's dict syntax as well. You should read the JSON specification at json.org to get an idea of it. Here's an example JSON snippet from my API:

```
1   {
2       "id": 3,
3       "created_at": 2023-08-25 06:36:35,
4       "updated_at": 2023-09-17 01:07:41,
```

```
5        "title": "Learn Python the Hard Way, 5th Edition (2023)",
6        "description": "The 5th Edition of Learn Python the Hard Way released in
         ↳ 2023.",
7        "price": 20,
8        "currency": "USD",
9        "currency_symbol": "$",
10       "active": 1,
11       "slug": "learn-python-the-hard-way-5e-2023",
12       "category": "Python",
13       "created_by": "Zed A. Shaw"
14   }
```

As you can see, this could easily be Python data, and it would work in many other languages. This syntax for key=value storage is very old, and many languages adopt it, which is why JSON is so easy for other languages to use.

The Problem

The CEO of the company told my boss—who told me—that the CEO thinks I'm not working hard enough. She read in *CIO Magazine* that watch time is the most important metric on YouTube—and since learncodethehardway.com has videos, that means it's exactly like YouTube. The CEO thinks I should measure the total watch time to prove I'm working hard. I immediately run into your team's office—wiping my nose repeatedly for some reason—and yell, "Quick! Watch time! Videos! Stat! Stop everything!" Then I run out, jump in my Tesla, and go golfing with the CEO to make sure she knows I still exist.

The team stops everything and has another meeting, and the senior developer tells you that they'll work on the problem, but also the CEO wants you to work on the problem to "send out as many feelers as possible on this synergy." Not sure what that means but looks like you're duplicating the work of the senior developer? Who cares—it's not your money; it's the investors' money!

My website learncodethehardway.com has a simple API for the courses I sell. Each course has modules, modules have lessons, and lessons have media. I'm fairly lazy, though, so I want you to calculate how much watch time all of my videos have. Your script should have the following features:

1. You'll have to discover the data and its rules on your own. The senior developer is too busy. *The Clue* provides a small starter that will let you get JSON output to analyze and discover each piece of data.

2. The script should output watch time (aka minutes of video available) per *course*, *module*, and *lesson* as individual CSV files.

3. I don't make enough money to have you thrashing my website with your buggy API downloader. You'll need to cache your results when you get them working. One key to getting this right is that all data has some kind of updated_at field that's updated when it changes.

Each API will tell you how to access it, so it's simply a matter of sorting out what you're getting back and how to analyze it. This exercise is intentionally vague so you have to figure it out. Figuring things out with limited information is a huge part of creating your own software.

The Setup

For this exercise you'll be using the `requests` project to access the API of learncodethehardway.com. You install it like normal:

```
1  conda activate lpythw
2  conda install requests
```

`Requests` is nice for accessing APIs, but be careful if you have to download anything large as it might have issues with buffering the entire download into memory at once.

The Clue

The learncodethehardway.com API is fairly simple and supports four URLs you can access:

- `/api/course`—The main URL to get a list of available courses
- `/api/module`—How to get information for a module
- `/api/lesson`—Information on individual lessons
- `/api/lesson_media`—Details on every media that lessons access, which is extracted with `ffmpeg`

When you access these APIs, they'll tell you their rules for accessing them. You can use this starter code to get going:

Listing 53.1: ex53.py

```
 1  import requests
 2  from pprint import pprint
 3  import sys
 4  import csv
 5
 6  api_url = "http://learncodethehardway.com/api/course"
 7
 8  # list all courses
 9  r = requests.get(api_url)
10  data = r.json()
11  pprint(data)
```

```
12
13   # get one course, full=true includes all modules
14   r = requests.get(api_url, params={
15       "course_id": 1, "full": "true" })
16
17   data = r.json()
18   pprint(data)
19
20   # remember with? use it with csv
```

Awesome API Tools

- FastAPI—A really great way to quickly generate one of these APIs

- AlpineJS—If you use *FastAPI* to make a JSON API and you make HTML pages, then Alpine is an easy way to access the JSON API and, oh, look at that, you have a web framework

- jq—An incredibly useful tool for querying and viewing JSON data

- curl—Useful to get data off websites from the command line. Try curl SOMESITE | jq to get easy pretty printing of JSON data

Study Drills

1. What other information about the media in the courses can you discover? What information is automatically dumped out of ffmpeg?

2. Find other APIs and try to work with them too.

Data Conversion with pandas

We'll now explore pandas, which is the main way data scientists work with data. It's also a useful project outside of data science, so it's worth using no matter what your future holds. The main things pandas provides are data conversion and a DataFrame structure, which is used by *many* statistics and mathematics applications. We'll explore the concept of a DataFrame in the later exercises.

In this exercise, you'll use pandas to take the CSV file you created to output various formats for your bosses. You'll also use a tool called Pandoc to generate this report. You don't *have* to use Pandoc, but it is an *insanely* useful tool for doing reports in various formats.

Introducing Pandoc

Pandoc's job is to take one text format and convert it to another format. It can take Markdown files and convert them to HTML, PDF, ePub, and many other formats. This means you can write reports in nice, easy to write Markdown and then convert them to any format that's required for the job. Need to submit a LaTeX file to a journal? Pandoc. Need to submit HTML to the web server team? Pandoc.

The Problem

I don't like your CSV files from the previous exercises. They're so unprofessional. I'm a lazy manager who doesn't have time to find a way to view them on my phone. I have Jira tickets to create with only titles! My boss is too busy playing golf with the CEO. What do you think we are? Workers? Pfft. That's your job.

You need to convert these CSV files you have to a few formats for me, my boss, and the CEO:

1. I want an Excel .xls file I can load into Microsoft Excel (aka Boomer pandas).

2. My boss wants an HTML file with the table in it that I can email and pretend I made it.

3. The CEO just wants a PDF with big numbers on it summarizing the total watch time available. Don't pester her with details! She has investors to defraud!

The best way to approach this problem is:

1. Use csv to open your CSV file from the previous exercise. Yes, you could just generate the document directly, but let's pretend that a senior developer is throwing these CSV files over the wall at you, so you're stuck with them.

2. You then use pandas to convert the loaded data directly to an .xlsx file.

3.   Once you have the pandas conversion working, you'll need to get it into the .xlsx file format.

4.   Use Pandoc to produce the reports to my boss and the CEO. Your script should output Markdown but use Pandoc to produce a PDF and HTML report.

5.   When running Pandoc, you should use the subprocess module to run it efficiently and control it with Python.

The Clue gives you almost 80% of this solution, but the real work will be the reporting requirements and using the CSV files you've been given. Keep in mind that this is a completely fake problem for *you*, but in real life you run into this kind of scenario *constantly*. You'll rarely get very clean data directly from another data source. Instead, you have PDF, .xls files, .csv files, raw JPEG image scans, or even weirder formats you've never heard of before. Becoming good at handling bad data is a *fantastic* way to get into data science. Data munging is something *everyone* needs, but many people don't particularly like to do it because it's "beneath" them.

The Setup

To use the pandas Excel output, you'll need to install openpyxl:

```
1  conda activate lpythw
2  conda install openpyxl
```

Once that's installed, the code in *The Clue* should work.

The Clue

This code does more than the previous code, but I feel you'll need more help to get the pandas part working so you can work on the reporting and analysis part:

Listing 54.1: ex54.py

```
1   import csv
2   from pprint import pprint
3   import pandas as pd
4
5   records = []
6
7   with open("ex53.csv") as csvfile:
8       reader = csv.DictReader(csvfile)
9       for row in reader:
10          records.append(row)
11
```

```
12   # do you analysis here
13
14   df = pd.DataFrame(records)
15
16   pprint(df)
17
18   df.to_excel("ex54.xlsx")
```

You have a few ways to approach this:

1. Load the CSV and just use plain old Python to do the analysis. After you get an analysis working, use `DataFrame.to_excel()` to output the results. This might be a good first step.

2. Skip ahead to Exercise 55 to learn more about pandas and use that to do the analysis. You'll eventually have to do this in a later exercise, so if you find this one is too easy, then start learning pandas now.

Study Drills

1. Can you round-trip your results and produce a JSON API with `FastAPI`? This is an advanced task, but if you can pull it off, you're winning.

2. How many other formats can you output with `pandas`? Try to produce a few more files.

How to Read Documentation
(Featuring pandas)

This exercise is going to teach two very important skills. First, you'll learn about pandas and its DataFrame construct. This is the most common way to work with data in the Python data science world. Second, you're going to learn *how to read typical programmer documentation.* This is a *far* more useful skill as it applies to every single programming topic you will ever encounter. In fact, you should think of this exercise as using pandas to teach you how to read documentation.

INFO For this exercise you are free to switch back to Jupyter to make exploration and documenting what you learn easier. If you then want to make a project using pandas, you can take what you learn with Jupyter to create it.

Why Programmer Documentation Sucks

There's a concept in painting called "the gestalt." The gestalt of a painting is how all of the parts of a painting fit together to create a single cohesive experience. Imagine I paint a portrait of you and create the most perfect mouth, eyes, nose, ears, and hair you've ever seen. You see each part is perfect and then you pull back, and when placed together...they're all wrong. The eyes are too close together, the nose is too dark compared to everything else, and the ears are different sizes. On their own, they're perfect, but when combined into a finished work of art, they're awful because I didn't *also* pay attention to the gestalt of the painting.

For something to have high quality you have to pay attention to the qualities of each individual piece *and* how those pieces fit together. Programmer documentation is frequently like this awful portrait with perfect features that don't fit together. Programmers will very clearly and accurately describe every single function, the nuances of every option to those functions, and every class they made. Then completely ignore any documentation that describes how those pieces fit together or how to use them to do anything.

This kind of documentation is everywhere. Look at Python's original SQLite3 documentation and then compare it to the latest version that finally has "how to use" placeholders. That's a fairly important topic you need for good security and it's...just casually ignored for about a decade?

Learning from this documentation requires a particular style of reading that's more *active*. That's what you will learn in this exercise.

How to Actively Read Programmer Docs

I won't force you to suffer through really bad documentation. Instead, you'll take a baby step and learn how to read documentation using the pandas documentation. The pandas documentation is good. It at least has a quick start guide to get you going, cookbooks, how-to guides, an API reference, and lots of examples. Everything is clearly described, but when you read it, you're still kind of lost because it's a lot of documentation spread all over with no clear guide.

This is where *active* reading comes into play, and it's something I've had you do for this entire course by *making you type in code and change it*. Reading programmer documentation actively means *you* have to type in the code as you read, change the code to find more, and apply what you learn to your own problems to learn *how* to use what you learn. Your goal with this process is to *find the gestalt the programmers ignored.*

Step #1: Find the Docs

The very first thing you should do is find the docs. You might laugh, but sometimes that's a difficult first step. Important questions to ask:

1. *Are you looking at the right version of the docs?* This is a *very* common problem in Python and JavaScript because sometimes the old documentation is more popular in Google than new documentation.

2. *Is this documentation a guide or an API description?* You need at least a guide and API documentation. You actually need more than that, but if a project has *only* API documentation, then you're going to have to work much harder to learn it. A guide is where you want to start.

3. *Is there a cookbook or how-to guide with lots of examples?* You've found a unicorn in the world of programming.

4. *What are the most interesting topics to you?* Do you have a specific pressing need? Is there a document covering this topic?

Step #1 with pandas

Let's go through the pandas documentation and answer each of these questions:

1. Yes, it looks like the documentation is the right version.

2. The /docs/ has both guides and API reference. You'll need the guide to follow and the API reference to look up specifics about things you use in your own projects later.

3. Yes, there's both getting started tutorials, which show you how to do various things, and a cookbook in the User guide with many quick examples.

4. *What are the most interesting topics to you?* In this exercise you'll focus on DataFrame, so any documents that cover that are useful. If you wanted to process many .csv files, then you'd look for documents explaining loading and saving .csv files.

Step #2: Determine Your Strategy

What do you do if most of these have "No" answers? What if the project only has autogenerated API docs and not a single document or example explaining how to *use* the API? First, do you *have* to use this pile of garbage? Life's too short to use software that not even the developers care about, so maybe just don't use it. If you really want to use it or have to use it, then you have two complementary strategies:

1. Find guides and example code other people wrote about the project
2. Choose your own small project that will use this project, and spend your time reading the API docs to get your project working

If the project has everything you need, then you have a couple different strategies:

1. Start with any cookbooks and how-to documents with many examples
2. Start with the guides that walk through each topic the project thinks is important
3. Start with the API docs anyway and try to make your own software using the API

These options are not mutually exclusive. Start with one option, and if it's not working, switch to another. Keep doing this until you understand enough to use the project or study further.

Step #2 with pandas

In the pandas example, we have everything we need *except* an overall guide telling us where to go, so that's why you need a strategy. I have three complementary strategies in this situation:

•   Start with the cookbooks and how-to documents and use them as a guide to dive deeper into related documentation.

•   Start with the deeper user guide and as you go through it read cookbooks and how-to documents to get practical examples.

•   Try to make something using the API reference. Sometimes this is the best strategy if you are *hot* to work on an idea, but don't get discouraged if it's too hard. If you get stuck, switch to the other strategies.

Step #3: Code First, Docs Second

This will seem counterintuitive, but when reading programmer documentation, you will have more success if you start with the code and then read about it. This works because the code is something you can experience and that experience gives you a better understanding of what's being said in the documentation.

Step #3 with pandas

Let's look at the 10-minute guide to pandas as an example. Right away there's this code:

```
1   import numpy as np
2   import pandas as pd
3   s = pd.Series([1, 3, 5, np.nan, 6, 8])
4   # this prints it in Jupyter
5   s
6   dates = pd.date_range("20130101", periods=6)
7   # print it in Jupyter
8   dates
```

This code is spread across multiple short descriptions about the code, so you type each example in first. Once it's working, change it around and *then* read the descriptions. This will make the descriptions easier to understand.

However, if you read the descriptions first, this is what you read:

```
1   Customarily, we import as follows.
2
3   Creating a Series by passing a list of values, letting
4   pandas create a default RangeIndex.
5
6   Creating a DataFrame by passing a NumPy array with a
7   datetime index using date_range() and labeled columns:
```

Those on their own or with a quick glance at the code make almost no sense. After you get the code working, these sentences help fill in gaps in your understanding. They also link to more documentation on what you just used.

Step #4: Break or Change the Code

After you get a piece of code working, take the time to break it so you can see how errors are handled. One *massive* blocker for beginners is deciphering the convoluted error messages programming languages produce. There's almost a weird art to reading them and using Google to find the answer. One of the ways to learn the "language of terrible errors" is to expose yourself to as many errors as possible on purpose so you can study them.

The second thing to do is ask if you can do something and then try to do it. You'll ask, "How do I give a `series` a different index?" Or, you might ask, "How can I pass a `series` to a `DataFrame`?" The kinds of changes you want to focus on are *combinations* of things you just learned.

Step #5: Take Notes

A key aspect of learning to code (or anything) is explaining what you've learned back to yourself. The best way to do this while you're working is to have a `notes.txt` file in the directory where you're putting the code you write. In this `notes.txt` file, write down questions you have, things you discover, and comments about what you're learning.

Another important part of the `notes.txt` file is *links*. You should be recording links to what you read or what you need to read as you work. This will help you later when you need to remember where you read about something.

Step #6: Use It on Your Own

The entire purpose of this last module is to move you from someone who *knows* Python to someone who can *use* Python to express their own ideas. After you feel you have enough understanding of the project, you should try to make something of *any* size with it. This is when you will switch to relying more on the API reference than the other documentation.

Step #6 with pandas

If you're stuck and can't think of anything to create, then take an example from the cookbook or how-to documents documentation and modify it to do something new. Maybe you have it load the data from a SQL database or change the data used.

Step #7: Write About What You Learned

When I think of painting, writing, and programming, I think of them as mediums for *articulating my automatic thoughts, experiences, and feelings so I can consciously understand them*. Painting helps me understand what I see. Writing helps me understand what I know and feel. Programming helps me understand how to do something.

I spend all day using my eyes to see the world, but it's only when I try to *paint* what I see that I start to consciously understand what I'm seeing. Painting forces me to consciously understand the automatic way my visual system processes the world.

Programming forces me to structure my understanding of how something works into logical steps and structures. After I turn a process or idea into code, I understand how it could actually work.

Writing helps me organize my almost random thoughts into a coherent conscious structure. The act of organizing all of my thoughts into an essay that makes sense and flows naturally helps me further understand my ideas.

More importantly, each of these mediums—painting, programming, and prose—force me to explore what I *don't know*. Externalizing my knowledge in these ways gives me a glimpse into my brain. I can look at a painting and say, "Well, it looks like I have no idea what this flower actually looks like." I can study code and see, "I clearly have no idea how this algorithm is supposed to work." I can read through an essay and see, "I really don't know how to explain what I'm feeling about this topic."

This is why you should write about what you've learned. You don't have to show it to anyone or be a good writer. Your writing doesn't have to be original. I'll tell you, 99% of all writing is *not* original. The point is not to impress other people with how clever a writer you are. The point is to explain to *yourself* what you know so you can see if you actually learned something.

Step #7 with pandas

For Step #7 I want you to write at least 8–10 paragraphs teaching someone else what you've just learned about DataFrames. How would you explain the DataFrame to someone who knows Python? What is your best advice on how to use it? Are there any things to avoid when using it?

Another option is to write your own curriculum to learn the pandas DataFrame. If you were to write a guide for someone else, what links should they read in order to best understand it? For each link, describe what they learn at that stage and how it relates to the previous link they studied.

A final option is to use Jupyter to create a notebook that demonstrates and explains everything someone else would need to learn. I suggest first writing a short version of the curriculum idea and then turning that into a structured notebook that follows the curriculum.

Step #8: What's the Gestalt?

The final step in this process is to ask yourself, "What's the big picture for this project?" This is a more abstract step and should fall out naturally from your writings and notes, but being able to summarize the project will give you a mental framework to hold everything else you learn.

Your understanding of the project might be different from the authors, but your description of the project is more for *you* than a general statement for everyone.

Step #8 with pandas

If I were to summarize the purpose of pandas, I might have several "gestalt statements":

- "pandas' purpose is to provide Python with higher-level features commonly found in other statistics and math languages like R, SAS, and Mathematica"

- "pandas gives an easier way to load, structure, and manipulate tabular data for analysis"

Am I right? What did you come up with? Does it help you understand pandas better?

Reading My pandas Curriculum

While it is useful for you to learn how to read documentation and devise your own curriculum, I also feel you might need one provided by me. The problem is, projects frequently change, and I want this course to last longer than the next version of pandas. To solve this problem, you'll need to visit https://learncodethe hardway.com/setup/python/ to get the latest updated curriculum.

Using Only pandas

I n this exercise you'll take the mess of random scripts you've made and create one clean tool that uses only pandas for the entire process. You'll do this for both the TTB beer statistics and the video watch time for my website.

Make a Project

It's time to get cleaned up and make a project for this exercise. You don't need to install this project, but it should have all the required project files, automated tests, a README.md, and the scripts necessary to run your tools.

The Problem

You've been promoted! I got tired of the senior developer who was only able to produce CSV files, and now you're in charge of my beer and video watch time empire. I want you to create a single tool that does everything you've learned from Exercise 51 to now. The solution I want should have all of the following features:

1. pandas to the bone. You should use pandas for everything you can including converting data, transforming it, and producing reports.

2. The TTB offers .xls files, so ditch the PDF parsing. What was I thinking?!

3. Your tool should handle command-line options that allow me to produce an HTML or PDF report for either TTB beer statistics or my website's watch time.

4. I want tests! Automated tests that hit at *least* 90% coverage or you're *fired*! Turn in your badge! Pack up your desk! You're not getting your $0 per month paycheck!

5. Don't crash my server! You should cache data from the TTB and my webserver so your tool runs fast.

6. I need an option to tell it to force download everything in case your caching doesn't work.

7. You'll get a bonus if you use Git to maintain your code, make your reports pretty, and come up with novel ways to show me the data.

Feel free to get creative with this project so long as you're using pandas to produce these reports.

The Setup

You should have everything you need to get this to work, but I highly suggest you create a new conda environment for this project:

```
1  conda deactivate
2  conda create ex56
```

Obviously you don't have to call it ex56. You could call it "beertime," "lastpaycheck," "señordev," "señora-boss," or whatever you want. The point is to have fun and don't take it too seriously…but also I'll fire you if you don't get it right.

Study Drill

1. This might be a tough drill, but see if you can make a web user interface for this project instead of a command-line tool. Don't worry if this is beyond your grasp, but attempting something beyond your skills is a great way to learn. I suggest checking out FastAPI and Alpine.js for a possible solution to making a user interface and API for it.

The SQL Crash Course

You can't do science without data, and the most widely used language for storing and managing data is SQL. Many "no-SQL" databases have some language that looks quite a lot like SQL. That's because—for all its faults—SQL is a fairly well thought out language for specifying the storage, querying, and transformation of data. Learning SQL basics can only help you in data science, but there's another important reason why I feel SQL is a great way to end the course:

> I don't want this course to *only* be about data science. I use data science *and Python* as a theme to teach the basics of programming. They are simply tools that help me with my goal of teaching you how to use a computer to express your thoughts and ideas.

SQL shows its face in *every* part of the technology industry and in many personal projects. Your phone has a 100% chance of having numerous SQLite3 databases on it. Your computers all have SQLite3 databases on them. You find SQL in web applications, desktop applications, phone applications, and even video games. If it's not in an application you install, there's most likely a SQL database somewhere between you and some other computer on the internet. Even if something doesn't use a SQL database, it is most likely using something that is very similar to one.

That means learning SQL will not only benefit you as a data scientist, but it'll also benefit nearly every aspiring programmer no matter what journey they take in the medium.

What Is SQL?

SQL is a language that enables the management and querying of a group of tables in a database using a *mostly* declarative structure. This is a large sentence to unpack, so let's break it down in small pieces:

- *"SQL"* is usually pronounced "sequel" as in *Batman Returns* was a terrible sequel to the excellent *Batman* with Michael Keaton.
- *"is a language"* means that there is a syntax similar in the same way Python or JavaScript have defined syntax that you must learn.
- *"that enables"* means it will allow you to control the data structures utilized in your database with that language.
- *"the management"* means you can use SQL to control not just what's *in* a table but also what defines a table and many aspects of how the database software operates.
- *"and querying"* means SQL also provides a way to extract data out of multiple tables to answer questions you might have. SQL's ability in this regard is so strong you can sometimes (*many* times?) replace complicated Python data science code with a few SQL queries.

- *"of a group of tables in a database"* means you aren't restricted to only one table at a time but instead can run SQL across many tables in the database. This also implies a major advantage of SQL over a system like pandas: relations. SQL isn't concerned with only the contents of a table but also how tables are related to each other.

- *"using a mostly declarative structure"* is tough to explain, but think of it as defining the results you want rather than explaining exactly how to get them. Rather than saying "for every row of the person table give me x,y,z," you'd say "give me x,y,z of the person table," and SQL figures out how to make that happen. Python by comparison is considered "imperative," which means you actually specify exactly how to generate the results you want.

- *"...mostly..."* means that while SQL is declarative, it also has certain situations where the order of statements matters. In a fully declarative language, the order of statements does not matter, which is why SQL is only *mostly* declarative.

Our next goal is to learn the initial SQL language and use it on a simple but fun data set, the European Central Bank's historic Euro exchange rate data.

The Setup

To complete these next exercises, you'll need to install `sqlite3` program, but there's a high probability that it's already installed on your computer. Open a Terminal window and type:

```
1  sqlite3 euro.sqlite3
```

This will start a prompt that's inside `sqlite3` and you can quit with:

```
1  .quit sqlite3
```

If that works, then you're done setting up `sqlite3`. If you do need to download it, then find the appropriate link for your OS on sqlite3.org.

The next thing you need is the data from the European Central Bank's historic Euro exchange rate data set. You can download the latest at https://www.ecb.europa.eu/stats/eurofxref/eurofxref-hist.zip.

INFO If this data is missing, you can refer to the https://learncodethehardway.com/setup /python/ link to see if I have an updated source for the data or an alternative `.csv` to use.

Once you download this file, you can unzip and save the `.csv` file inside to your work directory for this exercise.

Fixing and Loading

Depending on when you get this data, you might find that it has an additional trailing comma. That means it's *data munging time!* You'll need to write a small Python script that loads this .csv file, fixes the trailing column, and then writes a corrected one. As I've said many times, data you get from other sources almost *always* has some weird problems.

> *Hint:* You can remove the last column using Python's range syntax, row[0:-1].

I named my file fixed.csv. Once you've fixed the data to remove the trailing column, you can load it into sqlite3 like this:

```
1  sqlite3 euro.sqlite3
2
3  sqlite> .import --csv "fixed.csv" euro
4  sqlite> select count(*) from euro;
5  6331
6  sqlite>
```

I'm showing you the sqlite3 shell, so you don't type in the sqlite> as that's the prompt. You might also get a different number from 6331 depending on when you download the file.

You can then look at the rows available with the .schema command, which shows you how the table euro is defined:

```
1  sqlite> .schema euro
```

I'll cover more on SQL and schemas in the next exercise, but for now it's simply the rows of a table and the data types it contains.

Back Up Your Database

As you work, you'll want to make backups of your euro.sqlite3 database. You'll be making changes to it, and you won't want to go through reloading the entire database when you break it. To back up your database, do this:

```
1  sqlite3 euro.sqlite3 ".backup euro_backup.sqlite3"
```

To recover the database, you copy the file back:

```
1  cp euro_backup.sqlite3 euro.sqlite3
```

There are many more sqlite3 dot commands, so use the .help command to find out more, and read the SQLite3 CLI documentation.

Create, Read, Update, Delete

In nearly every container you use in programming there are four essential operations:

1. Create things in the container, *and* create containers

2. Read the things in the container, *and* read meta information about the container

3. Update the things in the container, *and* update the meta information about the container

4. Delete things from the container, *and* delete parts of the container's structure

If you look back at the Python io module, you can see files have all of these elements. You can open them, create them, update them, read from them, write new things to them, and get information about the file.

SQL and sqlite3 provide all of these capabilities to a database, its tables, and the contents of those tables. A good way to map from directories and files to a SQL database is with this structure:

- *database* is like a *directory*. The sqlite3 command gives you the ability to create a database (mkdir), create tables in the database (touch), and delete tables from the database (rm).

- *table* is like a file in a *directory*. SQL gives you commands similar to *Geany* or a text editor, which makes more sense once you realize...

- *row* is like a *line* in a *file*. If *Geany* is like SQL, then the rows in a table are edited similar to a text editor. You can add rows (lines), change the text in the row, delete the row, search for a row, etc.

Finally we can map the words "create," "read," "update," and "delete"–aka CRUD operations–to operations you would normally do to a file:

- *CREATE* maps to commands such as mkdir, cp, and touch, adding a new line in a text editor

- *READ* maps to commands such as ls, cat, and grep, searching for lines in a text editor

- *UPDATE* maps to mv (you're updating the name) and edits the contents of a line in a file

- *DELETE* maps to commands like rm and rmdir or deletes a line from a file

Once you understand this, you can start to map each of the main SQL commands to one part of the CRUD operations. If the links I provide to the SQLite3 documentation are not very helpful, then refer to Exercise 55 on reading documentation.

SELECT

The SELECT statement is the *READ* operation of SQL. Its purpose is to take a description of the kind of data you want and then scan through the table (or multiple tables) to gather the data. The result of running SELECT is actually another temporary table. Let's do a simple query of the ECB data to see how it works:

```
1  SELECT date, USD
2    FROM euro
3    WHERE date(date) > date('2023-01-01');
```

This will get every rate for USD after '2023-01-01' and print a large table with the results. Let's break down every part of this so you understand what it's doing:

1. SELECT starts the statement (also called a "command" sometimes).

2. date, USD are the columns you want from the euro table. If you are selecting from multiple tables, you can use the table's name like an object in Python: euro.date, euro.USD

3. FROM starts the list of tables you will be querying.

4. euro is the table you want date, USD to come from. You can specify multiple tables by separating them with a comma as in Python lists.

5. WHERE starts your selection criteria, which is a Boolean logic expression similar to Python's if-statement. This example has only one condition, but you can use AND or OR for more complex selections.

6. date(date) > date('2023-01-01') is because SQLite3 uses various date() functions to convert data to date objects for comparison. When you want to do date and time calculations, this is how you do it. This says "every row where date is *after* 2023-01-01."

7. Finally, end the statement with a ; (semi-colon). If you don't, you can get into trouble because SQLite3 is pretty bad at letting you abort commands you've messed up.

Study this and try many different conditions and results. Try to get different currencies and different time ranges.

Date and Time

You can read more about the SQLite3 Project date functions, but the main thing to understand is SQLite3 really only stores text (or, it used to be that way) and doesn't actually have a date type. Instead, you use functions to convert the data to a date before doing comparisons or date/time math.

The most common operations are:

*   date('2023-01-01')—turn this into a date.

*   datetime('2023-01-01 12:00:00.000')—convert this date+time stamp.

*   time('12:00:00.000')—convert only a time signature.

*   date('now')—the current date, also works with all three above.

- `date('now', '+1 day', ...)`—you can add as many modifiers to the date to set something specific. The `...` I have here isn't something you type; it's just my indicator that you can add more than one modifier.

An important thing to understand about date/time is programmers hate it, so it can cause problems. Here's what the SQLite3 Project documentation says as of 2023:

> The computation of local time depends heavily on the whim of politicians and is thus difficult to get correct for all locales. In this implementation, the standard C library function `localtime_r()` is used to assist in the calculation of local time. The `localtime_r()` C function normally only works for years between 1970 and 2037. For dates outside this range, SQLite attempts to map the year into an equivalent year within this range, do the calculation, then map the year back.

For most people, the date/time functions in SQLite3 should work if the time on your computer also works, but if you are using a different calendar, then you might need to confirm that SQLite3 actually gets the dates right before you rely on them.

INSERT

The `INSERT` statement is the *CREATE* operation of SQL. Using `INSERT`, you can add new rows to a table, similar to appending a new line to the end of a text document. Let's add a few more values of USD:

```
1  INSERT INTO euro (date, USD)
2    VALUES (date('now'), 1.090);
3
4  INSERT INTO euro (date, USD)
5    VALUES (date('now', '+1 day'), 1.087);
```

Once again, let's break these lines down so you can understand what they do:

1. INSERT INTO starts the insert statement.
2. euro is the table to append the new row.
3. (starts the list of *columns* you want to set. If you know the exact order of columns, you can skip this, but I rarely know all the columns and have to spell them out.
4. date, USD are the two columns we will set. Any columns not listed will get default values or null. You can also cause an error if a column is defined as not allowing null
5.) closes the list of columns.
6. VALUES starts the values section of the insertion.
7. (begins the list of data to insert. It will match the list of columns you give before VALUES in the same order.
8. date('now') is how you set this to today's date.

9.   `1.090` is a number for the USD column.

10.   `);` finally ends the list of data, and the `;` ends the statement.

The second line is almost the same except I use the SQLite3 date math to calculate one day ahead with `date('now', '+1 day')`. You can place as many additional calculations as you want after the first parameter.

You can use SELECT to see your data, but there's a problem with this data. The currency names are all referenced in the INSERT, so when you query this data, you get odd results:

```
1   SELECT * FROM euro WHERE date(date) > date('now', '-1 day');
2
3   2023-09-21|1.09|||||||||||||||||||
4   2023-09-22|1.087|||||||||||||||||||
```

The repeated | bars are empty columns since you inserted nothing for the remaining table columns when you said (`date, USD`) in the INSERT. That means each country has `null` for that day.

In the next exercise, we'll work on fixing this with "normalization," which is the process of cleaning up tables that don't work well with SQL.

UPDATE

The UPDATE statement will change the data in multiple rows and uses the same WHERE syntax that SELECT uses:

```
1   UPDATE euro
2     SET USD=100, date='2048-01-01'
3     WHERE
4     date(date) > date('2023-01-01')
5       AND USD=1.0808;
```

This is the first time I'm using an AND to do more complicated selection, but an UPDATE is similar to a SELECT combined with an INSERT even though it's not adding any new rows. Let's take this one apart so you can see what I mean:

1.   UPDATE starts the update statement

2.   `euro` is the table to change

3.   SET is how you assign new values, which means the syntax is different from INSERT, which used VALUES rather than `column=value`

4.   WHERE then comes from SELECT and indicates what rows to change

5.   `date(date) > date('2023-01-01')` says every row after 2023

6.   AND USD=1.0808 adds "and also has a USD rate of 1.0808"

7.   ; ends the statement

Use what you know of SELECT and UPDATE to undo what you just did. You'll need to first confirm this actually worked with SELECT and then use UPDATE to correct the values. Use a backup of your euro.sqlite3 to get possibly missing data you need for this restoration, but see how much you can correct without the previous data.

DELETE and Transactions

Finally, the DELETE statement deletes rows from a table. If you want to delete the rows where we set USD=100, we do this:

```
1    DELETE FROM euro WHERE USD=1.1215;
```

As with SELECT and UPDATE, the WHERE clause can take the usual Boolean forms of AND and OR. Let's break this one down quickly as well:

1.   DELETE FROM starts the delete statement.

2.   euro is the table to delete from. I highly recommend you delete from only one table at a time and instead use transactions (see first paragraph, top of next page) when you need to delete from multiple tables in one atomic move.

3.   WHERE, just like with SELECT and UPDATE, determines what rows to delete. While you should delete from only one table at a time, you *can* use multiple tables to determine what to delete.

4.   USD=1.1215 applies only to rows where USD is 1.1215.

5.   ; ends the statement.

There is one problem with this because what if you accidentally delete too much? You could also use UPDATE wrong and update too much. It'd be nice if you could add a "safety valve" that prevents the change from happening if it's not right. That's where transactions come in:

```
1    SELECT count(*) FROM euro;
2
3    BEGIN TRANSACTION;
4
5    DELETE FROM euro;
6
7    ROLLBACK TRANSACTION;
8
9    SELECT count(*) FROM euro;
```

If you run this, you'll see the count doesn't change. Make sure you have a backup, and then change ROLLBACK TRANSACTION to COMMIT TRANSACTION to see it delete everything.

Normally DELETE FROM euro would nuke your entire database with no warning. With BEGIN
↳ TRANSACTION you're making a "save point" where the work you want to do is protected. You can
do as much SQL as you'd like, and if you want to abort, you do ROLLBACK TRANSACTION. If you want
to commit, you use COMMIT TRANSACTION, and it'll work.

Transactions are very important when you have a sequence of changes that have to all work. Let's say
you're going to update 10 rows and then update another table, but this second update causes an error.
If you don't have a TRANSACTION, then your first 10 updates actually work, but now your database is
broken because the second update set failed. With a TRANSACTION you can abort when the second
update set fails and nothing happens.

Math, Aggregates, and GROUP BY

SQLite3 Project features a wide range of built-in math functions you can use to perform calculations on
your data. There are also many aggregate functions that perform calculations based on groups of rows,
which you can construct with a GROUP BY clause.

First you can use GROUP BY to group rows by a column. Try this:

```
1  SELECT date, USD from euro GROUP BY date;
```

That would give you the USD for each date, but that's not super useful. It's better if you combine GROUP
↳ BY with one of the aggregate functions like this:

```
1  SELECT count(date),
2      date, avg(USD),
3      min(USD), max(USD)
4    FROM euro
5    GROUP BY
6      date(date, "start of month");
```

That's a lot better as now we're grouping the results by month and getting the avg(), min(), and max()
of USD that month. Take a look at the year 2000. That's the dot-com bomb.

Let's break this last SQL statement down before I give you a final challenge:

1. SELECT starts your select statement.

2. count(date) will count up the number of rows with date values in each GROUP BY group.
    This means if any date is set to null, it will not be counted.

3. date, avg(USD) is still listing the columns, but it's on a new line. The avg(USD) will give the
    average rate of USD in that GROUP BY

4. min(USD), max(USD) then gives us the minimum and maximum. You can also add as after
    any of these to give them a name for reference in your query. If you did min(USD) as min,
    you could then use min in a WHERE clause. The column name would also change to min

5. FROM euro gets this data from the euro table.

6. GROUP BY tells SQL you want to group the results by some criteria.

7. date(date, "start of month"); will take the date and do math that moves it to the "start of month", although it seems to be off a bit and goes one day too far. This effectively gives you monthly grouping by converting all dates in a month to one day.

8. ; ends the statement.

To finish things off, I'm giving you the final task of using ORDER BY to sort the avg(USD) results from lowest to highest. You'll need to find the ORDER BY documentation, learn how to sort in different ordering, and use the as keyword to rename the column.

Python Access

The Study Drill for this exercise is simple to describe but possibly difficult for you to do:

Use Python to repeat all of the SQL shown in this exercise.

To accomplish this goal you'll need the code from the Python SQLite3 documentation, which describes in great detail how to use the module. You also know how to study documentation like this after Exercise 55, so leverage your skills when studying this library.

One thing you *must* do when solving this is use placeholder values in your SQL as described in *How to use placeholders to bind values in SQL queries*. If the link doesn't go directly to that section, then scroll all the way down to the bottom or search for the word "placeholders."

SQL Normalization

I n the previous exercise, we explored SQL basics using the European Central Bank's historic Euro data set. In this exercise I'm going to teach you about data modeling by reshaping this data into multiple tables to "normalize" it.

What Is Normalization?

Normalization is about reducing redundancy in your data set. You see some form of redundancy, move it into a separate table, and then link the two tables via an `id` column. It gets far more complex and theoretical, but this is the general idea. Doing this has a few advantages:

1. It reduces the size of your data, and reduced size generally improves performance (but not always).

2. It helps you understand the structure of the data possibly giving you better insights into better analysis.

3. It makes many queries faster because you can narrow searches to specific data you want, rather than always searching all of it (but not always).

4. It makes it easier to augment the data later since you can change the contents of a small isolated table rather than trying to change a giant table.

5. It helps find errors in analysis since you're forced to explain how two pieces of data should be related. Does a user have one purchase or many purchases? Does that mean a purchase has many users or only one user? Normalization highlights these kinds of mistakes and forces you to formalize an answer.

6. It makes you look like a real professional because you know what the word "normalization" means.

When you normalize a database, you follow a process that goes through different "levels" or "normal forms" of quality:

1. First Normal Form (1NF) has the goal of making one row and one column for every type and piece of data.

2. Second Normal Form (2NF) has the goal of moving redundant *discrete* data into separate tables based on their relationship to keys in the table.

3. Third Normal Form (3NF) requires that every piece of information in a row is only about the key of that row. This is where most people stop with normalization as further normalization can make the data more complicated than it needs to be for your application.

Let's take the ECB table and walk through normalizing it to second normal form (2NF). Going to third normal form (3NF) is not too useful in this data set.

First Normal Form

I'm a practical person, so I believe that if the data you have serves your purpose, then just use it. The ECB is perfectly fine if you want to know the price of the Euro versus other currencies. It's also a better data set if you want to make some graphs, do time-series calculations, and do other common financial analyses.

What happens if you want to create a database that stores *more* than the ECB data? That's where normalization starts to become useful. If you look at the ECB data, you'll see it has this design:

Date	USD	JPY	BGN	...
2023-09-19	1.0713	158.2	1.9558	...

Now imagine you need to start tracking which countries have discontinued their currency. It doesn't happen often, but it does happen. With this giant table you'd have to make a *new Boolean column for every currency.*

Date	USD	USD_done	JPY	JPY_done	BGN	BGN_done
2023-09-19	1.0713	0	158.2	0	1.9558	0

This makes my programmer brain scream in agony. What happens if you then have to track that country's full name for the currency? Again, you have to *make a new string column for every currency.* That hurts so much I won't even show you this eldritch horror of a table.

This kind of data is called "denormalized" because there is a lot of redundancy, but it's in the *schema* of the table, not so much the data. This is important to understand because in the original .csv there isn't much redundancy *in the data*. Each currency gets a column of unique data for each date. The redundancy is found in the structure of *each column*, which is why adding new information about each currency causes so many problems.

This is also why I say you want to remove redundancy of *discrete* data. A discrete piece of data is something where there is a limited number of items. There are only so many currency codes in this data, but the currency fluctuation numbers can be in any numeric range. The numbers are *not* discrete, so trying to reduce their redundancy will fail. The currency codes or if they are discontinued are discrete pieces of data, so you can remove their redundancy.

What if you try to fix this by creating a single column `currency`?

Date	currency	rate
2023-09-19	USD	1.0713
2023-09-19	JPY	158.2
2023-09-19	BGN	1.9558

Now we've fixed the schema repetition, but that shows us the *data* repetition. If you did this to the whole table, you'd get every currency repeated for every day. You could add the information I mention before with columns `discontinued`, `currency_name`, but those columns would also have repeated data in them for every date.

Despite this problem, this table is in first normal form (1NF) and is ready for the next stage. Another problem you would have to fix is any columns that have multiple data elements in them. Imagine if the data was like this:

Date	currency	rate
2023-09-19	USD	[1.0713, 1.588]
2023-09-19	JPY	[158.2, 257.8]
2023-09-19	BGN	[1.9558, 2.34]

This is actually tough to do in SQL, but here I've turned `rate` into a column that's containing two numbers. This would also need to be converted by extracting every number and making a new row:

Date	currency	rate
2023-09-19	USD	1.0713
2023-09-19	USD	1.588
2023-09-19	JPY	158.2
2023-09-19	JPY	257.8
2023-09-19	BGN	1.9558
2023-09-19	BGN	2.34

Implementing 1NF

In most normalization situations, you have to figure out how to use SQL to change the data, but our `euro` table in SQLite3 is too broken to use SQL. It might be possible, but it's far easier to change your Python `ex57.py` script so that it creates the table using Python SQLite3.

At this point in the exercise I want you to implement the 1NF table like this:

1. Change your `ex57.py` script so that it creates the table if it doesn't exist

2. Load the data as you've done before, but instead of writing a new `.csv`, you should use Python's `sqlite3` to write the data directly to the database

3. Your only goal at this stage is the 1NF table I describe earlier, but keep in mind that you'll change this script in the next section to create the 2NF version

4. The size of the data *explodes* once you do this, so consider stopping after a few hundred rows from the `.csv` to save time

Creating Tables in SQL

To accomplish this goal, you'll need to know how to `create` tables and `drop` them (delete). To create a table, use this syntax:

```
1  CREATE TABLE IF NOT EXISTS rate
2    id INTEGER PRIMARY KEY AUTOINCREMENT NOT NULL,
3    date DATE, currency TEXT, rate FLOAT;
```

The IF NOT EXISTS is optional. You should read the CREATE TABLE documentation to learn the full syntax, but this will create a table named `rate` that has the three fields you want: `id`, `date`, `currency`, and `rate`. The complicated INTEGER PRIMARY KEY AUTOINCREMENT simply says create an `id` that is a number that gets incremented automatically on every insert. Doing this means you *do not* include the `id` column when doing insert and instead let the database pick the number for you.

You'll also need to drop the table if it exists:

```
1  DROP TABLE IF EXISTS table_name;
```

The IF EXISTS is also optional in this. I recommend that you assume the database is fresh so you can drop the table and re-create it again each time you run. Otherwise, you have to do complicated loading logic that checks for existing data.

Second Normal Form (2NF)

You now have the data in this first normal form (1NF), and it repeats the currency names:

Date	currency	rate
2023-09-19	USD	1.0713
2023-09-19	JPY	158.2

Date	currency	rate
2023-09-19	BGN	1.9558

The next task is to create a new table that will hold information about currencies *only* and then link it back to the rates table. Now we have two tables like this:

id	date	currency_id	rate
1	2023-09-19	1	1.0713
2	2023-09-19	2	158.2
3	2023-09-19	3	1.9558

Notice here I've replaced the currency with a currency_id, which will reference the currency information in this table:

id	currency
1	USD
2	JPY
3	BGN

I've replaced the repetitive currency names with similarly repetitive numbers, but this is what you want. Remember, you're trying to remove *discrete* redundancy. The currency_id column could be any numbers, but the *currency names* are a fixed set. This will also allow you to then add more columns to the new currency table, which isn't easily done in the 1NF version of the table.

Implementing 2NF

There are two general paths you can take when implementing this schema:

1. Utilize SQL to "migrate" the database from one schema to another. In this path you write a sequence of SQL statements that transform the schema and data to the 2NF set of tables. This process is called a "migration," and it's essential in modern database development as it allows you to upgrade a production database without taking it down for very long.

2. Simply rewrite your ex57.py script to use this schema directly. Since you're loading this data for the first time, you can simply make the data better right away. This is the ideal situation since you can work on the data before it ever gets to production and avoid later painful migrations.

For this part of the exercise I'd like you to try both options. First, use SQL to change the data into the new two-table configuration. Then you should rewrite your ex57.py script to do it directly. This will help you understand how both options work and which one to use when you can use it.

To get you started, here's the SQL I used to do option 1:

Listing 58.1: euro_migrate.sql

```
1    DROP TABLE IF EXISTS currency;
2
3    CREATE TABLE currency (id INTEGER PRIMARY KEY
4      AUTOINCREMENT NOT NULL, currency TEXT);
5
6    ALTER TABLE rate ADD COLUMN currency_id INTEGER;
7
8    INSERT INTO currency (currency) SELECT currency FROM rate GROUP BY
9    currency;
10
11   UPDATE rate SET currency_id = currency.id FROM currency WHERE
12   rate.currency = currency.currency;
13
14   ALTER TABLE rate DROP COLUMN currency;
```

You could improve this with transactions, but it should work correctly as long as the data hasn't changed since I wrote it. If it did change, then fix my SQL. Let's walk through this euro_migrate.sql file one line at a time:

1. I first drop the currency table with a DROP command, but notice I add IF EXISTS. This makes sure your SQL will still run if the database is empty.

2. I then create the currency table with CREATE, but this time I don't have a IF NOT EXISTS. That's because the first line is dropping the table always.

3. I then alter the rate table with ALTER TABLE. ALTER TABLE is how you add or remove columns from a table, but it does have limitations, so read the documentation to study it.

4. Once the schema is how I like it, I INSERT INTO the currency table using rate as the source of the data. The SELECT currency FROM rate GROUP BY currency part can be run on its own (do it) to see what it produces. This "subquery" will produce the data we want, and then INSERT INTO will go through each result row and use that as an insert into currency

5. Once currency is updated, I can now migrate the original rate.currency to the new currency.id with an UPDATE command. This works like the SELECT, but it sets the rate. ↳ currency_id equal to currency.id for each row where rate.currency = currency. ↳ currency

6. Now that rate.currency_id points at currency.id, I can use another ALTER TABLE to drop the currency column from rate, and the conversion is complete.

Studying this one SQL file would be highly beneficial to you, so I recommend you open your `euro.` ↳ `sqlite3` file with `sqlite3 euro.sqlite3` and paste each line in one at a time. After you paste the line in, investigate the database with these commands:

```
1  sqlite> .schema rate
2  sqlite> .schema currency
3  sqlite> select * from rate;
4  sqlite> select * from currency;
```

This is how you inspect what's in the database, and it should help you to begin to understand what this SQL is doing.

Using Python

Migrations are very useful, but in your case it's far more beneficial to simply get the data right the first time. Studying data you have extracted to determine the best structure can save you mountains of pain later. To do this, you'll need to change your `ex57.py` loader script to now do the following:

1. Create the new schema with the `rate` and `currency` tables ready to go.

2. Instead of `csv.reader()`, use `csv.DictReader()`. This works the same but returns a dict, which has each column name in it as the keys. This is the secret to getting a list of all of the countries on each row.

3. Extract the `date` from the other data in the row. Now you have the `rate.date`, `rate.rate`, and `currency.currency` columns as keys and values in the `dict`

4. The keys of this dict are now your first insert into the `currency` table. You need to do this only once, so your first row from `csv.DictReader()` can be used to load the `currency` table.

5. Once you have your `currency` table loaded, you can query it again to get the `id=currency` text and place that in a new `dict` for reference while you build the `rate` table.

6. Finally, you process the rows inserting each `rate` and `currency_id`

What you may realize with this approach is that it ends up being *more* complicated than the SQL solution. You might try a middle approach that loads the `rate` table like before but then uses the SQL from the other solution to do the conversions.

Querying 2NF Data

We can now explore how you would query across these two tables using the advanced SELECT syntax. If I want all rates after January 1, 2023 for the USD, I'd do this:

```
1  SELECT * FROM rate, currency WHERE
2    rate.currency_id=currency.id
```

```
3    AND currency.currency='USD'
4    AND date(rate.date) > date('2023-01-01');
```

Let's walk through this query one piece at a time:

1. I do the SELECT * FROM as you learned before to select every column. If you want to narrow this down, you can name each column you want such as rate.date, rate.rate, ↳ rate.currency_id, and currency.id

2. Next I list the two tables I want to query, rate, currency, but if you don't connect these tables, you'll get weird results.

3. After the WHERE, I make this connection with rate.currency_id=currency.id. This tells SQL to match each row of rate to each row of currency via the rate.currency_id and currency.id columns.

4. AND currency.currency='USD' *also* (and) further narrows the results to only rows that match rows in currency where currency.currency is 'USD'.

5. Then we get to how SQLite3 handles dates. To do date comparisons, you need to apply the function date() or datetime() to both the column *and* the date you want to use. In this case, I use date(rate.date) > date('2023-01-01') to say "turn rate.date into a date and compare it to '2023-01-01,' which I also want to be a date()." You can read the SQLite3 Date and Time Functions documentation for the full list of possible functions.

If you do this correctly, then you should only get the rates for 2023 for the USD currency. What happens if you forget the rate.currency_id=currency.id? Try it, but use count(*) to see the difference in results:

```
1  sqlite> SELECT count(*) from rate, currency
2     WHERE currency.currency='USD' AND
3     date(rate.date) > date('2023-01-01');
4
5  7544
6
7  sqlite> SELECT count(*) from rate, currency WHERE
8     rate.currency_id=currency.id AND
9     currency.currency='USD' AND
10    date(rate.date) > date('2023-01-01');
11
12  184
```

The results without currency_id=currency.id are meaningless, and you can see you get *far* more results when you get it wrong. This is because SQL is merging the two tables in a useless way that has no connection between them. I actually can't think of why you would *want* to do this. You can also see that the rates don't make any sense. One day the USD 1.07, and the next it's 8.9?

Querying with Joins

Many people who use SQL *insist* that you can't use SQL without knowing everything about "joins." A SQL JOIN is a way to tell SQL how to search across multiple tables by joining the results together. The problem is most joins are more complicated versions of what you'd do with simple equality between tables, and many times a JOIN will give you unexpected results if you're not careful. This is especially true when you get into the more obscure joins like LEFT OUTER JOIN.

Let's look at that query again, but just use count(*) to see how many results are returned:

```
1   SELECT count(*) FROM rate, currency
2     WHERE rate.currency_id=currency.id
3     AND currency.currency='USD'
4     AND date(rate.date) > date('2023-01-01');
```

In my database I get 184 results. Now, let us do the same thing using JOIN:

```
1   SELECT count(*) FROM rate
2     JOIN currency ON rate.currency_id=currency.id
3     WHERE currency.currency='USD'
4     AND date(rate.date) > date('2023-01-01');
```

The result of this query is...184. It produces the exact same results, and the syntax is nearly identical. You're mostly moving one WHERE clause up to a JOIN currency ON clause, and for some reason that now makes you a "database expert."

There are other join options, but most of them produce results that are *probably* not what you want unless you really know what you're doing. These JOIN variants will return all of one or both tables, but fill in any missing data with null. I honestly have never once in all 30+ years of using databases wanted that. 99.99999% of the time I want data from some tables that's constrained by the data in other tables.

So what should you use? Use whichever one makes sense. I use the WHERE-only version because I know it will return exactly what I tell it to with no weirdness between databases or needing a Venn diagram showing me what gets returned. You might like JOIN because it looks "cleaner" or because you only have to mention only one table after FROM. Whatever your reason, just get good with what you choose and know about the other style.

Study Drills

Write more queries against the 2NF database that answer the following questions:

1. What's the average rate of USD for 2022?
2. What's the minimum rate of JPY for all years?

3.   Use what you know about UPDATE to make sure all rate.rate rows with rate == 'N/A'
     are set to null instead.

4.   Explain this SQL:

```
1  SELECT count(*) as total, currency.currency
2    FROM rate, currency
3    WHERE rate.currency_id = currency.id
4    AND rate.rate is null
5    GROUP BY currency.currency
6    ORDER BY total DESC;
```

Try to guess what it will do, and then study any keyword or syntax you don't understand at the official
SQLite3 documentation. Once you feel you understand it, run it to see if your analysis is correct.

Finally, why do I use count(*) instead of count(rate.rate)? How would you rewrite this using
JOIN instead?

SQL Relationships

O ur final exercise is going to cover the concept of relations in SQL. In technical terms every table is a relation, but we're going to be more specific and talk about tables that are connected to other tables in various ways.

One-to-Many (1:M)

A "relation" in SQL is a method of using id columns in tables to associate one table to another through a "one-to-many" or "many-to-many" relationship. In our ECB data we have a rate for each country and a currency that rate applies to. We can say the following about this relationship between rate and currency:

"A Rate has one Currency, and a Currency has many Rate."

In our 2NF version of the ECB data, the first part is modeled by placing a currency_id in the rate table so that each rate row has only one currency.id. This also implements the "Currency has many Rates" side since any query for a currency.id in rate.currency_id would pull up all the daily rates for that one currency.

One-to-Many in Python

I find it helps to understand these concepts if you see how they're typically implemented in Python. If I wanted to say "Rate has one Currency" in Python, I'd do this:

```
1   class Rate:
2     def _init_(self, date, rate, currency):
3       self.date = date
4       self.rate = rate
5       self.currency = currency
```

I simply create a single attribute and set it equal to the currency for this Rate. This connection is implemented by the rate.currency_id in the rate table, and in Python it's implemented using =.

On the other side of the equation we have "Currency has many Rates." To implement that in Python I do this:

```
1   class Currency:
2     def _init_(self, rates):
```

```
3       # rates is a list but...wait
4       self.rates = rates
```

In this example, `rates` is a list of `Rate` objects and maps to the SQL `rate` table.

One-to-Many Problem

I now have a problem, though. A `Rate` needs to be attached to each `Currency`, but the `Currency` needs a list of all the `Rate` objects. To understand what I mean, here is some broken code that attempts to create a `Currency` and a few `Rates`:

```
1  jan_usd = [Rate('Jan', 1.2, usd), Rate('Jan', 1.3, usd)]
2  usd = Currency(jan_usd)
```

Do you see the problem? I can't use the variable usd when creating the jan_usd list because it hasn't been created yet, and I can't create usd until I have the list of jan_usd filled. There are a couple ways to fix this, but let's see if you can figure this out.

Your job then is to invent a `Rate` and `Currency` class that can be created to model this database correctly. How will `Currency` get its list of rates? How will `Rate` get the `Currency`? Bonus points if you can actually load these objects out of the database using only the SQLite3 module. It's also acceptable to create the variables differently.

Many-to-Many (M:M)

The other kind of relation is a "many-to-many" relation, which would be phrased like this:

"A Rate has many Currency, and a Currency has many Rate.

This is actually incorrect, but if we did want to model this, we'd need a *third* table typically named `rate_currency`. This third table would have the `id` from `rate.id` and the `id` from `currency.id` in it like this:

rate_id	currency_id
1	1
2	2
3	3

Your currency table would stay the same, but your `rate` table would then change like this:

id	date	rate
1	2023-09-19	1.0713
2	2023-09-19	158.2
3	2023-09-19	1.9558

You delete the `currency_id` and move that to `rate_currency`, and now you can have any rate, on any day, be associated with any currency. You also need to give every row of `rate` its own `id` column. This is also *ridiculous* and not something you'd actually do since now the complexity of this database is far too high for almost no benefit. That doesn't mean many-to-many relationships are wrong; they're actually amazing, and you should use them where you find them. It's just that *this* one is really a bad choice. I'm only doing it here as a demonstration.

INFO You may notice that I don't use the English plural form when naming tables or talking about the tables. That's because English plural structure is all over the place, so using it reliably is inconsistent. The other reason is each table isn't considered a container of "rates," but rather a structure that is a "rate." You can think of the table as a class in Python, and each row as an object in Python. You wouldn't name your Person class "People" because it's not a container. Same goes with tables in a SQL database.

Many-to-Many Problem

I want to make sure you understand that doing this many-to-many transform on the ECB data is *wrong*, and the best way to make you understand this is to have you do the transformation and then use it. Turn your 2NF ECB database into a many-to-many monstrosity by writing a new migration and a new loader script.

I suggest starting with whatever gives you the most confidence. Are you feeling confident with Python but not SQL? Then create this many-to-many model in plain Python without the database. Are you feeling pretty good about your understanding of SQL? Then start by trying to write a migration that creates the many-to-many table. Or, maybe you like writing the loader? Then write a new version of the loader that creates the many-to-many model.

One-to-One (1:1)

There's one more type of relation called a "one-to-one" relation, but it doesn't come up very often. A one-to-one relation is typically written as:

One Rate has one Currency, and one Currency has one Rate.

This is also not correct for the ECB data, but if you were to create this, you'd simply put a `rate.currency_id` and a `currency.rate_id` so the rows are solidly connected from both sides.

The question to ask is: Why not just extend one of the tables with the new information? If every row of `rate` matches a single row of `currency`, then the two tables are essentially one table. You could just put the data in `currency` right into `rate` and save a step.

The reason you sometimes need this is because you can't change one of the tables. Maybe the `rate` table is too large for the database but you need some more information. Maybe the `rate` table is used by an old service that can't handle more columns in the table. You could even have an evil database admin who won't let you use ALTER TABLE on a production table. For whatever reason, one-to-one relations are usually used to extend a table when you can't using ALTER TABLE for some reason.

Attributed Relations

While one-to-many isn't very useful, attributed relations are incredibly useful when you need them. All an attributed relation does is add some additional information to the many-to-many table. In our `rate_currency` table it could mean adding an `updated_at` column to keep track of when this relationship was last updated:

rate_id	currency_id	updated_at
1	1	Jan 1, 2023
2	2	Jan 10, 2023
3	3	Aug 3, 2023

In this example, it's not very useful, but it is *very* useful when you have some piece of data that seems to not belong to either side of a many-to-many relation. Use an attributed relation any time you wonder, "Does the update time go on the `rate` or the `currency`?" It might be that what you want is to track the update time of the *connection*, and that works best on the joining table.

Querying M:M Tables

There really isn't anything different between a 1:M table query and an M:M query; you're just adding one more table that must be connected via `id` columns. Here's how I'd do it with this exercise's database:

```
1  SELECT count(*) FROM
2    rate, currency, rate_currency
3    WHERE rate.id=rate_currency.rate_id
4    AND currency.id=rate_currency.currency_id
5    AND currency.currency='USD'
6    AND date(rate.date) > date('2023-01-01');
```

I changed it from only `rate.currency_id=currency.id` to use the `id` columns in the new `rate_currency` table. Simply set all three tables equal, and you're ready to go.

How would you do this with `JOIN`?

```
1  SELECT count(*) FROM rate
2    JOIN currency
3      ON rate_currency.currency_id=currency.id
4    JOIN rate_currency
5      ON rate_currency.rate_id=rate.id
6    WHERE currency.currency='USD'
7    AND date(rate.date) > date('2023-01-01');
```

I honestly don't think this is any better than the other form. It's not worse, but I find the WHERE version to be more direct and easy to understand. You use whichever one you like.

Your Last Study Drill

Welcome to almost the end of the course. I hope you gained both knowledge and confidence while you studied with me. For your final Study Drill, I want you to go get the book *SQL for Smarties* by Joe Celko. This book was last updated in 2014, but SQL hasn't changed much since then, and Joe's book is the most comprehensive SQL book you can find. I believe that if you want to learn SQL, then completing Joe's book using SQLite3 will be all you need to fully understand it.

You may think I've taught you enough, and probably that will be true for a while, but you *will* run into situations where better knowledge of SQL can solve big problems for you. Even if your goal going forward isn't data science, the prevalence of SQL makes learning it well a highly valuable investment.

Advice from an Even Older Programmer

I magine it's 1820 and you want a nice portrait of your mother. You hear that paintings in pastel are all the rage and can be done quickly while still looking beautiful, especially in the candlelight you use to light your home at night. You contact an artist, and they come to your home, do some initial sketches of your mother, and then schedule return visits to complete the painting. Since the artist uses pastel, they can finish a very nice portrait in a record 6 hours of sitting, and make your mother look younger too. It also costs you only a week's salary, which is a bargain compared to an oil painting. Those are very expensive and can take months.

Decades pass, and your children want to have a nice portrait of you. It's 1840, and your children sign you up to sit for a photograph! It's so exciting because they look so real and they're so easy. You go to the photographer's studio and sit in a chair wearing your finest clothes, and the photographer takes the photo. The whole process takes maybe 30 minutes, with the photo taken in an instant. Within a few years even more ways to take photos are invented, and within a few decades photography begins to completely change the world, for better and worse. Eventually the pastel of your mother is long forgotten.

Today you (not the 1820s you) live in a world that photography made possible. You are looking at this course either on a computer screen that is a direct descendant of the early cameras or on a book that was printed using cameras. Your computer is also a direct descendant of photography, with the original process to create a CPU utilizing a process similar to developing film. Not only that, but your computer would not exist without the ability to utilize photography to exchange schematics, designs, documents, and many other artifacts necessary to construct all the equipment to make it. You are also most likely alive because of photography and painting, which helped pioneer modern chemistry manufacturing by companies like Bayer. Without the industrialized chemistry perfected on pigments, you would not have aspirin, antibiotics, X-rays, and photographs of DNA.

I firmly believe that photography created the modern world, and I believe that you are currently standing on the edge of a similar revolution in computing with the recent invention of Generative AI. It's very early, but technology such as large language models and Stable Diffusion are already useful technologies and only getting better. Eventually these technologies will feed into even better and more efficient technologies, in much the same way photography created the silicon wafers that now power the sensors in modern cameras. If these technologies continue to advance, then what happens to programmers?

Probably the same thing that happened to painters when photography sufficiently advanced. Before photography, you had to hire an artist if you wanted a memory of your mother, and all of those artists were out of work within one generation. Now it's odd to find an artist who can accurately paint a portrait. I believe programming will be very similar, where it will be odd to find a programmer who can actually code something from scratch without help.

If that's the case, then why bother learning to code? For the same reason I learned to paint a realistic portrait:

> There is more to programming than just getting paid to turn buttons cornflower blue for some billionaire.

I learned to paint because I felt like I would enjoy it, and I do immensely. I can easily take a photo, but painting gives me a unique experience that I can't get from taking a photo. I learned to code because I really enjoyed making a computer do things, and programming gives me an experience I can't get if I let a large language model do it for me. I code because I feel like I have to, not *just* because it pays the bills.

What does this mean for you as a new programmer? The story of photography and painting continues in the 1900s when painters realized they didn't *have* to do realistic paintings anymore. They could paint whatever they wanted, so they made paintings that reflected who they were and what they saw. Painting changed from a thing you did to pay the bills into a vehicle of human expression, which is what we consider *art* today.

I believe this will happen to programming soon as well. You'll see programmers being liberated from having to do mundane boring tasks like "make this button 20% larger." They'll instead be able to use computation to express their thoughts and feelings. Sure, people will still obviously do the boring work when they need money (and there's no shame in that). Many artists have painted a few cat portraits to pay the rent. But the vast majority of programming will change into a new art form for expressing yourself rather than just a boring job.

It's not something that will happen soon, but I hope this book prepares you for the change. Learning about data science is the first step to understanding how Generative AI models work. Understanding how this technology works will give you some control over the future of programming. Learning to code now is also the first step to creating the software you want to create. Maybe in the future everyone becomes some kind of indie game developer? Who knows, but you now have an amazing future ahead of you if you're willing to be flexible and embrace the new things that come along.

Until then, I'll be happy if you take what I taught you and get a job or create a small business. I don't want you to think I'm *against* programming as a job. After all, the artistic future of programming can't happen if you can't feed yourself.

Index

Page numbers followed by an italic "*t*" indicate tables.

Photo by Marvent/Shutterstock

VIDEO TRAINING FOR THE **IT PROFESSIONAL**

LEARN QUICKLY
Learn a new technology in just hours. Video training can teach more in less time, and material is generally easier to absorb and remember.

WATCH AND LEARN
Instructors demonstrate concepts so you see technology in action.

TEST YOURSELF
Our Complete Video Courses offer self-assessment quizzes throughout.

CONVENIENT
Most videos are streaming with an option to download lessons for offline viewing.

Learn more, browse our store, and watch free, sample lessons at
informit.com/video

Save 50%* off the list price of video courses with discount code **VIDBOB**